T0265847

SYMPATHY, SOLIDARITY, AND SILENCE

Three European Baptist Responses to the Holocaust

Lee B. Spitzer

Foreword by Reid S. Trulson

JUDSON PRESS
PUBLISHERS SINCE 1824
VALLEY FORGE, PA

Sympathy, Solidarity, and Silence: Three European Baptist
Responses to the Holocaust

Cover Photograph: "2020-03-04 ISRAEL 38 Jerusalem—Yad Vashem Museum Survivors" ©2020 Lee B. Spitzer. Used with permission.

Interior design by Crystal Devine.
Cover design by Lisa Delgado, Delgado and Company.

Library of Congress Cataloging-in-Publication data
Names: Spitzer, Lee B., author.
Title: Sympathy, solidarity, and silence : three European Baptist responses
    to the Holocaust / Lee Spitzer.
Identifiers: LCCN 2022014699 (print) | LCCN 2022014700 (ebook) |
ISBN
    9780817018351 (paperback) | ISBN 9780817082444 (epub)
Subjects: LCSH: Holocaust (Christian theology) | Baptists--Europe. |
    Baptists--Doctrines.
Classification: LCC BT93 .S68 2022 (print) | LCC BT93 (ebook) | DDC
    231.7/6--dc23/eng/20220606
LC record available at https://lccn.loc.gov/2022014699
LC ebook record available at https://lccn.loc.gov/2022014700

Printed in the U.S.A.
First printing, 2022.

Contents

Foreword

Sympathy, Solidarity, and Silence: Three European Baptist Responses to the Holocaust, is a must-read second book of Dr. Lee B. Spitzer's rooted in his Holocaust research. His book, *Baptists, Jews, and the Holocaust: The Hand of Sincere Friendship,* overturned the conclusions of earlier scholars that United States Baptists were largely silent in the face of anti-Semitism and the Holocaust in the 1930s and 1940s. His new work is a second *tour de force.*

Sympathy, Solidarity, and Silence covers the 1930s and 1940s but moves to a European context—to people directly involved as onlookers, protestors, rescuers, victims, or collaborators. Spitzer's meticulous research examines British, French, and German Baptist attitudes and actions regarding anti-Semitism and the attempt to exterminate the Jewish people.

While the breadth of Spitzer's research enables coherent themes to appear, its depth of detail prevents simplistic categorizations. Spitzer recounts heroic actions of love and sacrifice by Baptists on behalf of the Jewish people under Nazi occupation throughout Europe. Nevertheless, source materials support his unflinching assertion that "the whole Baptist family bears a responsibility to repent and seek reconciliation with the Jewish world." Such tensions arise when diligent research recognizes that documents require interpretation and that some details remain contradictory or inconclusive. Spitzer can therefore note "in an honest reappraisal of the Holocaust period, Baptists today may remember and honor Baptists who acted in solidarity with Jews during the Holocaust, while at the same time acknowledging the inconvenient truth that many Baptists failed to respond appropriately to Nazism."

Spitzer's work on Baptists and the Holocaust earned him a PhD degree in Theology from Vrije University (Free University) Amsterdam, in association with the International Baptist Study Centre. As a Baptist World Alliance (BWA) historian, Spitzer has compiled and indexed all the resolutions, manifestos, messages, and proclamations issued by BWA World Congresses from 1905 through 2015. Furthermore, he is a member of the Committee on Ethics, Religion, and the Holocaust Museum in Washington, DC. That academic and theological background positions him to make some observations that might elude other scholars.

Spitzer distinguishes "racialism" from "racism" and observes that the BWA resolution on racialism passed in Berlin at its 1934 World Congress was "the first and only organizational protest by an international religious body ever made against Nazi anti-Semitism within Germany during the Third Reich." His work with the BWA documents substantiates his observation that the Congress's racialism protest became the BWA's most widely disseminated statement from 1934 to the present and was the precedent for many subsequent racism resolutions.

Spitzer reintroduces the term "personality," the affirmation that "all people are made in the image of God and possess a soul, have dignity, and are of unlimited worth, and therefore deserve religious and political respect, freedom, and security." The 1934 BWA resolution on race relations ascribed personality to all people, thus affirming that Jews and people of color are made in God's image and deserve political and social equality and civil rights. That Baptist core conviction rebuked Nazi totalitarianism and anti-Semitism.

Spitzer examines the 1847 German Baptist confession of faith written largely by Julius Köbner, the Danish son of a Jewish Rabbi, and observes that it exhibited the "greatest degree of Jewish influence of any confession created by the Baptist movement throughout its entire history." The November 8-9, 1938, Kristallnacht burning of Torah scrolls and synagogues was part of the Nazi effort to create a German national and Christian movement that was devoid of any Jewish roots. Spitzer demonstrates how German Baptists totally revised their 1847 confession, removed Jewish influences, and produced the 1944 confession that conformed with Nazi anti-Semitism.

Sympathy, Solidarity, and Silence fuels remembrance, probes repentance, and challenges emboldened racism and anti-Semitism. And it is timely. It follows the 2017 Unite the Right rally in Charlottesville, Virginia, where protesters chanted slogans from Nazi Germany: "you will not replace us," "Jews will not replace us," and "blood and soil." It follows a 2020 study of millennials and Generation Z-age people in the US "showing that 63 percent of respondents did not know that 6 million Jews were killed in the Holocaust and 48 percent could not name a single death camp or concentration camp."[1] It also follows the 2022 call by the Council of the European Union to remember the victims of racist and anti-Semitic violence and to promote research and education on Jewish life, anti-Semitism, and the Holocaust.[2] This book is precisely the kind of rigorous research for which the European Council is calling amid the loss of historical memory and increased racism and anti-Semitism in both the United States and Europe.

Though outside the scope of its inquiry, the book prompts related questions such as: How does "the whole Baptist family" repent and seek reconciliation with the Jewish people? Do Baptists bear a similar responsibility regarding the Roma and LGBTQ people whom the Nazis likewise sought to exterminate? How does the church's struggle to remain faithful in the face of German Nazism inform the challenge it faces in Christian nationalism? How do people of faith find guidance when several of their core convictions collide?

Sympathy, Solidarity, and Silence should be required reading for Baptists. It has cautionary value for those who oppose racism, anti-Semitism, religious nationalism, and autocracy. It will be an enduring resource for all who seek deeper knowledge of the Holocaust, religion, history, politics, and the state in the 20th Century. Meanwhile, we eagerly await learning from Dr. Spitzer's additional Holocaust research that will extend the narrative about Baptists, anti-Semitism, and the Holocaust to Baptist fellowships in other European, North American, and Asian countries.

NOTES

1. Luis Andres Henao, "Holocaust survivors sound a call to action," *Philadelphia Inquirer* (April 29, 2022), A5.
2. See https://www.consilium.europa.eu/en/press/press-releases/2022/03/04/council-adopts-conclusions-on-combating-racism-and-antisemitism/.

The Call of the Past,
a Hope for the Future

*To make our way forward is to go back in history. To recover
past trauma is to awaken to the pain, and we cannot heal until
we see the narratives of the past renewed by faith and hope. We
cannot move forward by ignoring the past.*[1]

Makoto Fujimura, the author of the above quote, spoke with "a
German friend who confessed that he got so sick of rehashing Germany's Nazi past in school that as an adult he refused to return to
Auschwitz or to visit places with a painful past, including Hiro-
shima and Nagasaki." However, when faced with a contemporary
terrorist attack, "he realized that the past he was trying to avoid is
in front of us now, and that the only way to move forward is to first
recognize what happened in the history of trauma."[2]

This volume, by rediscovering the stories of how British,
French, and German Baptists responded to Jew hatred and persecution during the Nazi era, reveals both the achievements and failures
of Baptists during that period. Some Baptists may prefer to "let
sleeping dogs lie" and avert their eyes from a recounting of anti-Semitism and the Holocaust that shines a spotlight on Baptists in
particular. Other Baptists may be relieved to learn about the many
positive—and even at times prophetic or heroic—ways in which
Baptists challenged Hitler's hate-filled totalitarian regime. My intent is to help Baptists in the twenty-first century move forward
in a spirit of humility by honestly owning our past—the good, the
bad, and the ugly—and to gain wisdom from it. The Spirit of God

may, and does, speak through history, as the prophets of the Jewish Scriptures demonstrated so ably.

My aim as a historian is threefold. First, it is my goal to honor *truth-telling*. I seek to offer historical narratives that are accurate, fair, and thoughtfully arranged. Second, I believe that history is *coherent* (it is not merely a random set of unrelated incidents that have no meaning or significance), and that the meaningfulness of historical narratives can best be explored by identifying the themes that bind incidents to one another across time. Third, historical reflection, especially when it exposes evil, failures, and mistakes (whether intentional or not), offers opportunities for us all to reflect, repent, seek forgiveness, and perhaps subsequently experience reconciliation and healing.[3]

Our contemporary culture is sometimes disdainful of the past, judging it by current and supposedly more enlightened paradigms of justice, ethics, and philosophy. Such haughtiness and pride impose ideological screens that insulate us from the lessons of the past. It takes courage to be willing to open oneself up to the past and its periods of horrifying atrocity without flinching from its raw power to astonish, accuse, and assault our sensibilities. Abraham Joshua Heschel once posed a rhetorical question that strikes at my heart: "To live both in awe and consternation, in fervor and horror, with my conscience on mercy and my eyes on Auschwitz, wavering between exaltation and dismay?"[4] If Baptists are to face our past and receive the gift of transformational hope, we must embrace Heschel's paradoxical call to live an authentic intellectual and spiritual existence—and let history speak.

NOTES

1. Makoto Fujimura, *Silence and Beauty* (Downers Grove, IL: InterVarsity, 2016), 204.
2. Fujimura, 204.
3. See Desmond Tutu, *No Future without Forgiveness* (New York: Doubleday, 1999).
4. Abraham Joshua Heschel, *A Passion for Truth* (Woodstock, VT: Jewish Lights, 1995), xiv.

Acknowledgments

I am indebted to several scholars and institutions whose guidance and assistance have influenced my research on Baptists and the Holocaust in general and the writing of this work in particular. I wish to express my continuing appreciation to my two doctoral advisers, Dr. Henk Bakker and Dr. Parush R. Parushev, for their wisdom and encouragement, resulting in my receiving a PhD in theology from Vrije Universiteit in cooperation with the International Baptist Studies Center in Amsterdam in September 2016. They counseled me to divide my original research agenda in half—one focusing on Baptists in the United States (which was published as *Baptists, Jews, and the Holocaust* by Judson Press in 2017), and the other on European Baptists (the present volume).

Several libraries and archives provided assistance during my research. I would like to express appreciation to the American Baptist Historical Society (Atlanta, Georgia), the Andover-Newton Theological Seminary Library (then at Andover, Massachusetts, and presently located at Yale University), the Regent's Park College Library (Oxford, Great Britain), the Elstal Theological Seminary Library (Wustermark-Elstal, Germany), the International Baptist Studies Center Library (Amsterdam, Netherlands), the Southern Baptist Historical Library and Archives (Nashville, Tennessee), and Carolina University's George M. Manuel Library (Winston-Salem, North Carolina).

Deepest thanks to my wife, Dr. Lois Spitzer, an associate professor at Stockton University, and my most ardent supporter and reviewer. Special thanks to Rev. Dr. Ann Borquist, ABCUSA International Ministries global consultant, for her manuscript editing and feedback. As always, the editorial team at Judson Press has been a joy to work with.

Various scholars have provided ideas, feedback, assistance, support, and encouragement throughout this journey. Thanks to Reid

Trulson, Erich Geldbach, Paul Fiddes, Martin Rothkegel, Reinhard Assmann, Brian Talbot, Stanley Slade, William Brackney, William Shiell, Elmo Familiaran, Toivo Pilli, Mike Pears, Anniel Hatton, Franck Keller, Patti Duckworth, and Raisa Ostapenko—I appreciate you all! A word of appreciation, as well, to Elijah Brown, general secretary of the Baptist World Alliance, for welcoming me to the BWA's team as historian.

I am grateful to the Centre for Baptist Studies in Oxford Publications for granting permission to use material from my chapter "The British Baptist Union and the Nazi Persecution of Jews, 1933–38," published in *Peoples of God: Baptists and Jews over Four Centuries* (ed. John H. Y. Briggs and Paul S. Fiddes [Oxford: Centre for Baptist Studies, 2019]). Similarly, I am grateful to *Baptistic Theologies* journal for permission to use material from my article "The Nazi Persecution of the Jews and Scottish Baptist Indignation" (9, no 2 [Autumn 2017]).

A METHODOLOGICAL NOTE

European Baptist History from an American Vantage Point

In volume 1 of my Holocaust series, *Baptists, Jews, and the Holocaust*,[1] I covered the responses of Baptists in the United States to Hitler, his anti-Semitism, and the attempted extermination of the Jewish people. That book also covered the actions of the Baptist World Alliance, particularly in relation to positions taken at its World Congresses.

In this second volume, I consider how Baptists across Europe responded to the threat posed by Hitler, Nazi anti-Semitism, and the Holocaust. Due solely to space limitations, I focus on Baptists in Great Britain (including Scotland), France, and Germany.[2] In contact with their American colleagues, each of these national fellowships was challenged to clarify their stances on totalitarianism, Nazism, and anti-Semitism in light of Baptist core convictions, such as soul freedom and personality, separation of church and state, and democracy and freedom in both the civil and political spheres. Reflecting the secular political divide that defined the Second World War, German Baptists were soon alienated from their British, French, and American brothers and sisters. The fellowship between them was broken, and they found themselves on opposite sides of the ideological divide.

A key difference between European and American responses was contextual—unlike their American peers, European Baptists had to face Hitler's threats and assess their role in saving Jewish victims while under threat of losing their own freedom and independence. European Baptists were not only onlookers to the anti-Semitic campaigns of the Nazis but were also at times protestors, rescuers, victims, or collaborators. Accordingly, a comprehensive history of this period must incorporate not just institutional actions but the sometimes heroic—or tragic—stories of individuals, ministries, and local churches.

This book explores aspects of European Baptist history during the Nazi era from a distinctly American and English-language perspective (while not neglecting non-English sources). There are two reasons for employing this methodological strategy.

First, European Baptist history by necessity must take into account the continuous cross-Atlantic conversation, fellowship, and interaction that was a feature of the era. The Baptist World Alliance, headquartered in London and then Washington, DC, was dependent on both American financial support and human leadership. James Henry Rushbrooke, general secretary and then president of the Baptist World Alliance, though English, spent a great deal of time in the United States, cultivating relationships and strategizing with Baptist leaders. Rushbrooke's successor as general secretary, Walter Oliver Lewis, was an American who had served in Europe as the representative of the American Baptist Foreign Mission Society. The leaders of the European Baptist fellowships regularly met with and corresponded with their American counterparts, whose mission organizations often sponsored projects and ministries in their countries.

Second, a treasure trove of valuable English-language primary source documents (reports, articles, and communications) brings to light new facets of the narratives of British, Scottish, French, and German Baptists, which this study utilizes. During the 1930s and 1940s, not only did Baptist periodicals report extensively on what was taking place, but they also published English-language articles composed by French, German, Dutch, Norwegian, and other leaders. In addition, dozens of secular English-language newspapers and periodicals preserved stories and reflections by Baptists that provide fascinating insights into how Baptists struggled with the events and challenges of the Nazi period.

There is no previously published book that details how European Baptists responded to Nazi anti-Semitism and the Holocaust in cooperation and coordination with their partners in the United States. Bernard Green's *European Baptists and the Third Reich*

(2008) covers the same time period, surveying how European Baptists in each country institutionally survived World War II. Baptist responses to anti-Semitism and Jewish refugees and victims receive some attention but are not the primary concern. The same can be said for his earlier work, *Crossing the Boundaries: A History of the European Baptist Federation* (1999).

French Baptist writers, led by Sébastien Fath and André Thobois, have published works that preserve memories of Baptist responses to Nazism and the plight of Jewish refugees, but much of their research has not been readily available in English. This work pulls the various stories together, weaving them into a more contextual and comprehensive narrative.

Several quality books in German focus on how German Baptists sought to survive under Hitler's regime. The standard work is Andrea Strübind's *Die unfreie Freikirche: Der Bund der Baptistengemeinden im "Dritten Reich"* (1991). She published an English summary of her research in "German Baptists and National Socialism," an article in the *Journal of European Baptist Studies* (8, no. 3 [2008]). Other German historians, such as Roland Fleischer and Erich Geldbach, have also written about this time period. Building on their insights, this account provides a more *balanced and critical* assessment, exploring a consistent track record of German Baptist complicity that can only be described as deeply troubling for Baptists of conscience.

Much research has been done on "righteous Gentiles" who aided Jewish refugees and victims during the Holocaust.[3] A few of these studies cite Baptists. This work, based on primary sources, adds new details and context to this field of study.

NOTES

1. Lee B. Spitzer, *Baptists, Jews, and the Holocaust: The Hand of Sincere Friendship* (Valley Forge, PA: Judson, 2017).

2. In future publications, I hope to extend the narrative to Baptist fellowships in other European, North American, and Asian countries.

3. See, for example, David P. Gushee, *Righteous Gentiles of the Holocaust: Genocide and Moral Obligation*, 2nd ed. (St. Paul, MN: Paragon, 2003); and Mordecai Paldiel, *The Righteous among the Nations: Rescuers of Jews during the Holocaust* (New York: HarperCollins, 2007).

Baptist World Alliance World Congress Resolution 1934.7 "Racialism"

This Congress representing the world-wide, inter-racial fellowship of Baptists, rejoices to know that despite all differences of race, there is in Christ an all-embracing unity, so that in Him it can be claimed with deepest truth there is "neither Greek nor Jew, circumcision nor uncircumcision, barbarian, Scythian, bond nor free, but Christ is all in all."

This Congress deplores and condemns as a violation of the law of God the Heavenly Father, all racial animosity, and every form of oppression or unfair discrimination toward the Jews, toward coloured people, or toward subject races in any part of the world.

This Congress urges the promotion of Christian teaching concerning respect for human personality regardless of race, and as the surest means of advancing the true brotherhood of all people, urges the active propagation of the Gospel of Christ throughout the World.

INTRODUCTION

In the Track of the Storm

World War I devastated Europe on so many levels. Approximately 20 million soldiers and civilians perished, with a like amount of people wounded. On March 17, 1919, James H. Franklin, foreign secretary of the American Baptist Foreign Mission Society, arrived in Paris to "ascertain, if possible, what should be done to assist the evangelical churches in their reconstruction work after the great war," so that "in the track of the storm," Northern Baptists could mount a compassionate humanitarian response in coordination with other Baptists from across the world.[1]

Franklin toured two towns in northern France where "there were Baptist churches with substantial houses of worship before the towns were laid in ruins"[2] by German forces. The devastation to Baptist edifices deeply troubled Franklin. His travels reminded him of the historical experience of Baptists, who, like his Huguenot hosts, "suffered for freedom of conscience." He wrote, "My heart was greatly moved by the thought of the sufferings of these early Protestants, whose fight for religious freedom has blessed the entire world."[3]

One of Franklin's French hosts, Rev. Philemon Vincent (who lost two sons to the war), prophesied that the Great War would not be Germany's last offense: "This is the two hundredth time in history that the Germans have invaded France. They will come again!"[4] Franklin praised the courage of Baptists and other Protestants in the face of war. At a meeting with Franklin on April 23–24, 1919, the French and Belgian Baptist leaders expressed "their very earnest desire to see the work of reconstruction have the highest claim over any other interest."[5] That desire would become a core ministry of the Baptist World Alliance and the all-consuming calling of a young British pastor named James Henry Rushbrooke.

In 1920 J. H. Rushbrooke was called by the London Conference of the BWA to serve as its commissioner for Europe, with
responsibility to support the expansion of the European Baptist
movement and promote reconstruction and aid work, particularly
in the eastern part of the war-ravaged continent.[6] His call was preceded by a rigorous fact-finding tour of Europe, accompanied by
Northern Baptist Charles Brooks,[7] to assess the state of the Baptist
churches and the humanitarian situation throughout central and
eastern Europe. Their report to the London Conference contained
suggestions that became a precedent for how the BWA would respond to the future destruction of Europe after the Second World
War. Rushbrooke believed the London meeting was a milestone
for the BWA, for, as Bernard Green rightly judged, World War I
and the reconstruction crisis it engendered "created conditions in
which through the London Conference the Alliance found its *rai-
son d'être.*"[8] Another such purpose was the BWA's call to advocate
for persecuted Baptists. Baptist persecution in Romania became a
key issue discussed at the London Conference[9] and occupied Rushbrooke for the rest of his life—often diverting energy away from
the Jewish plight under Nazism.

Rushbrooke's 1920 tour provided him with an opportunity to
reestablish ties with the German Baptists. For more than twenty
years, Rushbrooke had a multilayered relationship with Germany.
He had studied in Germany and met his wife, Dorothea Getrud We-
ber, there. Rushbrooke's personal ties to Germany and his devotion
to Dorothea "became the inspiration for his deep desire in future
years to establish healthy Anglo-German relations . . . together they
devoted their energies to working and praying for forgiveness and
reconstruction in a defeated Germany and a shattered Europe."[10]
The tour also may have provided Rushbrooke's first personal encounter with the reality of European Jewish persecution. In a lecture he gave in November 1920, he revealed that he learned that in
"Buda Pesth [Budapest] the Jews were being killed."[11]

Like Rushbrooke, Walter Oliver Lewis was destined to make
his mark on the global Baptist movement. He was born in Stanber-
ry, Missouri, on February 22, 1877, and served in several Southern Baptist churches before joining the American Baptist Foreign
Mission Society in 1922. He earned doctorates from the Southern
Baptist Theological Seminary in Louisville, Kentucky, and the

University of Erlangen, Germany.[12] When Rushbrooke vacated the office of BWA general secretary in 1939 and became its president (succeeding George W. Truett, the venerable Texan Southern Baptist), Lewis was a natural choice to replace him. Together Lewis and Rushbrooke guided the BWA through the tumultuous period of World War II and the Holocaust.[13]

Lewis's ministry as the European special representative for the American Baptist Foreign Mission Society (ABFMS) of the Northern Baptist Convention (now known as American Baptist Churches USA) brought him to Odessa in southern Russia in January 1923. Lewis traveled to Odessa to help distribute much-needed household supplies, clothing for children, and other items for some thirty thousand people in need. He utilized Baptist churches, as well as other agencies, to distribute this humanitarian aid.

Just before leaving the city, Lewis experienced a chance personal encounter with "a Jewish woman who spoke German" that he never would forget. Decades later he recounted this conversation in the *Watchman-Examiner*, a leading Baptist newspaper in the United States. She reminded him of the imprisonment of Joseph and Joseph's conversation with another prisoner: "Joseph had predicted the butler would be released and begged him to remember his fellow prisoner. No doubt the butler promised to do what he could, but the record says that for two full years he never thought of his promise." Lewis recalled that the "Jewish woman expressed the hope that I would not forget the sufferings of the people of Russia when I returned to America."[14]

Lewis invoked this memory to urge Baptists to support relief efforts throughout Europe following the collapse of the Third Reich. Europe lay in ruins, displaced people needed assistance, and Baptist churches required rebuilding. Baptists throughout the continent were anxiously looking to the BWA to duplicate what it had done so well after World War I—distribute aid to Baptists in need, and through them, serve others requiring food, clothing, and supplies. For Lewis, displaced European Baptists were modern-day incarnations of the biblical Joseph, yearning to be remembered and helped.

Lewis's conversation with this Jewish woman in Odessa raises a potentially disturbing question. Did Lewis truly grasp her message and its plea? Like the gospel's Anna (Luke 2:36-39), was this Jewess prophesying to Lewis not to forget or not to be insensitive to a future need of her people, the Jews? Was she like Rachel, "weeping for her children and refusing to be comforted, because they are no more" (Jeremiah 31:15; Matthew 2:18, NIV)?

European Baptists and their institutions justifiably received compassionate attention from Baptists following the conclusion of the Second World War, but what about the Jews? What was the responsibility of Baptists to befriend, aid, and stand in solidarity with Europe's Jewish community during the Third Reich and the Holocaust? During the Nazi era, did Baptists, particularly in Great Britain, France, and Germany, reject anti-Semitism and exemplify the gospel of love and care for Jews in spite of the costs? Did Baptists *forget Joseph* or come to the aid of their Jewish neighbors?

"Two Growing Fires"

In the years between the two world wars, Baptists around the world were concerned about the emergence of totalitarianism. With the establishment of the Soviet Union in 1917, Communism was a key concern; later, as the National Socialist Party made progress in Germany, Nazism gained increased attention. Totalitarian ideologies, whether from left or right, were anathema to the Baptist core convictions of individual liberty, religious freedom, and separation of church and state (understood in various ways). Atheism was another consistent target of Baptist disapproval.

In his capacity as commissioner for Europe, Rushbrooke became increasingly involved in the challenges facing Russia during its famine of 1921–22,[15] including the Russian Baptist struggle for religious freedom.[16] On December 19, 1929, he spoke at a public mass meeting sponsored by the Christian Protest Committee in London, opposing the Soviet Union's persecution of Jews and Christians. On stage before about eight thousand people at the Royal Albert Hall, Rushbrooke acknowledged that both Jews and Baptists were global religious communities with a significant number of adherents in the Soviet Union and England.[17]

Energized by a predilection for peacemaking, Baptists in the early 1930s sought to promote international friendship, Baptist solidarity across national borders, and reconciliation between former military enemies. With an unidentified member of the German Baptist Union in attendance, the English Portsmouth and District

Baptist Union in October 1932 heard its president, Mr. W. C. H. Napier, declare that both atheism and communism were "disintegrating and destructive forces" dedicated to destroying faith, especially among youth. The Baptists of England and Germany needed to stand together in opposing this menace. The assembly composed a message, sending "their loving Christian greetings to all the Baptists of Germany, praying that grace, mercy, and peace may be with you all in our Lord Jesus Christ." The German leader promised the message of friendship would be circulated throughout the German Baptist Union.[18]

Within the German Baptist Union, there was also growing awareness of the rise of communism and Nazism. In a letter to the editor published in May 1942, English Baptist A. E. Flux recalled an encounter he had while visiting Germany in 1931. He "met a talented young Baptist leader who has since taken refuge in America." Most likely he spoke with Herbert Gezork (see Chapter 9). The German summarized the pre-Nazi situation Germany found itself in, from the perspective of its youth:

> Under the influence of the economic depression and unemployment, in face of the utterly hopeless outlook of a nation which is supposed to pay reparations for two more generations, the German young people are joining in great and increasing numbers the radical political parties, the Communists on the one side, still more the National-Socialists on the other side. It is the radicalism of despair, and you can imagine how extremely difficult it is for young Christians to stand between two growing fires, and to raise our voice for peace and understanding between the nations.[19]

The Baptist Union of Great Britain and Ireland promoted an international friendship hiking tour in the summer of 1932. Seventeen English young people partnered with two youths from Holland and seven from Germany and journeyed through Germany, Switzerland, and France. In the Black Forest of Germany, they talked about "the German people's attitude to the British, of the future of Hitlerism, and other topics of the day." The band just missed seeing Hitler in person at one of his campaign stops in Freiburg. The British guests were informed that German youth were following Hitler "in desperation—the desperation of unemployment and threatened starvation."[20]

Like their neighbors, German Baptists were so shaken by the weaknesses of the democratic Weimar Republic and the scary specter of atheistic communism advancing from the east, that the temptation to give a strongman and his party a try was difficult to resist. German historian Andrea Strübind concludes, "At the end of the Weimar Republic the German Baptists had found no uniform position in the debate about National Socialism. The opinions ranged from sharp rejection to active membership in the NSDAP"[21]—the Nazi Party.

The Fiery Furnace of Nazi Anti-Semitism

Basil Mathews, a popular English writer throughout the 1930s, was well regarded by Baptists in both Great Britain and the United States. In 1934 he published *The Jew and the World Ferment*, in which he lamented that German Jews were "in the fiery furnace of Nazi anti-Semitism." Hitler and his movement considered this small minority of citizens "a real curse for the German nation." He believed Europe and America needed to grapple with the Jews' "tormented yet hopeful present" in order to "discover how we, who are in our own land their neighbors, ought to act towards them."[22]

Mathews maintained that the Jewish situation could best be understood by recalling the history of European persecution of the Jews, and especially the ghettos created to segregate Jews from the dominant Christian society. Although some Jews had assimilated into European culture, discarding their religious heritage due to the allure of secularizing forces, others preserved a strong sense of Jewish identity. In spite of persecution, the Jewish people continued to gift humanity with "the knowledge of the oneness and holiness of God and of his will to guide man's personal and national life to a supreme end." This prophetic vision "of all human history under divine control" was in direct contradiction to the nationalistic totalitarianism of Nazism.[23]

The Christian tradition universalized the Jewish prophetic perspective based on its understanding of Jesus and his mission. Nevertheless, a significant question remained: how should Christians relate to the Jewish people in light of contemporary anti-Semitism? The answer may be found (although Mathews did not employ the term) in the Christian (and especially Baptist) concept of *personality*—the affirmation that all people are made in God's image and possess a soul, have dignity, and are of unlimited worth, and therefore deserve religious and political respect, freedom, and security. Mathews challenged Christians to examine their personal attitudes toward Jews, under the "burning searchlight of Christ's revelation of God as the Father of all men, with its corollary, which we are not always ready to accept, of human brotherhood."[24] Asserting that Christians must not ignore their Jewish heritage, Mathews posed a relationally focused set of questions: "We may not even know any Jews personally. But how many of us have never been guilty of a lack of friendship toward them at some time, or of slighting references to them in conversation? Have we ever attempted to understand them? Do we really regard them as children of the one Father of our worldwide human family?"[25]

The Baptists of the Union of Great Britain and Ireland, under the leadership of their general secretary, Melbourn Evans Aubrey,[26] were pondering the very same questions, in response to the rise of Adolf Hitler and the establishment of a Nazi government dedicated to fanning the flames of anti-Semitic prejudice in 1933.

NOTES

1. James H. Franklin, *In the Track of the Storm: A Report of a Visit to France and Belgium, with Observations regarding the Needs and Possibilities of Religious Reconstruction in the Regions Devastated by the World War* (Philadelphia: American Baptist Publication Society, 1919), foreword.

2. Franklin, 8.

3. Franklin, 25.

4. Franklin, 63.

5. Franklin, 102.

6. Ernest A. Payne, *James Henry Rushbrooke, 1870–1947: A Baptist Greatheart* (London: Kingsgate, 1954), 34–43; and Bernard Green, *Tomorrow's Man: A Biography of James Henry Rushbrooke* (London: Baptist Historical Society, 1996), 80–83.

7. Rev. Charles A. Brooks was the secretary of English-speaking Missions and Indian Work for the Northern Baptist Convention's American Baptist Home Mission Society. Green misidentified him as a representative of the Southern Baptist Convention's Foreign Mission Board; see Green, *Tomorrow's Man*, 68.

8. Green, 84.

9. "A Baptist Survey," *Birmingham Gazette*, July 20, 1920, 5.

10. Green, *Tomorrow's Man*, 27.

11. "Central Europe as It Is To-Day: Lecture by the Rev. J. H. Rushbrooke," *Hendon and Finchley Times*, November 19, 1920, 3.

12. Biography courtesy of Southern Baptist Historical Library and Archives, as found at the ABHS archive summary for Walter Oliver Lewis. See Walter O. Lewis Papers, RG1592 [Folder], American Baptist Historical Society, Atlanta, GA.

13. Payne, *James Henry Rushbrooke*, 44, who called Lewis "one of Rushbrooke's ablest and most devoted lieutenants."

14. Walter O. Lewis, "He Forgot Joseph," *Watchman-Examiner*, July 4, 1946, 702.

15. "Baptists and Russia—Dr. Rushbrooke's Appeal for Help," *Northampton Daily Echo*, June 8, 1922, 7.

16. "Baptists in Europe," *Kington Times*, June 10, 1922, 2.

17. "Religious Persecution in Russia," *Jewish Chronicle*, December 27, 1929, 22–23.

18. "Christianity and Communism—a Present Day Issue," *Portsmouth Evening News*, October 27, 1932, 3.

19. "Readers' Views—Despair Put Hitler in Power," *Derby Evening Telegraph*, May 27, 1942, 2.

20. "Hiking Towards World Peace—an Attempt at Promoting International Friendship," *Derby Evening Telegraph*, August 17, 1932, 4.

2. Andrea Strübind, "German Baptists and National Socialism," *Journal of European Baptist Studies* 8, no. 3 (May 2008), 8.

22. Basil Mathews, *The Jew and the World Ferment* (New York: Friendship, 1935), 9.

23. Mathews, 15, 25–27, 44–47.

24. Mathews, 152.

25. Mathews, 158.

26. Aubrey recommended Mathews' book in his column "Some Books," *Baptist Times*, November 22, 1934, 719–20: "Both for the story it gives of the Jews and their place in history, and also for the account of the present condition of Jewry, calling as it does for the sympathy and the thought of Christian people, I have found it of uncommon interest."

PART ONE

The Sympathy of the Baptists of Great Britain

CHAPTER 1

Leading the Protest

Facing the Nazi Flames of Persecution

Adolf Hitler was appointed to be the new chancellor of Germany on January 30, 1933.[1] Four days earlier, M. E. Aubrey surveyed the impressive social and political gains Jews had made in England and elsewhere: "The ghetto has disappeared in most countries. Jews are no longer segregated in quarters of great cities. They live side by side with Christians, serve in Legislatures and on public bodies, are accepted socially, and are admitted to our circles of friendship." Of course, Aubrey had no idea that Hitler would reverse all of these gains for Jews in Europe; instead, like Mathews, he imagined Jewish progress as an "opportunity" to share the Christian message with a remarkable people to whom Baptists owed a religious debt. Baptists should "promote friendships and open the way for the offering of the Christian Gospel."[2] Aubrey urged Baptist churches to consider creating "Friends of Israel" committees, sponsor "discussion groups on Judaism and Christianity," and offer "resistance to any anti-Jewish feeling in the neighbourhood."[3]

On March 30, 1933, both the *Watchman-Examiner* (the premier independent Baptist newspaper in the United States) and England's the *Baptist Times* published their first reports on the Nazis' persecution of the Jews. The latter's article summarized what many British Baptists felt throughout the 1930s:

> The accounts of the ill-treatment of Jews in Germany came as a shock to the world. . . . The persecution of the Jews is a recurrent blot upon the pages of history, but Germany has stepped back hundreds of years and has tarnished a glorious past.

2

Nothing but evil can come of the Hitlerite policy in stirring the passions of the people against the Jewish race. The consequences may be and ought to be very severe. It is no use talking of brotherhood while Jews are dragged through the streets, their property destroyed, their bodies maltreated, even when their lives are spared. The responsible authorities in Germany should put on sackcloth and ashes, and lament and seek forgiveness. We hope that the entire Christian Church will unite in protest against these outrages. The Jews have our sympathy. They have earned their right to be recognized as equals in the foremost nations of the earth.[4]

Following April's anti-Jewish boycotts in Germany, the *Baptist Times* lamented that "hundreds of thousands of Jews in Germany . . . have not only been deprived of their means of livelihood, but their passports are being taken from them, so that they cannot leave the country to make a living elsewhere."[5] In its next issue, the paper exposed the goal of the "anti-Semitic campaign" that was "ruthlessly and relentlessly being carried out against the Jewish" citizens: "Herr Hitler is well on the way to the achievement of his ideal of a purely Aryan State."[6] Rejecting assertions that reports of Nazi persecutions were exaggerated, it took a critical stance against Nazi anti-Semitism: "The inflammatory anti-Jewish speeches of Herr Hitler and his lieutenants have been well known for months. Now we have the legislation of the Hitlerite Government expressly designed to deprive Jews of their livelihood on no other ground than race. We repeat that Germany is incurring indelible shame."[7]

The Baptist Union of Great Britain was also upset about the plight of German Jews from the first outbreak of persecution. The issue of the "treatment of Jews in Germany" was brought to Aubrey's attention in early 1933.[8] The 1933 assembly in Glasgow, Scotland (meeting on May 2–4), unanimously approved a resolution on "Freedom of Conscience" that was moved by J. H. Rushbrooke, now the BWA's general secretary. The delegates voted to "deplore the action of Governments in denying freedom and the full rights of citizenship to well-disposed subjects on the grounds of race or of religious or political beliefs, and abhor all methods of repression and persecution."[9] A more explicit protest was approved by Northern Baptists in the United States at their convention at the end of May 1933. It deplored "outbreaks of race hatred and discrimination, as seen in our own country, and in the persecution of Jews in Germany."[10]

The Union's Council, dismayed by new manifestations of anti-Semitism, urged its membership "who work where there are many Jews to remember that they are of the race that gave us our Master and our Bible, and in love to serve them for His sake."[11] Rushbrooke acted in this spirit when he returned to his former congregation, Derby's St. Mary's Gate Baptist Church, for their 142nd-anniversary service on May 7, 1933. In his sermon, he dismissed German allegations that accounts of Jewish persecution were "merely anti-German propaganda." Having recently traveled to Germany, he confirmed that "the Jews in Germany were suffering peril, pain and death, and under the law no Jew could earn a decent income."[12] At the end of 1933, Union President R. Rowntree Clifford urged Baptists to give sacrificially toward assistance for Jewish and Jewish-Christian refugees "in this emergency, until schemes for permanent settlement elsewhere have been framed."[13]

Baptists across the country also responded, often within ecumenical and civic contexts. On May 10, 1933, more than five hundred people filled the Hendon town hall to protest attacks against German Jews. Rev. W. Rufus Jones, pastor of the Hendon Baptist Church, was among the leaders of the meeting. The audience unanimously voiced support for a resolution expressing "its abhorrence at the persecution and discrimination under which the Jews of Germany are suffering, and in the name of humanity appeals to the German Government to take such measures as will cause such persecution and discrimination to cease."[14] A similar meeting took place in Southport, outside of Liverpool. Non-Jewish clergy and civic leaders, including Rev. P. T. Thomson, pastor of Duke Street Baptist Church, denounced Germany's persecution of Jews before an interfaith audience. They passed a resolution virtually identical in language to the one passed in Hendon.[15] Aubrey also represented Baptists at public protests. On June 27, 1933, he joined other religious and political leaders for a major rally at Queen's Hall "to protest against the treatment of the Jews in Germany."[16]

Trading Fire with German Baptists

J. H. Rushbrooke opposed the initial waves of Nazi anti-Semitism while also supporting the German Baptist Union's intention to host the 1934 BWA World Congress in Berlin. In April 1933 he told the *Baptist Times* that "so far as his personal observation was concerned, public order in Germany appears now to be undisturbed." The *Baptist Times* was uncomfortable with this remark, adding that due to Nazi control of the press, "under such conditions it would be difficult for any visitor to form an impression of the state of the country as a whole. It is admitted even in the Government Press that regrettable incidents have taken place."[17] The editor denied it was publishing "atrocity propaganda" in their coverage of events in Germany. To the contrary, he said, "The inflammatory anti-Jewish speeches of Herr Hitler and his lieutenants have been well known for months. Now we have the legislation of the Hitlerite Government expressly designed to deprive Jews of their livelihood on no other ground than that of race."[18] Two weeks later the paper decried the German government's "instructions for the degradation of Jews to second-class citizens."[19]

The German Baptists traded fire with the *Baptist Times* in an effort to blunt its criticism of the Nazis. The German Baptist newspaper *Wahrheitszeuge* justified the Nazi campaign to unify "the entire nation on the basis of National Socialism" and brushed aside other issues as "mistakes" and "non-essentials." It made no mention of Jewish persecution and certainly offered Jews no sympathy. The *Baptist Times* shot back, "Our brethren are mistaken in their view that British judgment is based on mere incidents. . . . Anti-Semitism is fundamental to the Hitler policy; the uncompromising and violent language in which hate of the Jews has been preached by the Nazis for over ten years explains the outrages that have occurred. We condemn this hostility towards an entire race expressed not merely in deeds of violence but in the considered legislation and administration of the present German Government."[20]

British Baptists worried that the "Nazification of Protestantism" was not purely a matter of polity but also an expression of an anti-Semitic Nazi worldview. Not only were the Nazis guilty of "brutal anti-Semitism," but they intended to corrupt Protestants by setting "aside the canon of the Scriptures by excluding the Old

Testament. . . . The Nazi-controlled Church is to be strictly German—racial and militarist. Christianity is to be officially identified with doctrines of hate and violence."[21]

The *Baptist Times* tried to clarify its position by stating that it was "not concerned with particular cases of persecution of the Jews" but rather with the "whole trend of [Nazi] national policy."[22] Two weeks later the paper published a response by German Baptists from the pages of the *Wahrheitszeuge*. As would be the pattern throughout the Nazi era, German Baptists ignored the plight of the Jews and defended the Nazi regime's efforts to restore German national pride and power: "For we are German Baptists, and thanking God for it, we will be and remain so in the future."[23]

In rebuttal the *Baptist Times* asserted that a protest against Nazi anti-Semitism was not an expression of anti-German sentiment: "Our plea for justice for the German Jews does not mean that we are in favour of injustice to any other section of Germans. Our protest does not imply any anti-German spirit. We should have taken the same position had the treatment of the Jews been the work of any other country." The editorial also repudiated expressing exclusivist national pride in church life, asserting that "there is a nationalism which is a deadly enemy to Christianity." Based on Baptist historical core convictions, it concluded, "Our faith compels us to stand for freedom, not simply for the freedom for the Jew who is of German birth, but for the German who is not a Jew."[24]

Meanwhile, speaking before the Assembly of the German Baptist Union, Rushbrooke stressed Anglo-German Baptist solidarity and affirmed the "high spiritual level" of the proceedings. However, "references to the political changes in Germany were inevitable, and it was evident from first to last that the overwhelming majority of German Baptists' welcome the Nazi Government with the Chancellorship of Herr Hitler, chiefly on the ground that it has averted the peril of atheist-Communist domination."[25] While the *Baptist Times* noted the League of Nations' discussion on the emigration of Jewish refugees fleeing Hitler's persecution,[26] Rushbrooke praised German Baptists' relief efforts "for sufferers of their own race in the U.S.S.R."[27] He reported that during a visit to the United States, he sensed that the "American attitude, which a few months ago was strongly adverse to the Hitler regime, has become almost friendly. The anti-Semitic doctrine of the Nazis is still sternly condemned, but the action of Germany in leaving the Disarmament Conference and the League of Nations is regarded with approval rather than resentment."[28]

At the end of November 1933, Rushbrooke affirmed that Berlin would host the 1934 BWA Congress. Although "certain aspects of German policy" might "operate against a full attendance," the "claims of Christian fraternity" with German Baptists carried greater weight within the executive committee. Rejecting Berlin would "have the appearance of a definite slight to the German Baptists." Rushbrooke relegated the Nazi treatment of Jews to secondary status: "It was also felt to be unfitting that differing opinions concerning the policy of Governments should be allowed to check our expression of Christian unity through the Congress, or to interrupt a fraternal co-operation which has been maintained for so many years. At precisely such a time as this, the hand of fellowship should be firmly grasped." The oppression of German Jews could not compete with the "hopes and desires of the German brethren." He assured Baptists that they "would be welcomed by a Union of fellow-believers, which has an honourable past, and we trust, under the blessing of God, a great future."[29] This was precisely what German Baptists would say at the 1934 congress—with Adolf Hitler being the embodiment of God's blessing!

British Baptist Concerns

In January 1934 Rushbrooke went on the offensive with a full-page newspaper invitation to the congress. Berlin was "singularly appropriate" for an international meeting intended to demonstrate the unity of the Baptist witness to the world.[30] At the annual assembly of the National Free Church Council, Rushbrooke warned against the "giant evils" of the day, which included "the terrific forces of nationalism, and of racialism, the enslavement of man by man."[31] The *Baptist Times* took umbrage at the *Christian Century*'s criticism of Berlin as the venue. It declared, "Baptists do not play fast and loose with their fundamental principles. In accepting an invitation to Berlin or to any other city, Baptists are not likely to compromise the spirit of liberty which is their vital breath."[32]

Rushbrooke also penned a determined defense of Berlin as the congress's site. Although some Baptists had "expressed apprehension on the ground of the political situation," British Baptist attendance would buttress the witness of German Baptists. The alliance had negotiated with the Nazi government to ensure that there would be full freedom of discussion during the congress even though "such subjects as 'nationalism' and 'racialism' are in our programme." While silent about German Jews, Rushbrooke shared that German Baptists would not be in "peril" if they attended the congress in Berlin; he even worried about the repercussions they might face if the meeting was moved elsewhere! He argued that "democrats and internationalists" should travel to Germany to investigate for themselves how the Nazi revolution was impacting Germany to better understand their own countries' problems.[33]

Speaking at the Baptist Union's 1934 assembly in support of a resolution honoring the centenary of J. G. Oncken, the founder of the German Baptist movement, Rushbrooke bemoaned that "in Oncken's country to-day this is a testing time, a time of terrible trial, a time of challenge. I want to be able to tell our brethren there that the Baptists of the world are with them."[34] The assembly prayed that "the countrymen of Oncken may stand fast in the truth, the freedom, and the power of the Gospel, and in unswerving and undivided loyalty to the One Head of the Church."[35] However, that freedom had already been diminished: "The Young People's Union of the German Baptists was dissolved at the beginning of February. . . . The State now makes the demand to control the physical and political training of the young, and it is in deference to this demand that Baptist and other Free Churches have dissolved their young people's unions."[36]

Doubts continued to circulate about the ability of the congress to conduct a truly free conversation about Nazi persecution of the Jews and interference in church life. Echoing German Baptist talking points, Rushbrooke asserted that "in the main the items of the programme are not such as to raise any delicate questions. They are religious—dogmatic, devotional, missionary." So why was there a need to negotiate at all about the congress's discussions? The topical concerns of the congress had been set before Hitler rose to power. However, considering recent developments in Germany, it was now "desirable that the German Government should be fully informed." Rushbrooke admitted that "the findings of an international Baptist Commission might not accord with dominant German opinion," and thus the BWA needed reassurances from the German authorities that "liberty of speech" would be respected.[37]

The *Baptist Times* opposed "the Aryan race theory" that prevented Jewish believers from serving as pastors[38] and wrote approvingly of the powerful Barmen Confession.[39] Rushbrooke passed along reassurances from the German Baptists, who claimed "the conditions in our country are altogether quiet and orderly, so that there is absolutely no reason why the Congress should not take place."[40] Aubrey relayed concerns he heard in the United States regarding German Baptist responses to the Nazi campaigns against Jews and the Protestant churches: "There is a definite impression, right or wrong, in America that our German brethren have not allied themselves as definitely as they might have done with that section of German Protestants who have resisted the encroachment of the State on the province of the Church, and are in danger of missing one of the great historic opportunities of bearing witness to our Baptist Faith and Tradition."[41]

Just two days before the opening session of the Berlin congress, J. C. Carlile penned an editorial expressing his reservations about how German Baptists were responding to Nazism: "It is well known that a number of our people in Germany have not been very enthusiastic in their protests against the attempts to force all religious bodies into a Nazi Church. It is difficult to get accurate information, but there are doubts concerning the stability of our young people among the German Baptists." He prophetically asserted that "Baptists by conviction and tradition are opposed to the State control of religion. They stand for liberty and for the sacredness of personality. Their witness is worldwide and cannot be silenced by any nation, even though some adherents of the Baptist communion may waver in their allegiance and be attracted by the glamour of the religion of Nationalism."[42]

Carlile considered the congress to be "the acid test of modern Baptists." Baptist "silence" on the Nazi persecution of Jews would constitute "a betrayal of principle and lack of fidelity to those truths for which our sires did not hesitate to sacrifice their lives." He also feared that any protest might be interpreted as a "criticism of Herr Hitler and his Government," which "might result in disabilities, perhaps persecution, of the German Baptists." Not wishing to be accused of interfering in the internal affairs of another country, Carlile subverted his commitment to Baptist core convictions by writing that if German Baptists "prefer Adolf Hitler, it is not for us Baptists to object."[43] Carlile hoped that German Baptists would "realize that they do not stand alone but have the support of an international fellowship that knows no limitation of country, colour or race."[44]

The Berlin Congress from an English Perspective

The *Baptist Times* covered the Berlin congress in detail. The opening night's plenary speech by Canadian John McLaurin encouraged German Baptists to live up to Baptist core convictions, and as an olive branch of unity, extended "the fullest sympathy, help and partnership with our German brethren in their present trials, as they make their stand for our ancient truth that the Church of Christ shall be subject to the one Lord and not dominated by any earthly power, secular or ecclesiastical." He forthrightly addressed "the racial problem" facing the congress: "Racial animosities are sharper and more explosive to-day than ever in the immediate past, and in every land where our Churches are established they are called on to act as messengers of peace and goodwill, in the name of Him who broke down the middle wall of partition between East and West; brown, yellow, black and white."[45]

Commission reports on nationalism and racialism repudiated German Baptist positions and surely did not please the Nazi authorities. Sweden's N. J. Nordstrom echoed the Barmen Declaration's denial of the supremacy of the state over the church and applied it to Baptists: "Baptists confess Jesus Christ as their supreme authority in all religious and moral matters. Loyalty to Christ must precede every other loyalty. . . . The Church of Christ can never become an instrument for nationalistic aims and purposes without losing its power and failing in its mission to the world."[46]

England's C. E. Wilson presented the Racialism Commission's report, coyly denying that the proposed racialism resolution was "an attack against any persons or nations"—even though the anti-Semitic actions of the Nazis were clearly repudiated. Echoing Barmen, the report asserted that "a colour or racial bar to the worship and fellowship of the Church is a monstrous denial of the Lord—a violation of the very essence of His teaching." It addressed anti-Semitism as a sociopolitical phenomenon outside of the ecclesiastical sphere, a perspective lacking in the Barmen Confession. The report lamented "the long record of ill-usage of Jews on the part of professedly Christian nations" and considered "such injustice to be a violation of the teaching and the spirit of Christ."[47]

During the twelfth plenary session on August 10, Norwegian leader A. T. Ohrn formally moved that the resolution on racialism be adopted, and the motion was seconded by Wilson. Adopted unanimously, the racialism resolution's historic and courageous rejection of both anti-Semitism and other forms of racial prejudice was clear and prophetic:

> This Congress deplores and condemns, as a violation of the law of God the Heavenly Father, all racial animosity, and every form of oppression or unfair discrimination toward the Jews, toward coloured people, or toward subject races in any part of the world. This Congress urges the promotion of Christian teaching concerning respect for human personality regardless of race and as the surest means of advancing the true brotherhood of all people, urges the active propagation of the Gospel of Christ throughout the world.[48]

The racialism resolution was the first and only organizational protest by an international religious body ever made against Nazi anti-Semitism within Germany during the Third Reich. British newspapers across the nation covered the report's adoption and quoted the resolution's key provisions.[49] Rev. Charles Dyer, pastor of Hope Baptist Church in Plymouth, was an eyewitness to the historic proceedings. He was saddened by how "abjectly the State Church had submitted to Adolf Hitler" and was appalled by the "praise of Hitlerism" offered by "representatives of the Reich Bishop." Dyer praised Aubrey for proclaiming that God was neither German or English, and not "Aryan nor Semitic." He appreciated his fellow Englishman, Rev. Gilbert Laws, who rejected the Hitler salute by raising his arm at a higher angle to bring "greetings of the Baptists of Great Britain and Ireland to the Baptists of the world in the Name that is above every name." He approvingly quoted from the racialism report, including the sentence that deplored "the ill-usage of Jews."[50]

M. E. Aubrey found it "difficult" to "order his impressions" of the congress. His "misgivings" about Berlin as a venue were not fully allayed; despite freedom of speech within the congress halls, "it was too much to expect that the German Press should reproduce our resolutions on Church and State, on Race, on Nationalism, on Freedom, and on War." Aubrey praised German Baptist leader Simoleit as a "great Christian gentleman" and expressed the hope that under his continued leadership, German Baptists "will never, as a denomination, forsake any essential principle of our Baptist faith."[51] But in the same issue, the paper expressed astonishment over Simoleit's announcement that copies of the *Baptist Times* would not be sold in Germany because Carlile's August 2 column was deemed to be "offensive to the German people."[52]

Other British Baptists left the congress with varied impressions. Sheffield Baptist minister Rev. Joseph Robinson Renshaw watched Hitler process to the Reichstag during Hindenburg's memorial service, and said, "Whatever we [British] may think, there can be no doubt that the Germans are full of confidence in the Hitler regime, and are trusting him absolutely."[53] Rev. H. V. Little strongly believed that English and German delegates were overwhelmingly against war.[54] Harrogate's Rev. Reginald Kirby, though impressed by Germany's progress, nevertheless sensed "the absence of real freedom." "Alas," he said, "the German people are not free. Naziism makes that impossible, I am afraid."[55] An anonymous Baptist pastor was "terrified" by what he witnessed: "Hitlerism is a violation of the very laws of God."[56]

On the other hand, Rev. F. C. Spurr acknowledged the German perspective on "the delicate question of persecution, particularly that of the Jews." Spurr "heard a good deal about this Jewish question from Bavaria to the Rhineland, and if only half of it is true, then there is very distinctly another side to this question, of which our English newspapers have given us no account."[57] Rev. W. L. Cassie, pastor of the Castlegate Baptist Church, thought it was "a pity" that the English "do not hear more in our own country of the positive social and moral achievements of the Hitler regime."[58]

At its November 1934 meeting, the British Baptist Union's Council endorsed the key resolutions of the 1934 congress, including the one on racialism.[59] Over the next eight decades, the congress's racialism protest would become the BWA's most widely disseminated statement, and it has served as the precedent for many subsequent racism resolutions.

Baptist-Jewish Friendship

The British Jewish perspective on the BWA Congress was originally published in the *Jewish Chronicle*. While applauding the Baptist condemnation of anti-Semitism, it recognized that the Nazis permitted the congress to take place for their own political ends. Tourism income generated by the congress supported Germany's economy, and the German press was prohibited from reporting any news disapproved by the authorities. The newspaper approved of the racialism report but was uncertain about the German Baptist position regarding Jewish rights: "To no people, said the Report, was Christianity more indebted than to the Jews. Despite the presence at the Congress of German Baptists, who endeavoured to defend Nazi policy, the Reports on Nationalism and Racialism were unanimously adopted. Perhaps the manful reply of the General Secretary of the Baptist World Alliance, Dr. Rushbrooke, to whom the Jewish community already owes a debt of gratitude, went home."[60]

For Christmas 1934 the *Baptist Times* published a devotional that noted that the "problem of the personality of Jesus is renewed in every age." *Personality*, as a Baptist core conviction, served as a rebuke of Nazi totalitarianism and anti-Semitism. The devotional asserted, "Christianity has a Jewish background which cannot be left out of the picture."[61]

Covering the conflict between the German Christian and Confessional factions of the Evangelische Kirche in Deutschland (the German Lutheran Church), the *Baptist Times* sided with the latter, who opposed efforts to "abolish the Old Testament and to de-Christianise the New Testament." The paper quoted a critique of German Christian theology: "It makes a god out of race and blood, nationality, honour, and liberty. . . . Such idolatry is anti-Christ."[62]

Rushbrooke spoke on Nazi anti-Semitism at a London forum sponsored by the Society of Jews and Christians in London's Essex Hall on April 1, 1935. He "received an especially warm welcome" from the Jewish community, and "several of the speakers taking part in the discussion referred appreciatively to his speech at the Berlin World Congress and to the Congress resolution condemning anti-Semitism."[63] Rushbrooke confessed that Baptists were spiritually indebted to Jews and offered "the hand of sincere friendship" to the Jewish community on behalf of all Baptists:

> "When," said Mr. Rushbrooke, "as spokesman of my own communion at Berlin, I condemned in that city 'the placing of a stamp of inferiority upon an entire race,' it was not merely as a Baptist, but in the name of all instructed Christians that I spoke, and when our Congress passed its resolution—unanimously, in Berlin—deploring and condemning 'as a violation of God the Heavenly Father all racial animosity, and every form of oppression or unfair discrimination towards the Jews,' we expressed a judgment that, while we would apply it to men of every race, carries with it that special application a unique warmth of sympathy and a unique strength of just resentment, evoked by the knowledge of recent and continuing oppression and suffering. To my Jewish brothers and sisters under such conditions I extend the hand of sincere friendship."[64]

Rushbrooke's expression of friendship with the Jewish people was echoed by other English Baptists. Child's Hill Baptist Church in north London invited Rabbi I. Livingstone to speak about "The Position of the Jew in Germany" on Monday, October 12, 1936. The Baptist pastor, E. K. Alexander, welcomed the rabbi as a "friend" and assured him that "all who had gathered were with him and his race in the intolerable persecution which they were suffering in Germany, and he regretted to say even in this country. All recognised their indebtedness to the Jew and Judaism." The rabbi reported that "the Nazi leaders were simply obsessed with a fanatic anti-Semitism which caused them to make the Jew responsible in general for every misfortune which had ever happened or was ever likely to happen, and in particular, for all German troubles." Alexander responded by hoping that his members "would help all to a more practical sympathy not only with the Jewish race, but with all persecuted races in the world."[65]

Another fine "gesture to the Jews" was received by A. Newman, the rabbi of a synagogue in Leicester in December 1936. The local Baptist congregation sent a warm message—"the first of its kind in Leicester," that echoed some of Rushbrooke's sentiments:

In view of the pain given you by the crime of anti-Semitism in Germany and in this, our own country, we, the Christian community, worshipping the one God at Uppingham Road Baptist Church, Leicester, send greetings to our Jewish brethren in this city; and we would be happy to send our Minister to meet your Congregation to bear personally to you our sincere and grateful expression of our debt to Jews past and present, and of our fellowship with you in the one God and in our common humanity.[66]

Ongoing Persecution and Baptist Protests

While desiring the friendship of their Jewish neighbors, British Baptists did not wish to politically isolate Germany. In May 1935 the *Baptist Times* praised Hitler's foreign policy speech but also criticized the leader: "Hitler [regards] the Jews as Germany's misfortune and the pressure upon them is to be increased. All the friends of Germany regret the persecution of German Jews."[67]

British Baptist ambivalence toward developments in Germany was evident during the second International Old Testament Congress, which took place in Göttingen on September 4–10, 1935.[68] Six British Baptists were in attendance, including H. Wheeler Robinson, who spoke on the "Hebrew Conception of Corporate Personality."[69] The *Baptist Times* reported that "signs and noticeboards denouncing the Jews" could be seen, but he judged that "it would be wrong to suppose that the official attitude towards the Jews represents the attitude of Germans generally." However, the correspondent recounted a conversation with a Jewish jeweler who wistfully wished he could escape the persecution Jews were experiencing.[70] In the following issue, the newspaper sadly admitted, "Some strange infatuation seems to lure Herr Hitler to disaster. The increased persecution of the Jews is a scandal and disgrace to civilisation."[71]

Following the dramatic December 30, 1935, resignation of James G. McDonald, the high commissioner for refugees for the League of Nations, the *Baptist Times* highlighted the diplomat's frustration over "the Nazi persecution of Jews and persons who are supposed to be Jews and others who have anything to do with

Jews." The paper wondered how a "great and intelligent people" could harm "a race that has shown such brilliance of intellect and endurance of adversity."[72]

Henry Townsend, president of the Baptist Union, lodged a protest against Nazism on April 27, 1936. He accused European Protestants of failing to embrace the deep logic of the individualism and personality: "If Luther had worked out the implications of the priesthood of every believer, and pressed on to a German Free Church and a free democracy, he would almost certainly have changed the political history of Germany, and made impossible the Kaiserism of 1914 and the Nazi paganism of 1936." He derided Europe for its "rejection of what we call the Christian value of the individual." Communist and Nazi totalitarianism "rest on contempt for the value of the individual as taught by Jesus."[73]

John Charles Carlile, editor of the *Baptist Times*, declined an offer to submit an article to a German publication because of Germany's Jewish situation: "My view is that the treatment of the Jews and now the Catholics, by the authorities in the Germany I loved and honoured, is such an offence against humanity that it should be condemned in every possible way."[74] Carlile argued that a country that persecuted Jewish children in their own homeland was unqualified to have political control over other peoples. He declared, "Germany must answer the indictment of the moral sense of Europe concerning her treatment of Jewish children, part of her own population, and of the children of Christians, estimated at not less than half a million, who are said to be polluted by having had one or two ancestors who were non-Aryan."[75]

In September 1936 the *Baptist Times* observed, "Germany is still engaged in a desperate attempt to stamp out the Jewish element of her population. Children in secondary schools are submitted to a refinement of persecution."[76] In November Aubrey endorsed the efforts of the Save the Children Fund to relocate German Jewish children and encouraged churches to sponsor "Jewish and Christian" child refugees. He emphasized the persecution faced by Jewish school children: "Part of the school curriculum consists of anti-Semitic diatribes, and the child is compelled to listen to the grossest and most shameful accusations leveled against its Jewish forebears."[77] The struggles of Germany's Jews elicited Aubrey's sympathy, sorrow, and a desire to respond through deeds of mercy.

In contrast, Ernest A. Payne rationalized German Baptist "complacency and indifference" due to the youthfulness of the movement (even though it was a century old), and their desire to be accepted within German society: "The present régime, from whatever motives, has secured for our German friends greater freedom and, as they think, greater opportunity, than ever before."[78] Payne's defense of the German Baptists aroused protests, with one letter writer stating, "Baptists in the country and America are seriously exercised by the attitude of German Baptists towards the persecution of Evangelical Christians and of the Jews."[79] In rebuttal, Payne cautioned, "It is good for us to listen carefully to anything that Christian men from Germany have to say to us, and whether we accept their views or not, it is incumbent on us to believe in their sincerity."[80]

Rushbrooke had just such an opportunity in Germany in mid-summer 1937. However, he declared that during the discussions in Hamburg, Berlin, and Königsberg, "it was obviously out of the question that visitors from abroad should enter upon the discussion of acute controversial issues within the land, with many of which the German Government is closely concerned," and so he and his companions "limited ourselves to declarations of principle, including the historic Baptist claim of religious freedom, and refrained from entering upon details of the inner situation." In a letter intended for Hans Kerrl, the German minister of the Ministry of Ecclesiastical Affairs, Rushbrooke expressed the BWA's support for "liberty even for those not of our faith and order" and reaffirmed the 1934 BWA Congress resolution.[81]

Descending toward Doom

Kristallnacht was the nadir of 1938 for the German Jewish people, but even before that terrible night, European Jews faced prolonged persecution and terror. In its first issue of the new year, the *Baptist Times* highlighted the predicament of Romania's "unfortunate Jews [who] are to be cleared out of their jobs in industrial, journalistic and professional life. They are, in fact, being given notice to quit the country."[82]

Following the March 1938 *Anschluss* (annexation) of Austria, the Cricklewood Baptist Church in north London informed the rabbi of the Cricklewood Synagogue that the church needed to "do something to show their sympathy with the Jews in their persecutions." The church hosted a "service of intercession" on April 20 and invited the rabbi to speak before an audience of both Jews and Christians. At the conclusion of the service, an offering was taken that raised over £6 (approximately $95 today), before which the Baptist pastor Rev. R. W. Hobling "asked specifically that Jews should refrain from contributing as they had no doubt already done their duty."[83]

The Baptist Union passed a clear resolution about German Jews at its 1938 assembly. Moved by Aubrey, it read in part, "Especially do we regret and condemn the persecution to which the Jewish race and descendants of the Jewish people are being exposed in Germany and some other lands in Europe, in view of which we ask His Majesty's Government to consider measures for alleviating their sufferings and for promoting that international action which alone can meet so difficult a problem."[84]

Aubrey continued to advocate for German Jewish (and Jewish-Christian) refugee children. He lamented that "while Jews in this and other countries have done wonderful things in helping their co-religionists, and even Jewish Christians (many of whom, I am told, turning back to Judaism as a result), relatively few Christians appear to have any sense of responsibility for those of their own faith who, at great cost to themselves, have suffered for their convictions and are now suffering for their race."[85]

Aubrey sought to mobilize Baptist support for an ecumenical day of prayer on July 17 for those persecuted for "the faith and race of their fathers." He admonished his readers not to forget the "Jews, whose welfare and lives are imperilled [sic], usually through no fault of their own except that they belong to their great race and cling to their ancient creed."[86] Aubrey signed a letter supporting the prayer event, which promoted intercession for "Jews, who as Jews are outlawed and treated with brutality; Jewish (i.e.—'non-Aryan') Christians, equally the victims of this racial hatred and Christians under Nazi attack," in support of "the ending of the oppression of the Jews and the full recognition of spiritual liberty."[87] Although it is not possible to know how many Baptist congregations participated, the *Boston Guardian* reported that Rev. A. M. Bignell offered "special prayers for the Jews in Central Europe" at the Sunday service of the Baptist church in Sutterton.[88]

The appeal was timely, for the same issue of the *Baptist Times* quoted England's chief rabbi, who declared that "anti-Semitism is sweeping all over the globe and . . . the door of nearly every country is barred and bolted against them. . . . In Germany, anti-Semitism is part of the new Nazi religion."[89] Aubrey devoted his next column to this issue: "In Germany both Jews and Christians are being cruelly harassed. . . . The same State of things obtains in Austria where the number of Jews is 200,000. We hear pitiful stories of their treatment and plight. . . . When we are told of such things we British Baptists, whose forbears fought for the emancipation of the Jews in this land, feel our blood boil."[90]

Columnist Arthur Porritt focused his anger on the failure of the Evian Conference, where country after country "expressed their sympathy with the half-million persecuted Jews in Germany and Austria, but nearly all have pleaded the inability of their nations to do anything effectual for their relief." Exasperated, he concluded, "If nothing can be done for these sadly unfortunate Jews and non-Aryan Christians who are the victims of racial hate, civilisation confesses its bankruptcy."[91]

Curiously, Aubrey offered a more positive interpretation of the unfruitful negotiations. Even more surprising was Aubrey's comparison of Jews in Palestine and Nazism. While making clear that there was "no defence of German action" against the Jews, he observed, "The religion of 'race and soil' which Hitler is inculcating in Germany is borrowed from the Jews who always insisted on purity of race—the Chosen People—and their right to Palestine—the Promised Land. It is sheer irony that, while protesting against these ideas in Germany, they are expressing them in Palestine by hurling bombs into the midst of Arabs."[92]

In the autumn of 1938, Chamberlain's appeasement initiative and the Munich agreement received considerable attention from English Baptists. Carlile applauded the prime minister for adopting the Christian ethic of "going the second mile."[93] Porritt repeated Mussolini's characterization of Chamberlain, "a flying messenger of peace."[94] Aubrey praised Chamberlain for "giving to the world an example of restraint and readiness to take risks to avoid war."[95]

However, not all the news emanating out of the Continent was encouraging. Returning from a trip to Germany, Rev. Charles Dyer came away from a conversation with a teenage Jewish boy thinking,

"It was a sad thing to be a Jew in Germany today and even worse in Austria."[96] Porritt wrote about Jewish suffering in Fascist Italy— a first for the *Baptist Times*. He asserted that "all post-War migrant Jews are to be expelled from Italy within the next six months. Moreover, Jews, native or immigrant, are not to be allowed to hold posts in educational institutions under Government control after October 16." He sadly surmised that "Italy is shedding the last vestiges of her former Liberalism, for Jews were emancipated when Italy attained her freedom and unification."[97] Porritt referred to conquered Czechoslovakia as a "martyr nation."[98] Aubrey made an appeal for the Thanksgiving Fund to assist "Christians of Jewish blood who have been expelled or have escaped from Germany and Austria and now Czechoslovakia."[99]

On November 3 the *Baptist Times* reported that in Frankfurt, Jewish deportees were only "permitted to take what they can carry." The article contended that considering "the most diabolical persecution" in Germany, "it would be far more humane to shoot or to poison all of the Hebrew stock."[100]

The Fires of Kristallnacht

The fires of Kristallnacht erupted on the evening of November 9, 1938, and continued throughout the next morning. Hundreds of Jewish synagogues, homes, and cemeteries were destroyed, thousands of Jewish-owned establishments were attacked, and Jews were both arrested and killed. The entire world responded with protests, and the Baptist Union participated in that wave of outrage.

The British Baptist Union's Council met on November 15–16, 1938, just one week after Kristallnacht. The council's immediate and forthright response to the German situation predated the Northern Baptist resolution by two full weeks and the statement by the National Baptist Convention, U.S.A., by some three weeks. These American declarations no doubt were influenced by the British protest, which stated that the members of the council

> deeply deplore and condemn the harsh and vindictive measures, unworthy of a strong nation, which have been taken against Jews in Germany, and express their concern that this may seriously prejudice the prospect of improved relations between

our two countries. In declaring their sympathy with the Jewish people in their sufferings they respectfully ask the Prime Minister to represent to the German Fuehrer and Chancellor the disappointment and distress caused to the people of this country by recent happenings, and to request the parties to the Munich agreement to consult together, and with other Powers, before further divergencies of sympathies and hopes manifest themselves, in order that the work of appeasement which was then begun may be carried forward.[101]

The *Baptist Times* expressed amazement that a country as cultured as Germany could indulge in such barbarity; the "news from Germany filled all Europe with sorrow and indignation" because "racial hatred and hysteria seemed to have taken complete hold of otherwise decent people." Coming so soon after Munich, the publication admitted, "The strongest argument against concessions to Germany will be her inhuman persecution of Jews and religious minorities."[102]

Aubrey's November 17 column was almost entirely devoted to Kristallnacht. He noted that "we all have been moved to indignation by the suffering inflicted on the Jews in Germany." On behalf of Baptists, he said, "Our sympathy and desire to help go out to the Jewish people" and he called for donations for refugee resettlement. He expressed confidence that "the race that has outlived so many Empires that have persecuted it will outlive Nazi-ism [*sic*]." Nevertheless, he also hinted that he was troubled by the renewed determination of Germany to "make things worse for those we seek to help."[103]

Arthur Porritt had the last word on Kristallnacht in the November 17 issue, declaring, "The inhuman decrees against Jews announced on Saturday give one the impression that the Nazi leaders are despising the shame and even glorying in the disrepute Germany has brought upon herself. These anti-Jew barbarities are, after all, the natural outcome of the rancorous racialism instilled into Germans by Herr Hitler."[104]

The following week, Porritt approvingly cited global protests against Germany and encouraged churches to take offerings for suffering Jews. He also noted that "money will not solve the German-Jew problem" and explored the issue of resettlement possibilities for Jewish refugees. Sadly, he observed, "World condemnation is not apparently causing the Nazi Government any misgivings. In defiance of the outraged conscience of the world, the despoiling of Jews continues, and new harsh enactments against them are being put into operation."[105] He asserted that "at least 50,000" Jewish children "must be brought out of Germany at once."[106]

Kristallnacht represented an implicit critique of the efficacy of British Baptist protests (in the form of resolutions, expression of concerns, dialogues, and debates) against Nazi totalitarianism, interference with religious organizations, and the persecution of its Jewish citizens. Despite all the published articles, pious pronouncements, and expressions of sympathy for the Jewish people, Nazi anti-Semitism and its acts of oppression grew unabated between 1933 and 1938. The inability of the world to execute an adequate response to Kristallnacht served as a call to action for the Baptist Union in Great Britain. Refugee children, including Jews, would be the main beneficiaries.

NOTES

1. An earlier version of the rest of this chapter was published as Lee B. Spitzer, "The British Baptist Union and the Nazi Persecution of the Jews, 1933–1938," in John H. Y. Briggs and Paul S. Fiddes, eds., *Peoples of God: Baptists and Jews over Four Centuries* (Oxford: Centre for Baptist Studies, 2019). Permission to reuse this material was granted by coeditor Paul S. Fiddes.

2. M. E. Aubrey, "Our Jewish Neighbours," *Baptist Times*, January 26, 1933, 59.

3. M. E. Aubrey, "God's Chosen Race," *Baptist Times*, February 2, 1933, 75.

4. "Germany's Disgrace," *Baptist Times*, March 30, 1933, 205. Also quoted in Keith W. Clements, *Baptists in the Twentieth Century: Papers Presented at a Summer School July 1982* (London: Baptist Historical Society, 1983), 97. For a comprehensive overview of the *Watchman-Examiner's* coverage on Hitler, Nazism, anti-Semitism, and the Holocaust, see Lee B. Spitzer, *Baptists, Jews, and the Holocaust: The Hand of Sincere Friendship* (Valley Forge, PA: Judson, 2017), 87–113.

5. "Jews in Germany," *Baptist Times*, April 6, 1933, 223.

6. "The Jews in Germany," *Baptist Times*, April 13, 1933, 243.

7. "Conditions in Germany," *Baptist Times*, April 20, 1933, 258.

8. M. E. Aubrey, "Peace and Other Problems," *Baptist Times*, March 23, 1933, 187. Two previous assessments of Aubrey's leadership, Ernest A. Payne, "The Baptist Union 1897–1947," *Baptist Quarterly* 12, no. 8 (October 1947): 267–74; and Michael Goodman "A Faded Heritage—English Baptist Political Thinking in the 1930s," *Baptist Quarterly* 37, no. 2 (April 1997): 58–70, do not cover his attitudes and activities related to the Jewish people, anti-Semitism, or Nazism.

9. *The Baptist Handbook for 1934* [covering 1933] (London: Baptist Union Publication Department, 1934), Public Resolutions—Freedom of Conscience, 195.

10. *Annual of the 1933 Northern Baptist Convention*, Minutes Item 223, Resolution VII—"Race Relations," 238–39.

11. Baptist Union Council, "Approach to the Jews," *Baptist Times*, April 26, 1934, 303.

12. "Pastor Returns to Derby for Church's 142nd Anniversary: Dr. J. H. Rushbrooke on Jewish Persecution," *Derby Evening Telegraph*, May 8, 1933, 6.

13. "Christmas and German Refugees," *Baptist Times*, December 21, 1933, 890. The campaign was successful; see "German Refugees," *Baptist Times*, February 8, 1934, 93.

14. "Hendon—Jews Persecuted: Town Hall Demonstration of All Sections against German Oppression," *Hendon and Finchley Times and Guardian*, May 12, 1933, 20.

15. "Southport Sympathy for German Jews: Mass Call for Action," *Lancashire Evening Post*, May 19, 1933, 4.

16. "A Nazi State," *Baptist Times*, June 29, 1933, 439; "The Nazi Persecution," *Baptist Times*, July 6, 1933, 453. On the participation of Conservative Party members in this rally, see Harry Defries, *Conservative Party Attitudes to Jews 1900–1950* (London: Frank Cass, 2001), 119–20.

17. "Dr. Rushbrooke's Visit to Germany," *Baptist Times*, April 20, 1933, 259.

18. "Conditions in Germany," 258.

19. "The Persecution of the Jews in Germany," *Baptist Times*, May 4, 1933, 298.

20. "German Baptists and 'The Baptist Times,'" *Baptist Times*, May 18, 1933, 345. The newspaper reviewed *Mein Kampf* in "Hitler's Creed," *Baptist Times*, August 3, 1933, 523.

21. "Nazi Christianity," *Baptist Times*, June 29, 1933, 434; see also "Hitler and the Church," *Baptist Times*, July 6, 1933, 453.

22. "German Baptists," *Baptist Times*, August 17, 1933, 533.

23. "German Baptists and 'The Baptist Times,'" *Baptist Times*, August 31, 1933, 589.

24. "German Baptists and Ourselves," *Baptist Times*, August 31, 1933, 589; see also "The Jews," *Baptist Times*, September 7, 1933, 607.

25. "The German Baptist Meetings," *Baptist Times*, September 7, 1933, 598.

26. "Jewish Refugees in England," *Baptist Times*, October 5, 1933, 667; see Gwilym Davies, "The Jews at Geneva," *Baptist Times*, October 12, 1933, 693; and "The League of Nations," *Baptist Times*, October 19, 1933, 707.

27. "German Baptists Helping," *Baptist Times*, October 12, 1933, 688.

28. "Dr. Rushbrooke in America," *Baptist Times*, November 16, 1933, 777.

29. J. H. Rushbrooke, "Fifth World Congress," *Baptist Times*, November 30, 1933, 819.

30. J. H. Rushbrooke, "What the Baptist World Congress Does and Means," *Baptist Times*, January 11, 1934, 31.

31. J. H. Rushbrooke, "National Council of Evangelical Free Churches—Presidential Address," *Baptist Times*, March 15, 1934, 181.

32. "What Is the Matter with 'The Christian Century'?", *Baptist Times*, April 19, 1934, 277.

33. J. H. Rushbrooke, "Baptist World Congress Meeting in Europe," *Baptist Times*, April 5, 1934, 243.

34. "J. G. Oncken," *Baptist Times*, April 26, 1934, 298.

35. *The Baptist Handbook for 1935* [covering 1934] (London: Baptist Union Publication Department, 1935), Special Resolution on the "Centenary of the Formation of the First Baptist Church at Hamburg under the Rev. J. G. Oncken," 188; "Resolutions Passed at the Assembly—Johann Gerhard Oncken," *Baptist Times*, May 17, 1934, 362.

36. "Christian Youth Organizations in Germany," *Baptist Times*, April 19, 1934, 279.

37. "The World Congress," *Baptist Times*, May 31, 1934, 394.

38. "Canterbury and Berlin," *Baptist Times*, June 14, 1934, 431.

39. "The Barmen Confession," *Baptist Times*, June 14, 1934, 431.

40. "Berlin Baptist Congress," *Baptist Times*, July 12, 1934, 501.

41. M. E. Aubrey, "In America—Berlin 1934," *Baptist Times*, July 12, 1934, 499.

42. J. C. Carlile, "The Dilemma of Berlin," *Baptist Times*, August 2, 1934, 545.

43. Carlile, 545.

44. Carlile, 546.

45. "Baptists in Berlin," *Baptist Times*, August 9, 1934, 566.

46. Marguerite Williams, "Baptist Parliament of Nations. Berlin Congress," *Baptist Times*, August 16, 1934, 582.

47. Address by C. E. Wilson on "Racialism," in *Fifth Baptist World Congress: Berlin, August 4–10, 1934*, ed. J. H. Rushbrooke (London: Baptist World Alliance, 1934), 65–67. For a comparison between the Barmen Confession and the 1934 BWA Resolution on Racialism, see Lee B. Spitzer, "Baptists, Barth, and the Crisis of Conscience Initiated by the Emergence of Nazi Anti-Semitism," *American Baptist Quarterly* 34, nos. 3–4 (Fall and Winter 2015; actually published April 2017), 343–62.

48. BWA World Congress Resolution 1934.7 "Racialism," in *Fifth Baptist World Congress*, ed. Rushbrooke, 17. See also "Baptist World Congress Resolutions: Racialism," *Baptist Times*, December 20, 1934, 934.

49. See "Baptists in Berlin Denounce Ill-Usage of Jews by Christian Nations," *Nottingham Journal*, August 9, 1934, 1; "Baptist Congress Deplores Ill-Usage of Jews," *Sheffield Daily Independent*, August 9, 1934, 1; "Baptists Condemn War on Jews," *Leeds Mercury*, August 11, 1934, 3; "Baptists Condemn Anti-Semitism," *Belfast News-Letter*, August 11, 1934, 8.

50. Charles Dyer, "With Baptists in Berlin—Facing Facts and Hitlerism," *Western Morning News and Daily Gazette*, August 10, 1934, 3; see also his second article, "Church Unity in Germany," *Western Morning News and Daily Gazette*, August 13, 1934, 2.

51. M. E. Aubrey, "Berlin, 1934: Some Impressions," *Baptist Times*, August 16, 1934, 579.

52. "'The Baptist Times' Banned in Berlin," *Baptist Times*, August 16, 1934, 583; see also "Freedom of the Press in Germany," *Baptist Times*, August 23, 1934, 600; "Liberty of the Press in Germany," *Baptist Times*, August 30, 1934, 613; and "The 'Times' Banned in Germany," *Baptist Times*, August 30, 1934, 615.

53. "Saw Hitler—Sheffield Minister's German Visit," *Daily Independent*, August 14, 1934, 7.

54. H. V. Little, "No War before a Plebiscite Has Been Taken—World Baptists Cheer Speech in Berlin," *Western Daily Press and Bristol Mirror*, August 15, 1934, 5.

55. "Germany under Hitler's Rule—Harrogate Minister's Impressions of Visit to Berlin," *Yorkshire Evening Post*, August 16, 1934, 9.

56. Hannen Swaffer, "Baptists—& Hitler," *Daily Herald*, August 17, 1934, 12.

57. Frederic C. Spurr, "In a Small German Town," *Baptist Times*, August 23, 1934, 598.

58. "Impressions of Germany," *Berwick Advertiser*, September 6, 1934, 3.

59. "The Baptist Parliament," *Baptist Times*, November 29, 1934, 864.

60. "The Baptists in Berlin" and "Anti-Semitism Strongly Condemned," *Jewish Chronicle*, August 17, 1934, 8; cited in "A Jewish View of the Berlin Congress," *Baptist Times*, September 20, 1934, 662.

61. "The Problem of Bethlehem," *Baptist Times*, December 20, 1934, 933. For contemporary treatments of *personality*, see F. Townley Lord, "Some Modern Views of the Soul," *Baptist Quarterly* 5, no. 2 (1930): 66–73; and "The Achievement of Personality in a Material World," *Baptist Quarterly* 8, no. 5 (1937): 227–35; as well as Arthur Temple Cadoux, *A New Orthodoxy of Jesus and Personality* (London: Ivor Nicholson and Watson, 1934); and "W. W. B. Emery, "Freedom and the Free Churches," *Baptist Times*, May 16, 1935, 379.

62. "Dr. Karl Barth's Future," *Baptist Times*, March 14, 1935, 209.

63. "Jews and Christians," *Baptist Times*, April 4, 1935, 257.

64. "The Evils of Arrogant Nationalism," *Jewish Chronicle*, April 4, 1935, 30. Rushbrooke recommended that all Baptists study the resolutions in "Think Internationally," *Baptist Times*, April 11, 1935, 279.

65. "The Jew in Germany," *Times and Guardian*, October 16, 1936, 9.

66. "Baptists' Friendly Gesture," *Jewish Chronicle*, December 11, 1936, 18.

67. "Herr Hitler's Speech," *Baptist Times*, May 30, 1935, 411; "Jews in Germany," *Baptist Times*, August 15, 1935, 601.

68. See Norman Porteous, ed., *Second International Congress of Old Testament Scholars at Göttingen, September 4–10* (London: T&T Clark, 1935). The congress took place in a context of Nazi anti-Semitism, which impacted the proceedings; see Karl Loning and Erich Zenger, *To Begin With, God Created: Biblical Theologies of Creation* (Collegeville, MN: Liturgical Press, 2000), 3.

69. Walther Zimmerli, *Old Testament Theology in Outline* (Louisville, KY: John Knox, 1978), 227; see H. Wheeler Robinson, *Corporate Personality in Ancient Israel* (Philadelphia: Fortress, 1973, rev. ed. 1980).

70. "Two Generations in Germany," *Baptist Times*, September 26, 1935, 698.

71. "The Cloud over Germany," *Baptist Times*, October 3, 1935, 713.

72. "German Jews," *Baptist Times*, January 9, 1936, 27.

73. Henry Townsend, "Religion, Revolution and Democracy," *Baptist Times*, April 30, 1936, 335.

74. "Dr. Carlile and the Jews," *Baptist Times*, February 20, 1936, 136.

75. J. C. Carlile, "Germany and Mandates," *Baptist Times*, August 8, 1936, 609.

76. "Is the World Going Mad?" *Baptist Times*, September 10, 1936, 681.

77. M. E. Aubrey, "The Plight of Children in Germany," *Baptist Times*, November 12, 1936, 859.

78. Ernest A. Payne, "The German Church Conflict," *Baptist Times*, July 29, 1937, 568.

79. E. Amos, "Baptists and Germany," third letter, *Baptist Times*, August 5, 1937, 584.

80. Ernest A. Payne, "Baptists and Germany," *Baptist Times*, August 12, 1937, 600.

81. J. H. Rushbrooke, "With the German Baptists," *Baptist Times*, August 5, 1937, 589.

82. Arthur Porritt, "The Unfortunate Jews," *Baptist Times*, January 6, 1938, 7. For Rushbrooke's concern for Baptists, see "Rumania: The Baptist Position," *Baptist Times*, January 6, 1938, 14. For a Jewish perspective on Rumania, see "The Position of the Jews," *Yorkshire Post*, February 7, 1938, 5.

83. "Baptists' Sympathy with Jews," *Jewish Chronicle*, April 29, 1938, 17.

84. *The Baptist Handbook for 1939* [covering 1938] (London: Baptist Union Publication Department, 1939), Public Resolutions—Religious Liberty, 214–15.

85. M. E. Aubrey, "Non-Aryan German Children," *Baptist Times*, May 19, 1938, 383.

86. M. E. Aubrey, "Religious Persecution," *Baptist Times*, July 7, 1938, 522–23.

87. "Religious Persecution," 524.

88. "Sutterton," *Boston Guardian*, July 20, 1938, 13.

89. Arthur Porritt, "A Wave of Anti-Semitism," *Baptist Times*, July 7, 1938, 527.

90. M. E. Aubrey, "Germany," *Baptist Times*, July 14, 1938, 543.

91. Arthur Porritt, "Civilisation on Trial at Evian," *Baptist Times*, July 14, 1938, 547.

92. M. E. Aubrey, "The Evian Conference," *Baptist Times*, July 21, 1938, 563.

93. J. C. Carlile, "The Politics of the Second Mile," *Baptist Times*, September 22, 1938, 714.

94. Arthur Porritt, "Popular at Last," *Baptist Times*, September 22, 1938, 719.

95. M. E. Aubrey, "The International Situation," *Baptist Times*, September 29, 1938, 731.

96. "Victims of Militarism—Visit Impressions of Plymouth Minister," *Western Morning News and Daily Gazette*, September 27, 1938, 5.

97. Arthur Porritt, "Italy and the Jews," *Baptist Times*, September 8, 1938, 687.

98. Arthur Porritt, "Our Debt to the Czechs," *Baptist Times*, October 6, 1938, 751; see also Porritt's "After Munich," *Baptist Times*, October 20, 1938, 787.

99. M. E. Aubrey, "Non-Aryan Refugees," *Baptist Times*, October 13, 1938, 763. The appeal was apparently somewhat successful; see M. E. Aubrey, "Relief Funds," *Baptist Times*, October 27, 1938, 803.

100. "The Curse Never Came upon Israel Before," *Baptist Times*, November 3, 1938, 826.

101. *Minute Book of the Council of the Baptist Union of Great Britain and Ireland, April 1938–March 1939*, November 15–16, 1938, Meeting, Agenda Item XVI, "The International Situation and the Prime Minister's Action in the Cause of Peace," 490–92. The resolution was published in "The International Situation: Resolution Passed by the Council of the Union," *Baptist Times*, November 17, 1938, 864. For the texts and background stories of the Northern Baptist and National Baptist statements, see Spitzer, *Baptists, Jews, and the Holocaust*, 148–51 and 358–59. The Southern Baptist Convention did not publish a specific response to Kristallnacht.

102. "What Has Happened to Germany?", *Baptist Times*, November 17, 1938, 862.

103. M. E. Aubrey, "The Plight of the Jews," "The Undying Jew," and "A Meeting of Protest," *Baptist Times*, November 17, 1938, 863.

104. Arthur Porritt, "Like Pages Out of 'Jew Suss,'" *Baptist Times*, November 17, 1938, 867.

105. Arthur Porritt, "A World Aghast" and "Half-a-Million Homeless Jews," *Baptist Times*, November 24, 1938), 887.

106. Arthur Porritt, "Save the Jewish Children," *Baptist Times*, December 1, 1938, 907.

CHAPTER 2

The Arrival of Jewish Refugees

Welcoming Jewish Refugees—Stories of Benevolence, Generosity, and Shame

Within days of Hitler's ascension to power in 1933, British Jewish community leaders were aware of the plight of German Jews. During the Nazi era, about 120,000 Jewish refugees relocated permanently to the British Isles.[1] Jewish business owners organized fundraising campaigns to support German Jews who desired to immigrate to Great Britain and other destinations. The British government did not wish to be financially responsible for Jewish refugees, and the Jewish leadership agreed to an unprecedented commitment to "undertake a financial commitment to support Jews whose numbers, financial means or length of stay could not be predicted with any degree of accuracy."[2]

During the slow build-up to full genocide (1933–38), the Nazis systematically restricted Jewish participation in German society, stripping Jews of civil rights, citizenship, and the ability to hold jobs. Not knowing the future, many German Jews sought to remain in the country and to accommodate themselves to these anti-Semitic measures. For its part, the Anglo-Jewish community continued to raise extraordinary sums to meet the needs of Jewish refugees, while its "welfare and immigration services functioned almost routinely until November 1938."[3] Kristallnacht changed everything, reigniting the sense of crisis in a dramatic way.

In a front-page editorial on Kristallnacht on December 15, 1938, J. C. Carlile condemned Germany's "well authenticated instances of appalling cruelty on the part of official German representatives in their treatment of little children. . . . The conscience of the world has been shocked by the treatment of Jews in Germany." He quoted a British military officer who described specific atrocities, including: "concentration camps" where "words cannot describe the conditions. It is the Egyptian bondage over again." Carlile declared, "It is impossible for a nation to act as Germany is acting toward the children of the Jews and to be received on equal terms by other nations. Terror reigns wherever Hitler rules." He concluded by soliciting a Christmastime "freewill offering" from the country's Baptist churches, noting that even "a £5 note would save the life of a child," and announced that the newspaper would launch the campaign by donating £100. "For the sake of Mary's Child, let us help the children of Mary's race."[4]

M. E. Aubrey also considered the meaning of Christmas in light of the post-Kristallnacht struggles of German Jews. He thanked God that war had been averted, and he surmised that "even while our thoughts go out in sympathy to suffering Czechs and Jews we realise that, if the war with which we were threatened had come, their plight would have been immeasurably more bitter." More helpfully, Aubrey dedicated the annual "Crown Fund" offering to "those Jewish refugees, especially Christians of Jewish blood, whose dark sorrows do not yet even seem to have touched the minds of Christian men as did the tragedy of the dispossessed Czechs." He promised to personally donate 20 crowns and hoped to raise £5,000 by New Year's Day 1939.[5]

"The Jews: What Can We Do?"

J. H. Rushbrooke found himself in a very awkward position following Kristallnacht. While the Baptist Union condemned the travesty, the BWA merely recited the 1934 resolution, refraining from committing itself to "any specific course of action on behalf of Jews."[6] On February 2, 1939, he published in the *Baptist Times* a comprehensive response to the Jewish situation in "The Jews: What Can We Do?" Admitting, "The tragic situation of the Jews . . . is literally appalling," he asserted, "Private benevolence cannot cope" with the pressing needs of persecuted Jews, considering the sheer numbers of potential refugees involved:

Germany is making life intolerable for over half a million persons. Italy has followed her example, though the number of Jews in that country is small. Already there are indications that Czechoslovakia will be forced to follow the German lead. Hungary is almost certain to do the same. Rumania has made beginnings—at present comparatively mild—with anti-Semitic legislation. The most serious possibility of all is that Poland, with three-and-a-half million Jews, will follow the German precedent.[7]

Rushbrooke brushed aside criticism that the BWA had not spoken loudly enough, claiming, "In the face of an immense catastrophe, mere denunciation is vain." This brought the author to the article's key question: "What can we do?" Rushbrooke advocated that Baptists focus on assisting Jewish-Christians (non-Aryans), and even more specifically, Baptists from a Jewish background: "Among these Jewish Christians are many Baptists, and it would seem right and natural that we should acknowledge an exceptional responsibility for helping these."[8]

Rushbrooke personally made several attempts to facilitate immigration applications of Jewish Baptists. His responses to cases of need were predicated on the specific circumstances of each person's journey. In December 1938 Rushbrooke agreed to provide a personal "guarantee" for a special couple's financial "maintenance" during their interim stay prior to their ultimate emigration to the United States. Rushbrooke identified Dr. Walter Eisen as a forty-two-year-old "Jew by race . . . imprisoned in a concentration camp as a non-Aryan, and only on condition of his leaving the country can his release be obtained." His wife, who also possessed her doctorate, was willing to accept domestic work.[9] That same month Rushbrooke received a request from German Baptist leader Paul Schmidt on behalf of a "non-Aryan" woman. The woman's pastor provided an ambivalent recommendation, causing Rushbrooke to exclaim that he was unable to help because "thousands of refugees" were seeking entry and the government was "examining the cases with utmost care."[10]

Most sadly, it appears that Rushbrooke, whose wife's family lived in Germany, was also powerless to save members of his own extended family. In a brief letter to W. O. Lewis dated March 20,

1939, he confided that he had "learned today by telephone that Mrs. Rushbrooke's sister has just died. We think the end has been hastened by her distress that her daughter, married to a Jew, is under orders to leave the country immediately."[11] There is no update on the fate of Mrs. Rushbrooke's niece or her Jewish husband in Rushbrooke's archived correspondence.

How then should Baptists serve immigrant Jews? Rushbrooke suggested several options—hosting children, hiring women for domestic work, or providing housing for married couples and helping them find employment. He encouraged individuals to contact the Baptist Union or the BWA for referrals to other organizations "that are dealing with the refugee problem."[12] Rushbrooke referred many of the refugee cases that came to his attention.[13] Southern Baptist missionary D. G. Whittinghill wrote Rushbrooke requesting help for a "Jewish friend in Rome [who] has recently lost his position in one of the Banks." He even had a cousin in London—a potential sponsor.[14] Rushbrooke responded, "The difficulty is that this sort of application comes in every day, and many of the cases are extremely painful. There are organizations for dealing with them, and I am quite ready to use any personal influence I can. But we have a problem flung upon us by recent continental legislation and administration that is already straining our resources and will strain them to the utmost. Pray count upon me to do anything I can."[15]

So-called non-Aryan Christians—persons of Jewish ancestry who self-identified as Christian (through baptism or church membership)—often found themselves in particularly tenuous situations. Neither fully accepted by the Jewish community nor always embraced by Christian churches, they had no natural support systems to turn to when forced to emigrate from Germany or occupied countries. For example, Dr. Ernst Langfelder initiated correspondence with Rushbrooke in January 1939, requesting assistance in escaping Vienna to live in Teschen, Poland: "As a non-Aryan Christian, I carry the bitter lot of the Jews in Germany."[16]

Rushbrooke gave his information to an interdenominational committee for "Protestant Non-Arians [sic],"[17] while also contacting in vain the Polish embassy in London to secure him passage.[18] Langfelder, in despair, asked for help in getting to England or any other country that would take refugees[19] and supplied an autobiographical sketch in the hope that Rushbrooke might "find it possible to support my application." One sentence in Langfelder's life story is most poignant: "I have lost my material existence and have been compelled to leave my beloved wife over me being Evangelical, but of non-Aryan origin."[20] They divorced to protect her and their daughter in case of his arrest by the Nazi occupiers. On April 6 the German Emergency Committee stated it would provide assistance to Langfelder if £1 per week could be raised and suggested creating an annuity for Langfelder's lifetime needs. On April 25 Rushbrooke admitted he could not raise sufficient funds, but did offer to send a one-time donation of £1 designated for Langfelder if the committee committed itself to assisting him.[21]

Langfelder never escaped Vienna. On May 27, 1942, he and his sister, Julia, were "deported to the occupied Soviet Union . . . in Transport Train 204 with about 1,000 other Jews. They were murdered in the Maly Trostinec death camp near the city of Minsk on June 1, 1942." Somehow, his wife, Gertrude, and some other family members managed to survive the war.[22]

Funding Compassion for Suffering Jews

At its November 1938 meeting, the Baptist Union's General Purposes Committee discussed the plight of non-Aryan Christians. Aubrey noted that Conrad Hoffman, representing the International Missionary Council and its Jewish Relations Committee, "was very anxious that the Baptist Union should give a very definite lead in the matter of succoring these persecuted people," and Aubrey hoped the Union would make a "very strong appeal on their behalf to the Churches generally."[23]

No one on the committee objected to the idea of fundraising, but logistical issues caused concern. E. B. Walling observed that "the difficulty at the moment was that people did not know to whom to send their gifts with the best advantage." Grey Griffith "referred to the fund being raised by the Rev. Harcourt Samuel, pastor of Ramsgate Baptist Church, and wondered whether any new fund could be linked up with that."[24] Samuel, himself a Jewish Baptist, was the treasurer of the German Hebrew Christian Fund, an initiative of the International Hebrew Christian Alliance, which sponsored hotels in London for refugees.[25] J. R. Edwards preferred collaborating with the British Mission to the Jews, whose chairman and secretary were also Baptists. Aubrey suggested that the Union create a designated fund, and the matter was referred to the Finance Committee, which met on December 15. The committee only agreed to fund a mailing to the Union's churches and clergy, which would include a reprint of Aubrey's *Baptist Times*'s column and a cover letter from the secretary.[26] Nevertheless, the response was encouraging; Aubrey announced that 3,676 crowns were donated in just a little over a month![27]

At the Union's Moral and Social Questions Subcommittee meeting on February 7, 1939, Aubrey "reported that there was great readiness in the Churches to help Baptist Jewish refugees from Germany, the principal difficulty being to obtain Government permits for the entry of such refugees into England." Rushbrooke was asked to inquire if Baptists in the United States might be open to refugee resettlement.[28] A week later the subcommittee heard that Rushbrooke was pursuing the matter, while T. G. Dunning "outlined the action already taken to help Baptist Jews in Germany, many of whom were in desperate need." It was suggested that offerings raised for Czech Baptists might be diverted to "meet extreme cases of hardship amongst the Jewish Baptists."[29] In fact, Czech Baptists had already received via Rushbrooke an unspecified donation from British Baptists "ear-marked for Jews."[30]

In March 1939 Dunning urged British Baptists to rise to the challenge of assisting Baptist Jews. He graphically portrayed the "pathetic" overall situation, saying "the thought of life in a concentration camp fills our German Baptist Jews with dread, and the break-up of families due to the pogrom is a terrible domestic tragedy." He then asked, "How can we help?" Dunning urged British Baptists and their families and churches to assist these Baptist Jews through acts of kindness: "Just recently, by the mere giving of £10, a noble German Baptist of Vienna was saved from a concentration camp." He then listed specific Baptist Jews who urgently required immediate assistance, such as "Mr. H., a Baptist of Vienna resident in Belgium. Deprived of German passport. Must leave Belgium by July next."[31]

Baptist clergy and churches across England supported the Lord Baldwin Fund for Refugees.[32] Rev. F. C. Bryan, speaking during the Bristol Free Church Federation's annual meeting, promoted the offering with enthusiasm: "The way in which we respond to the appeal on behalf of Central European refugees will be the acid test of whether or not the people of Great Britain still have the qualities of the Good Samaritan. . . . Life for them is a sheer nightmare unless they can escape abroad."[33] Bryan specifically warned that of the one million refugees on the continent, most were Jews, and if these Jews did not "escape abroad the future held no prospects for them."[34]

Rushbrooke preferred that Baptists send their relief donations to the Baptist Union. He admitted to the Cinderford Baptist Church that the BWA did not have a "special fund for Jewish Refugees." By giving to the Union, it would "be clear that it represents a Baptist contribution" to Jewish suffering. He was concerned that "many of our people contribute directly to Lord Baldwin's Fund, and the effect of this might be to suggest that Baptists as such are not pulling their weight."[35]

Rushbrooke also passed on a donation of £55 he received to the Christian Council for Refugees from Germany and Central Europe, directed toward "the assistance of Jewish Christian refugees."[36] This donation may have come from the Northamptonshire Baptist Association, which in a gesture of concern for the plight of Jewish-Christian refugees, sent Rushbrooke a series of small donations from its churches and individual members in April and May 1939.[37] Rushbrooke confirmed that these gifts would be passed on by the Christian Council to the German Emergency Committee, which had the Nazi government's authorization to handle "all questions affecting Christian Jews."[38]

Baptist churches hosted ecumenical events for the benefit of Jewish refugees. Leicester's Victoria-road Church hosted an "Act of Fellowship" for Jews and Christians, with both the Baptist minister and Jewish rabbi speaking. An offering was taken for "the Jewish Fund for Refugees."[39] Similarly, Rev. Henry Cooper, the secretary of the International Hebrew Christian Alliance, urged Baptists to volunteer for refugee work and reminded them that "some Hebrew people join Baptist churches. They are by race, as interpreted by the Führer, Jews, but they are Christian in faith."[40]

In its first issue of 1939, the *Baptist Times* published "a pathetic appeal" from a German Jewish woman and her two Baptist daughters who were seeking to emigrate to England and work as domestics: "Help us come to England in some domestic service. I am 49 years old, healthy, and a first-rate cook. My eldest daughter, 22 years old, was in England for a year; she speaks French, German and Italian. The younger, a great lover of children, 17 years old, also knows these languages except Italian. Both would like to get into homes and to earn their bread by work."[41]

A. G. Parry and Jewish Immigrants

British Baptists responded to the plight of Jewish refugees in various ways. In addition to raising funds for humanitarian aid, passing resolutions, and having their leaders respond prophetically, many churches supported the British Society for the Propagation of the Gospel among the Jews, also known as the British Jews Society.[42] The society regularly advertised in the *Baptist Times* and solicited donations to continue its outreach and humanitarian assistance to Jews.[43] Rev. Arthur George Parry, a Baptist pastor, served as general secretary and was personally involved in facilitating the welcoming and care of German Jews fleeing Hitler. Parry regularly lectured on topics like "The Problem of the Jewish Refugee."[44]

One such arrival was Klaus Gräupner (later anglicized as Kenneth Graupner). His father abandoned the family to protect them, but he was unable to escape Nazi wrath, and "he died in a concentration camp in 1940." Following Kristallnacht, Kenneth's mother reached out to the British Jews Society, and Parry became personally involved. In 1939 Parry "had a houseful of young men from Germany, Austria, and Poland—effectively a private orphanage." Parry met Kenneth and his brother at a train station on the German border and accompanied them to facilitate their new lives in England:

> So I arrived in England in February 1939. We lived in West Norwood, south London. My brother . . . was ten and was boarded out with a Cornish Baptist minister whilst I stayed with Mr Parry. The Society's offices where Mr Parry worked were near Theobald's Road in Holborn, so I went to a grammar school in North London. Somehow I acquired English without trying; they got me to play cricket—once! When the schools broke up for summer and war was declared on Sunday 3rd September 1939, all the children and their teachers in London had been evacuated, but none of the teenagers living with Mr Parry.[45]

Graupner eventually earned his PhD, married an English woman, and enjoyed a reunion with his mother and sisters in 1951.

The relocation of Kenneth Graupner is but one example of a successful outreach on the part of British Baptists. On another occasion, Parry and Rushbrooke collaborated to aid a Jewish refugee. On March 31, 1939, Rushbrooke referred a married couple to Parry—Paul Iglasz, a Polish "tailor by trade, Jew by race, and a Baptist," and his wife, Jozefa ("an Aryan Pole, and a Baptist"). The Germans had cast Paul out of Germany in October 1938, and he and his wife were residing in Posnan, Poland, waiting to immigrate.[46] Rushbrooke had previously corresponded about Iglatz with Paul Schmidt and Paul Levertoff, a messianic Jew in England.[47] In the letter to Schmidt, Rushbrooke stated that Iglatz "has been a Baptist for 38 years, and . . . all of his family are Baptists."[48] Parry responded quickly; four days later he informed Rushbrooke that he knew of a possible sponsor family and would "make the application to the Home Office immediately after Easter."[49]

Kindertransport Stories

In response to the tenuous situation of over sixty thousand Jewish children in Germany and Austria, the Kindertransports were an effort to extricate and relocate these youths to England and other countries. Between 1938 and 1940 about twelve thousand children were rescued, with nearly ten thousand coming to Great Britain.[50] Jewish leaders involved with the British Kindertransport effort strenuously sought to protect the Jewish identity of the children, especially when placed with Christian host families:

> Many refugee children were boarded in the homes of caring Christian families, where they adjusted to their new surroundings and to their hosts. Others fared less well and felt isolated and abandoned. Among Christian hosts were those who sought actively to proselytize Jewish children, despite their knowledge that this was prohibited by the Movement [for the Care of Children from Germany], and some of them were successful in their endeavors.[51]

The *Baptist Times* published a column on one of their readers who decided to house two "little Jewish children made to suffer terribly because of the wicked persecution of Jews."[52] Readers certainly would have been encouraged by the *London Daily Mirror*'s report concerning Inga Enoch, an eleven-year-old German-Jewish Kindertransport child who found a new home in Bryn Smith Marchog, Wales. The child mastered Welsh, enabling her to capture "a prize for recitation" in a startlingly brief time. She attended the local Baptist church's Sunday school. Rev. H. Thomas extolled Inga's virtues: "She's simply marvellous. I've never known anybody to pick up Welsh so quickly." Inga herself stated, "I often sing and recite in the Sunday school. I like the Welsh language. It is very like German."[53]

Unfortunately, not every Kindertransport experience involving Baptist sponsors worked out positively. At least one situation was disastrous.

Susi and Lotte Bechhöfer, the twin daughters of Rosa Bechhöfer, were among the youngest Kindertransport children to arrive in Great Britain. Their Nazi father left the family before they were born on May 17, 1936, and Rosa gave them up after failing to secure permission to emigrate to the United States. After spending time in a Jewish children's orphanage in Munich, on May 16, 1939, the girls left Germany and made it to London two days later. They had been assigned to live in Cardiff, Wales, with a Baptist minister and his wife, Rev. Edward and Irene Mann, who were childless. The tragic nature of this arrangement is recounted by Susi in her autobiography, *Rosa's Child*.[54]

Moved by Kristallnacht, the Manns qualified to host a Kindertransport child through the German Jewish Aid Committee because there were not enough Jewish homes available.[55] Rev. Mann persuaded the committee that "there was no possibility whatsoever of Susi and Lotte being baptized in the name of Jesus Christ" because Baptists did not practice infant baptism.[56]

Upon their arrival in Cardiff, the twins progressively lost their ability to converse in German, and the Manns' "subtle campaign of attrition was allowing their Jewish roots likewise to pass into oblivion." Their names were Christianized to Grace (for Susi) and Eunice, while a "new, non-German, non-Jewish life was forged for the twins."[57] The Manns introduced the girls to Christianity, and they became involved in the activities of their Baptist church.

The family's inner dynamics were destructive and even evil. Lotte's health deteriorated due to a brain tumor in 1945, and she was sent to North Wales to live in a Christian boarding school, leaving Susi (now Grace) isolated at home. Rev. Mann isolated Susi from her peers and prohibited friendships, and he became "more and more besotted, and eventually obsessed" with her.[58] When she became a teenager, the abuse turned sexual in nature, with his wife ignoring the situation and not coming to Susi's aid.[59]

Despite Mann's continued harassment, Susi escaped her abusive home by attending nursing school, later marrying Alan Stocken, and having a child.[60] She rediscovered her original name and Jewish identity, sought out biological family in Germany and the United States, learned that her biological mother had perished in Auschwitz in 1943, and made psychological peace with her upbringing and even her substitute parents. Most interesting, she never did renounce Christianity even while embracing her rediscovered Jewish heritage.[61]

A Welsh Baptist Pastor Confronts Anti-Semitism

Twelve miles north of Cardiff, Wales, sits the small village of Pontypridd. On April 23, 1939, the pastor of the Hawthorn Baptist Church in Pontypridd preached a sermon featuring a most provocative title: "The A.B.C. of Jew-Baiting."[62] Rev. Richard Jones acknowledged that while "we are concerned, and rightly so, with racial and religious Persecution overseas, signs are not wanting that all is not well at home."[63]

In his forthright and hard-hitting message, this courageous preacher rejected the myth that the struggle between the Nazis and England represented a conflict between German anti-Semitism and British philo-Semitism. In fact, anti-Semitism was also being manifested throughout British society, prompting him to ask if prejudice against Jews (and blacks) was becoming "respectable-ised." It was time for Baptists to recognize with sorrow that "in this country, anti-semitism is gaining ground."[64]

Jones suggested that "Jew-baiting" thrived on the A.B.C. of "arrogance, brutality and credulity." Prideful Christian *arrogance*, which "prepares the way for the persecution of the Jews" must be replaced by a humility that recognizes that Christians "have nothing worth while that did not come to us through a Jew." The writers and prophets of the Old Testament were Jews, as was Jesus—"A

Jewish maiden gave Him to us." Even the New Testament and the Christian faith are Jewish gifts, for "the first Apostles were all Jews, and it was a Jew who brought the Gospel to our own continent." In light of the accomplishments of Jews like Einstein, Freud, and Ehrlich, Baptists should "go down on our knees each night and thank God for this great Race."[65]

In like manner, *brutality* against Jews must cease. It is easy to "blame" others because of one's own misery and troubles, and so feel the urge to harm them. This impulse must be resisted, because Jews don't deserve to be anyone's scapegoat—"The fault, dear Brutus, is not in our Jews, but in ourselves, that we are underlings."[66]

The third source of anti-Semitism was ignorance and the willingness to "believe in insufficient evidence" concerning spurious accusations against the Jewish people. Such *credulity* leads people to recirculate religious falsehoods such as that Jews "sacrifice Christian children in their ceremonies" and desecrate the elements of the Lord's Supper. Secular slanders, such as Jews controlling governments or financial systems, are claims only foolish prejudiced people can entertain. The preacher declared, "Anti-Semitism—hatred of the Jewish people—is based on a lie, and a deliberately engineered one."[67]

Jones concluded his sermon by noting that anti-Semitism "cannot stand the light." He urged his members "to expose the falsehoods which lie at the root of anti-Semitism—to strike in the name of Christ at every thought, at every word, at every deed, which contributes to this injustice." Looking to a future threatened by potential war, Jones offered a prophetic wish:

> In this anti-Semitic insanity which once again is lifting up its ugly head, and threatening the peace and prosperity of our world, let it be recorded in the history of the future that one empire remained sane, the British Empire, that one empire opened wide her gates to Jehovah's ancient people, that one empire welcomed her refugees, that one empire helped her in her day of trouble, that one empire gave her back her National Home in Palestine, as she had promised and as God has promised, that one empire fought her battles, that one empire loved her well, that "for the sake of Mary's child" that empire stood with those of Mary's race, and the Lord Jehovah blessed that empire evermore.[68]

While British Union leaders usually focused on Germany's anti-Semitism, Jones courageously sought to apply Jesus' question to the problem of contemporary anti-Semitism in his own country, in accordance with Jesus' question: "Why do you look at the speck of sawdust in your brother's eye and pay no attention to the plank in your own eye?" (Matthew 7:3, NIV).

This prophetic yet pastoral approach led Jones to take on one of the giants of the Baptist Union—Rev. Frederic C. Spurr, who had published "The Jewish Question" in the *Baptist Times* on June 1, 1939. Depending on who was posing the question, references to the "Jewish Question" often contained a negative overtone, the assumption being that the existence of a Jewish community was in some fashion problematic. Spurr stated that he had donated to the Baldwin Fund and opposed "the Nazis as much as anyone. This wholesale, indiscriminating terror is revolting to all decent men." Nevertheless, he felt that the issues surrounding the "Jewish Question" deserved "balanced" treatment, which in the end meant that Jews needed to take some responsibility for ending the prejudices lodged against them.[69]

Jones challenged Spurr's opinions, including the classic "greed" charge, by asking, "Is the prejudice against Jews 'on social and economic grounds' altogether justified?" Then came a second question: "Is this country as free from anti-Semitism as it thinks?" If so, how could one explain "the pig's head which was nailed to the door of a London synagogue during Passover week . . . ?" Reacting to Spurr's criticism of Zionism, Jones speculated that prophecies of the Old Testament prophets could have been easily "denounced as Zionistic propaganda" if they had been proclaimed in contemporary England. Jones closed with a moving thought: "Whatever else 'National Home for the Jews' may mean, a 'Home' is surely a place one can turn to in time of trouble."[70]

Spurr did not directly reply to Jones, but he did clarify his stance three weeks later: "Anti-Semitism is a dangerous disease which must be stamped out. It is inhuman, and definitely *anti*-Christian. I am sure a concerted effort in Britain on behalf of understanding would clear away the poisonous fog which now envelops many."[71]

A Unique Gift for Jewish Children

A most generous Baptist response to the ongoing struggles of the Jewish community to serve Kindertransport children happened one year after Kristallnacht. Samuel Ashby, a Baptist layperson, purchased, refurbished, and then donated a school building to the Jewish community of Shefford, a town about fifty miles north of London. The children had to be evacuated from the capital city to protect them from the German air force's bombing raids.

On Wednesday, November 15, 1939, the Clifton Fields Infants School was recommissioned for its new purpose at a public ceremony. For the donor, the occasion "realised a dream dear to his heart of showing kindness to the Jews." The ceremony was moderated by Rev. J. Cornish, pastor of the Shefford Baptist Chapel. The Jewish community was represented by Dr. A. Levene (Jewish secondary school headmaster), his wife, and Dr. J. Grenfeld (secondary school headmistress). Cornish "voiced his admiration for the Jewish race, spoke of their persecution and sorrows, and in their present distress and poverty he criticised the authorities for the absence of any provision for the education of the young people." On Ashby's behalf, he "presented Dr. Levene with the key of the school." Levene expressed gratitude for the generous gift and for the town's welcome of them. The need was great; some 250 children had been relocated to the Shefford area and desperately needed a permanent educational facility.[72]

Ashby's brother, Martin, a Baptist minister, "spoke of his brother's great admiration for the Jews and of his realised wishes on this present occasion." In an interview with the newspaper, Samuel Ashby revealed his motive behind the extraordinary gift: "I love the Jews and I have always done all I could to help them. I am a Christian and like to copy my Master, Who [sic] was a Jew. I hate Hitlerism and its oppression of the Jews."[73]

Ashby's gift to the Jewish community in Shefford had a lasting impact. On Christmas Eve 1942, Dr. Levene shared a lengthy tribute in the *Bedfordshire Times and Standard*. He celebrated the "record of three years' work of good will among Bedfordshire folk." While Jews in Germany and surrounding countries had been "shamefully ill-used," in England Jews "met with sympathy, kindness, and understanding"—especially in Bedfordshire. Levene credited this marked openness to the region's history of "having given refuge to the French Huguenots" and other factors that facilitated "the broad stream of friendship and tolerance, hatred of all forms of oppression, and real empathy with suffering." He mused, "Perhaps it was only at Shefford in Bedfordshire that such a large-hearted soul as that of the late Samuel Ashby could alone flourish—a man who purchased a school and a house to help accommodate many helpless Jewish refugee children, thus making a gesture unique in the story of evacuation in this war."[74]

Refugee Journeys

Following Kristallnacht, Baptists were most receptive to hearing the dramatic experiences of German refugees who had succeeded in fleeing Nazi persecution. Many of the speakers were Christians by faith and Jews by birth (in whole or in part). These testimonies sensitized Baptists to the consequences of Nazi anti-Semitism and reinforced their hopes that Jews might be open to Christianity.

Miss Gertrude L'Arrange, for example, shared her testimony at the Redhill Baptist Tabernacle in Surrey County, southwest of London, on June 16, 1939. Her mother was a "Christian Jewess." Gertrude embraced Christianity after "Hitler's persecution" made her "realise that Christ and Satan do not walk together." Despite studying to be a vocalist, her religious awakening caused her to forsake secular entertainment. She concluded by singing, "Down from His glory, ever living story, My God and Saviour came."[75]

Church audiences were open to politically analytical presentations from refugees. Oscar Stern, a Czech Jewish-Christian, spoke at an ecumenical event supported by both Anglican and Free churches. Born into a Jewish family, he accepted Jesus through a Salvation Army presentation in New York City when he was fifteen years old. He was subsequently "disinherited by his people." Back in East Prussia, Stern participated in "the fellowship of a little Baptist Church. Then came the beginning of Hitlerism." He was imprisoned and later fled to Czechoslovakia, but "when he thought he was once again a free citizen, came the Nazi swoop and he was again fleeing for his life."[76]

Stern offered a threefold critique of Nazi Germany. The "first Germany" supported Hitler and his military aggression. The "second Germany" was "composed of those millions whose consciences would not sanction much of what was going on but who were silenced by fear of concentration camps." The "third Germany" was populated by non-Aryans, and especially Jews, whose "humiliation" and desolation was total. "Hitler wished to rid himself of the Jews and the Nazis were prepared to massacre them, hence the wave of Anti-Semitism." Stern reminded his fellow Jesus followers that "world Jewry was in distress and needed the hand of fellowship and love."[77]

Two weeks later Stern provided a grim picture of the Nazi attacks against German and Polish Jews, who were facing "a cold, ruthless, and brutal process of extermination." Speaking to a packed crowd at the Torquay Baptist Church on November 18, 1939, Stern argued that Nazi anti-Semitism must be rejected by Christians. Stern cited imminent danger to the 3.5 million Polish Jews, who were "starving to death." He was concerned that Catholic, Orthodox, and even Protestant clergy leaders in Poland, Rumania, Hungary, and Austria were anti-Semitic, and even England was challenged by "this curse of racial discrimination that has long been turned against the Jew." Thousands of Jews sought refuge from German persecution but were faced with an "awful situation"—countries were not willing to take them in, and if they remained under Nazi control, they faced extermination.[78]

British Baptist openness to Jewish Christian refugees during the wartime years was illustrated in a remarkable manner when Poynton Baptist Church called Mrs. Lisa Goertz to serve as their interim pastor in August 1942.[79] Not only was she a woman (which in and of itself would have made the call notable), but she was also a Jewish disciple of Jesus who had "escaped from Germany after Gestapo oppression and torture."[80] Goertz's life in Germany, her broken marriage, her eventual personal commitment to Jesus, and her escape to England are all recorded in her autobiography, *I Stepped into Freedom*.[81]

While Goertz "was happy and content" to minister to "between 150 and 200 people" each week, she continued to struggle with an interior issue: "There was still bitterness in my heart and hatred against the Nazis."[82] Sadly, by July 1943 Goertz's tenure came to a close. Church records indicate that "she had decided to take up full-time war work in an attempt to relieve her distress at the loss of loved ones in Axis territory at the hands of the Nazis," but Goertz claimed that she had undertaken that job well before she left the church, and she cited her desire to attend Bible training school primarily for "Hebrew Christians of German descent" in Leicestershire as the reason for her departure—with the church's blessings.[83]

NOTES

1. Amy Zahl Gottlieb, *Men of Vision: Anglo-Jewry's Aid to Victims of the Nazi Regime 1933–1945* (London: Weidenfeld and Nicolson, 1998), 1.

2. Gottlieb, 13–14. These Jewish organizations also gave support to non-Jewish (Christian) refugees and had a strong relationship with James McDonald (61–62).

3. Gottlieb, 49.

4. J. C. Carlile, "Christmas and the Jews," *Baptist Times*, December 15, 1938, 961–62.

5. M. E. Aubrey, "The Crown Fund," *Baptist Times*, December 15, 1938, 962–63; "The Crown Fund" *Baptist Times*, December 22, 1938, 983. See also A. J. Sherman, *Island Refuge: Britain and Refugees from the Third Reich, 1933–1939* (Berkeley: University of California Press, 1973), 184–85.

6. "Baptist World Alliance and Anti-Semitism," *Baptist Times*, January 5, 1939, 2; see Lee B. Spitzer, *Baptists, Jews, and the Holocaust: The Hand of Sincere Friendship* (Valley Forge, PA: Judson, 2017), 415–17.

7. J. H. Rushbrooke, "The Jews: What Can We Do?", *Baptist Times*, February 2, 1939, 90.

8. Rushbrooke, 90.

9. J. H. Rushbrooke to C. B. McAlpine, December 6, 1938, Angus Library and Archive, Regent's Park College, Oxford, England.

10. J. H. Rushbrooke to Paul Schmidt, December 5, 1938. Baptist World Alliance Correspondence Box 15 A–L (January–June 1939), Angus Library and Archive. This case was not resolved because the German Baptists claimed they could not find the original request and the woman's name; see W. D. Kassul to J. H. Rushbrooke, January 1939, Angus Library and Archive.

11. J. H. Rushbrooke to W. O. Lewis, March 20, 1939, Angus Library and Archive. Lewis's written response was caring but did not offer any practical assistance: "It is sad to think that there is so much of that kind of trouble in Europe and the end is not yet in sight. I hope Mrs. Rushbrooke may not be unduly depressed by this sad news." W. O. Lewis to J. H. Rushbrooke, April 10, 1939, Angus Library and Archive.

12. Rushbrooke, "The Jews: What Can We Do?", *Baptist Times*, February 2, 1939, 90. Margaret Cowell provided a report on several secular British organizations helping Jewish refugees in "The Refugees—How to Help," *Baptist Times*, March 30, 1939, 246.

13. For example, Rushbrooke passed the case of Julian and Max Schmal on to the German Emergency Committee; see J. H. Rushbrooke to German Emergency Committee, January 13, 1939, and January 16, 1939, Angus Library and Archive.

14. D. G. Whittinghill to J. H. Rushbrooke, January 14, 1939, Angus Library and Archive.

15. J. H. Rushbrooke to D. G. Whittinghill, January 14, 1939, Angus Library and Archive.

16. E. Langfelder to J. H. Rushbrooke, January 5, 1939, Angus Library and Archive. Translated from German original text.

17. J. H. Rushbrooke to E. Langfelder, January 12, 1939, Angus Library and Archive.

18. J. H. Rushbrooke to Polish Ambassador, January 12, 1939, and reply January 14, 1939, Angus Library and Archive.

19. E. Langfelder to J. H. Rushbrooke, January 20, 1939, Angus Library and Archive.

20. E. Langfelder to J. H. Rushbrooke, March 10, 1939, Angus Library and Archive. Translated from German original text.

21. Silva Deutsch (German Emergency Committee) to J. H. Rushbrooke, April 6, 1939, and J. H. Rushbrooke to Silva Deutsch, April 11, 1939; Silva Deutsch to J. H. Rushbrooke, April 15, 1939; J. H. Rushbrooke to Silva Deutsch, April 25, 1939, Angus Library and Archive.

22. "Ernst Langfelder Biography," Salzburg Stumbling Blocks, accessed February 4, 2021, http://www.stolpersteine-salzburg.at/en/places_and_biographies?victim=Langfelder,Ernst.

23. *Minute Book of the Council of the Baptist Union of Great Britain and Ireland, April 1938–March 1939*, November 15–16, 1938, Meeting, General Purposes Committee, 502.

Aubrey had met with Hoffman on September 12, 1938, "concerning the present unhappy position of many thousands of Non-Aryan Christians" (353).

24. *Minute Book of the Council of the Baptist Union*, 502–3.

25. German Hebrew Christian Fund Advertisement, *Baptist Times*, March 9, 1939, 193. See "Harcourt Samuel Reflects on 100 years of the Hebrew Christian Alliance of Great Britain," May 22, 2015, https://jewinthepew.org/2015/05/22/22-may-1966-harcourt-samuel-reflects-on-100-years-of-the-hebrew-christian-alliance-of-great-britain-otdimjh/.

26. *Minute Book of the Council of the Baptist Union*, December 15, 1938, Finance Committee Meeting, 584–85.

27. M. E. Aubrey, "From the Secretary's Chair," *Baptist Times*, February 9, 1939, 103.

28. *Minute Book of the Council of the Baptist Union*, February 7, 1939, Moral and Social Questions Sub-Committee Meeting, 651–52. D. M. Albaugh "presented the case of European refugees as it concerned the work of our missionary societies" at the Northern Baptist General Council meeting on April 12, 1939. The council ignored the plight of Jewish refugees but agreed to cooperate with the American Committee for Christian German Refugees. See *Minutes of the General Council of the Northern Baptist Convention*, April 12, 1939, Item 4591, 7; *Annual of the 1939 Northern Baptist Convention*, Report of the General Council, Section 9—European Refugees, 39.

29. *Minute Book of the Council of the Baptist Union*, February 15, 1939, Moral and Social Questions Sub-Committee Meeting, 725.

30. H. Prochazka to J. H. Rushbrooke, January 4, 1939, Angus Library and Archive. Some of this money may have come through Southern Baptists. See J. H. Rushbrooke to E. P. Buxton, January 23, 1939.

31. T. G. Dunning, "Helping the Refugees," *Baptist Times*, March 16, 1939, 204.

32. Lord Stanley Baldwin launched the fundraising campaign bearing his name on December 8, 1938. The fund assisted Jewish refugees and "non-Aryan Christian refugees." About £522,000 was raised; see Gottlieb, *Men of Vision*, 119–20; Judith Tydor Baumel-Schwartz, *Never Look Back: The Jewish Refugee Children in Great Britain, 1938–1945* (West Lafayette, IN: Purdue University Press, 2012), 92. *Baptist Times* criticized the home office for restricting "the admission into this country of refugee Jews with regulations that are almost prohibitive" in "A World Problem," *Baptist Times*, January 12, 1939, 27.

33. "Lives as a Sheer Nightmare: Great Tragedy of the Refugees," *Bristol Evening Post*, May 8, 1939, 8.

34. "Civic Service at Tyndale Church," *Western Daily Press and Bristol Mirror*, May 8, 1939, 5.

35. R. S. Burnett to J. H. Rushbrooke, January 24, 1939; and J. H. Rushbrooke to R. S. Burnett, January 26, 1939, Angus Library and Archive.

36. John Hope Simpson (Christian Council for Refugees from German and Central Europe) to J. H. Rushbrooke, May 9, 1939, Angus Library and Archive.

37. Northamptonshire Baptist Association to J. H. Rushbrooke, April 24, 1939; May 4, 1939; May 15, 1939, Angus Library and Archive.

38. J. H. Rushbrooke to Northamptonshire Baptist Association, April 26, 1939, Angus Library and Archive.

39. "Fellowship of Jews and Christians," *Baptist Times*, February 23, 1939, 142.

40. "Who Are the Non-Aryans?" *Baptist Times*, February 16, 1939, 125; see also his letter to the editor, January 26, 1939, 64.

41. "A Pathetic Appeal," *Baptist Times*, January 5, 1939, 5.

42. See Mitchell Leslie Glaser, "A Survey of Missions to the Jews in Continental Europe 1900–1950" (PhD diss., Fuller Theological Seminary, 1998).

43. See advertisement, *Baptist Times*, January 2, 1941, 1; January 12, 1939, 21; and March 9, 1939, 184.

44. "Baptist Tabernacle," *Kent and Sussex Courier*, February 24, 1939, 13.

45. Glaupner's recollection is archived online by the BBC; see "The Story of a German Jewish Refugee," (Article ID: A4910096) posted by Ron Goldstein, August 10, 2005, http://www.bbc.co.uk/history/ww2peopleswar/stories/96/a4910096.shtml.

46. J. H. Rushbrooke to A. G. Parry, March 31, 1939, Angus Library and Archive.

47. See J. H. Rushbrooke to P. Levertoff, January 25, 1939; P. Levertoff to J. H. Rushbrooke, January 26, 1939, J. H. Rushbrooke to Mrs. P. Levertoff, January 27, 1939, Mrs. P. Levertoff to J. H. Rushbrooke, January 30, 1939, Angus Library and Archive.

48. J. H. Rushbrooke to P. Schmidt, January 25, 1939; and A. G. Parry to J. H. Rushbrooke, April 4, 1939, Angus Library and Archive.

49. Parry to Rushbrooke, April 4, 1939.

50. Baumel-Schwartz, *Never Look Back*, 5; and Gottlieb, *Men of Vision*, 102, 125.

51. Gottlieb, *Men of Vision*, 129.

52. "League of Little Friends Column," *Baptist Times*, January 5, 1939, 16.

53. "Refugee, 11, Got Prize for Welsh," *London Daily Mirror*, January 5, 1940, 6.

54. Jeremy Josephs with Susi Bechhöfer, *Rosa's Child: The True Story of One Woman's Quest for a Lost Mother and a Vanished Past* (London: I. B. Tauris, 1999). See pp. 3–16 for the story prior to landing in England. Her father's name was Otto Hald, as she discovered late in life (76).

55. Josephs, *Rosa's Child*, 17–22. The Manns did have a friendship with a Jewish refugee couple, the Vellishes, who helped acclimate the girls upon their arrival in Cardiff (24).

56. Josephs, 26.

57. Josephs, 27–28.

58. Josephs, 31–38.

59. Josephs, 43–46.

60. Josephs, 48–66.

61. Josephs, 67–159.

62. Richard Jones, "The A.B.C. of Jew-Baiting," Wales: Hawthorn Baptist Church, 1939, https://www.bethelbaptisthawthorn.org/history. Jones served as pastor from 1930 to 1964.

63. Jones, 2.

64. Jones, 2.

65. Jones, 4–5.

66. Jones, 6.

67. Jones, 6–7.

68. Jones, 8.

69. F. C. Spurr, "The Jewish Question," *Baptist Times*, June 1, 1939, 430. Louis Golding demolished Spurr's argument regarding Jewish responsibility for eradicating Christian prejudice in his Open Forum letter to *Baptist Times*, June 22, 1939, 484.

70. Richard Jones, "The Jewish Question," in Our Open Forum, *Baptist Times*, June 8, 1939, 444.

71. Frederic C. Spurr, "The Jewish Question," in Our Open Forum, *Baptist Times*, June 29, 1939, 504.

72. "Shefford Baptist's Gift to Jews," *Biggleswade Chronicle and Bedfordshire Gazette*, November 17, 1939, 4.

73. "Shefford Baptist's Gift to Jews," 4.

74. A. Levene, "A Record of Good Will," *Bedfordshire Times and Standard*, December 25, 1942, 4.

75. "Redhill Baptist Tabernacle," *Surrey Mirror and County Post*, June 16, 1939, 4.

76. "The Forward Movement," *Leighton Buzzard Observer*, October 24, 1939, 7.

77. "The Forward Movement," 7.

78. "Torquay Story of Nazi Atrocities: Mass Persecution of Jews Described by Refugee," *Torquay Herald and Express*, November 9, 1939, 3.

79. I am indebted to Robert Parkinson for alerting me to this story in *Finding a Friend: The Baptist Encounter with Judaism* (Oxford: Whitley, Regents Park College, 2020), 21–22.

80. Eric Younghusband, *Abundant Harvest: The History of Poynton Baptist Church from Early Beginnings Up to 1970*, Poynton Baptist Church, PDF booklet, undated, 9, accessed March 22, 2022, https://www.pbc.org.uk/ourstory/#ourjourney-section.

81. Lisa Goertz, *I Stepped into Freedom* (London: Lutterworth, 1960). Ruth Moriarty reviews Goertz's spiritual journey and ministry in a recorded sermon, accessed March 21, 2022, https://www.mixcloud.com/pbcsermoncast/treasures-from-our-past-lisa-goertz-1st-female-minister-of-pbc-ruth-moriarty/.

82. Goertz, 48.

83. Goertz, 49–51.

CHAPTER 3

The Baptist Union during World War II

Longing for Peace

The year 1939 marked a transition for Great Britain and its Baptists. Not yet at war due to the Munich Agreement, disturbed by Kristallnacht, and uncertain about the future, Baptists throughout Great Britain had many unanswered questions on their minds. Welsh Baptist Gwilym Davies, writing in the *Baptist Times* for its first issue of 1939, poignantly asked, "Was there ever in history anything more cruel than the outbreak of 'anti-Semite cannibalism' in Germany?"[1]

During the annual assembly on May 1–4, the pain of Kristallnacht still troubled the hearts of the fellowship. Incoming president P. T. Thomson denounced Nazism in a forceful way that would not soon be forgotten by his audience: "Of all the obscene creatures spawned by anti-Christ, none surely was more revolting than the philosophy . . . in the German mind which endows a race, a State, a culture, based on nothing but animal blood, with a life of its own, and in the process reduces the individual to a nonentity, a no-being." Cardiff Bible College's principal, T. W. Chance, while opposed to Hitler's racial doctrines, nevertheless held out hope that if Baptists "proclaim the Gospel with the same zeal and fervor as he [Hitler] proclaimed the racial ideals as a means of restoring Germany, we should witness a revival of religion without parallel" in that country.[2]

Speaking nearby before the Birmingham Rotary Club, Rushbrooke lauded the English for promoting "personal freedom and the dignity and worth of the individual." He warned that the British were "in collision with the German State on questions of policy and strongly opposed to what was presented by National Socialism with its cruel racial persecutions," but added that his hearers should not "drift into hatred of the German people."[3]

The assembly approved a resolution condemning Germany's aggressiveness while applauding England's attempts to secure negotiated "guarantees of non-aggression." A second resolution expressed "sympathy with all who in any land are suffering for conscience' sake, and especially with their Baptist brethren in Europe and Asia." They reasserted their "demand for complete religious liberty as alone compatible with the dignity of human personality."[4] However, they were silent on the liberation of suffering Jews.

Aubrey thereafter departed for Canada and the United States, in anticipation of the BWA World Congress in Atlanta. He commented that many Americans were wary of "European entanglements" even though most despised both Communism and Fascism. If England was forced into conflict, it could not necessarily count on the United States to join in, since "America has her own tremendous problems"—including "anti-Semitic agitation (mixed up often, with elementary forms of Nazi-ism [sic] and Fascism)."[5]

Aubrey played a most visible role at the World Congress; his debate with the German Baptist Paul Schmidt is covered in Chapter 8. Aubrey issued a memorable warning to the delegates, and in particular, the Americans. As an illustration, Aubrey described how a New Yorker remained in denial as his weather instrument, a barometer, indicated a hurricane was going to hit Long Island. He wrote a letter to the manufacturer, brought it to his mailbox, and when he turned around—both the barometer and his house had been hit by the storm! Aubrey then related it to present circumstances: "Less than a generation ago freedom seemed assured in countries in which it has now been swept away. And are there no mutterings in our own countries from which we should take warning? Has America no people who dabble in Fascism, Nazi-ism [sic], and anti-religious Communism? We should do well to give heed to the signs of the times."[6]

During the summer of 1939, Gwen D. Hoult, daughter of the Baptist pastor in Spalding, traveled to Germany for two weeks. She recounted a troubling conversation regarding the "Jewish Question." Her German counterparts asked her to imagine being a

German soldier following the Great War and to have Jews refuse her a job so she could eat. "Wouldn't you feel a longing to get rid of these Jewish managers who would turn a man away to starve?" Hoult replied that the British considered Jews to be "clever" while the Germans insisted they were "swindlers." Naively, she then inquired, "But why must you torture them?" They replied, "The Germans do not love their enemies."[7]

At the same time, Dr. T. J. Dunning, secretary of the Young People's Department of the Baptist Union, organized a delegation of fifteen young people who toured Austria, Romania, and Hungary with the aim of fostering relationships with Baptists. They were led by Rev. F. C. Bryan, pastor of Tyndale Baptist Chapel in Bristol. He engaged in personal conversations with ordinary people who defended Nazi philosophy and policies. Concerning Jews, he was told, "We don't want them. Send them anywhere, to England, Palestine, or just put them on the sea. Anything, anywhere. They are a plague to us."[8]

Two of the youth from Spalding shared their experiences in their local paper. In Vienna Dorothy Walden and Barbara Pearson recalled that the group was welcomed by the Baptist Church and by Hans Rockel, a leading German Baptist figure. Presumably he was present to ensure that the British youth would hear a defense of German Baptist life under Hitler. During the tour, it was "impossible to get away from the political situation." The presence of Hitler was everywhere. The plight of Austrian Jews also came to their attention. The group learned that in the near past, about 40 percent of Vienna's population were Jews who recently "have felt the full weight of the persecution against them. Their twelve synagogues have been destroyed by bombs, their shops are nearly all closed; on all public buildings, parks, cinemas, even wayside seats the words 'Juden forboden' (Jews forbidden) appear. They seem to be completely crushed and broken."[9]

From Peace to Wartime

In late August 1939, J. H. Rushbrooke dispatched an appeal to Canadian and American Baptists, requesting that they "pray that war may be averted and peace preserved, and that confidence and co-operation may replace suspicion and fear."[10] Within two

weeks a second letter acknowledged that "British Baptists, returning from Atlanta, find themselves ranged behind their Government
in support of war." Rushbrooke expressed support for his prime
minister's assertion that the British were going to war against "evil
things—brute force, bad faith, injustice, oppression, persecution."[11]
He added that the war should not prevent Baptists from remaining in fellowship with their German coreligionists. Unity among
Baptists across political dividing lines was a core conviction of the
BWA from its inception in 1905. In like manner, Aubrey shared
his "affection and deep regard" for the German Baptist leadership,
"Dr. Simoleit and the rest, whom we all honour for their character and work even if we find ourselves on opposite sides in this
quarrel."[12] Nevertheless, as peace transitioned into wartime, the
fraternal ties between the British and German Baptists frayed, as an
adversarial relationship replaced their historical friendship.

A special gathering took place at Christmastime in the Upton
Vale Baptist Schoolroom. Almost one hundred German, Austrian,
Czech, and Polish refugees, most of them Jewish, had escaped from
"Nazi persecution" and were fortunate enough to have made it
to Torquay, a town in southwest England on the English Channel. The community had welcomed them, offered various forms
of humanitarian assistance, and called for more "private hospitality" to alleviate needs. One person at the Christmas party observed, "The amount of tragedy represented in this room is almost
unthinkable."[13]

In April 1940 Sir John Harris, a venerable anti-slavery advocate, penned a passionate defense against Hitler's "race-hatred."
He wrote, "The doctrine has been set forth in all its crude brutality
by Hitler, and it covers all people of color, including Jews, Asiat-
ics, and Africans." Harris's intersectionality should have resonated
with Baptists who were familiar with the 1934 and 1939 BWA
Congress resolutions on racialism.[14]Although references explicitly
linking the nineteenth-century abolitionist campaigns to the protest
against Nazi anti-Semitism in British Baptist documents during the
Holocaust era are lacking, in 1940 an African American Baptist
leader, Lacey K. Williams, coined an original and evocative phrase
that graphically expressed the spiritual kinship between slavery and
the persecution of Jews during the Nazi era. He declared that African Americans, as the progeny of slaves, "have felt and known the

pangs of a suppressed, chained personality" and so therefore were willing to fight against the Nazis.[15]

The 1940 Annual Assembly of the Baptist Union took place in London, and its delegates approved a resolution expressing their support for the war. Not realizing that five years of terrible carnage lay ahead, the delegates imagined a coming peace that would "ensure respect for human personality, for the freedom of peoples, for law, and for the pledged word."[16]

Rev. Percy W. Evans delivered the president's address and focused on the theme of "personality." He provided a pertinent and inspiring summary of its meaning while showing, by implication, why Baptists had to reject Hitler's totalitarian philosophy and its ill-treatment of the Jews:

> The modern disregard for the sacredness of human personality arises from the fact that we do not set men in the revealing light of their relationship to God; men are viewed as producers or consumers, citizens or warriors, voters or taxpayers, but there is no inherent sacredness in any of these relationships, and ultimately no valid reason can be given why the ordinary man should not be treated as a means to an end, and sacrificed for the advantage of others more numerous or more strong than himself.[17]

Although the oppression of the Jewish people was always front and center in the Nazi agenda, after the start of the war, Baptists began to reimagine the contours and stakes of the wartime conflict. The Nazi threat was conceived as a titanic struggle between an idolatrous Nazi social order and Christianity. The plight of the Jews was demoted to an example of the evils of Nazi racialism. This shift was illustrated by Rev. James Greenwood's presidential address at the Yorkshire Baptist Association meeting, which took place two weeks after the general assembly. Greenwood proclaimed, "The avowed aim of the leaders of the Totalitarian States is to destroy Bible Christianity, and to organise life on principles fundamentally antagonistic to it." McMaster University (Toronto) professor Laurence Henry Marshall stated that "Nazi philosophy rejected Christ and the Christian moral standard." There existed a "Nazi conscience" that permitted any kind of immoral strategy or tactic in the furtherance of the German agenda. Examples included "lying propaganda and the brutal treatment of Jews, the suppression of free speech, the claim that the German race was a lordly race above other races of mankind, and destined to rule the world."[18]

Both Lewis and Rushbrooke represented the BWA at the 1940 Annual Meeting of the Northern Baptist Convention in Atlantic City, New Jersey. Rushbrooke confessed that many people were guilty of denial and "unreal thinking" during the rise of totalitarianism in the 1930s, and admitted that "some Baptists have been among the most obstinate in the refusal to face facts." He cited Jewish suffering as an example of the larger issues facing Baptists:

> We heard the voices of dictators glorifying war and mocking at the idea of personal liberty. We saw the youth of the totalitarian States lined up enthusiastically behind the dictators. We saw the terrible consequences in inhuman cruelty inflicted upon Jews and others. Still we closed our eyes; we would not see the imminent peril to freedom of thought and faith and life. The truth is, we had lost our belief in the grim reality of sin, and we tried to persuade ourselves that some things were too bad to happen.[19]

For Rushbrooke, the war against Germany was justified because every Baptist had the responsibility to ensure freedom and the survival of *personality* for future generations: "freedom, justice, the framework of society that allows personality—these are not private, they are human concerns" worth fighting for, so that "brute force and treachery shall not prove the decisive factors in the world's life."[20] In October 1940 Rushbrooke declared that the retreat of religious freedom was most evident in Germany, "where the totalitarian principle worked from the first not only in the direction of crippling the relatively weak churches, e.g., by breaking up their youth organisations and incorporating the young people in the Hitler Jugend, by silencing their witness on public questions, and by a rigid control of all their publications." Rushbrooke added a further comment in parentheses: "(The destruction of synagogues was also a flagrant example of religious persecution, though its deeper motive was race hatred.)"[21]

In his 1940 Christmas letter, Rushbrooke found solace in the arrival of refugees in England: "The presence in our midst of Dutchmen, Czechs, Poles, Norwegians, Jews and others, is a constant reminder that the cause Britain defends is not merely her own." Noting that "mankind is one," he concluded that "the Golden Rule must govern the relations of societies, including States, no less than of individuals."[22]

Jews, Christians, and Personality

Throughout 1941 most of the war news was discouraging for Great Britain. British Baptist clergy and scholars sought to lift the spirits of the faithful. "Hitlerism must and will be defeated," declared Pastor H. G. Ball to the membership of Trinity Baptist Church in Gloucester. Even though the Nazis "desired to exterminate the Jews . . . God's Word said they would be preserved. The Jews will long outlive Hitler." God would "bless" the United States and England because of their "kindness to God's chosen race."[23]

On May 29, 1941, H. Wheeler Robinson spoke to the Society of Jews and Christians in Oxford. He suggested that Jews and Christians shared a common reliance on the "prophetic consciousness as the 'Land's End'[24] of human personality where man can best look on the ocean of God." The prophets proclaimed God's "justice" and "mercy" when they found themselves in "times of social evil." The current conflict had "brought Jew and Christian closer together," for both "assert the dignity and worth of the personality to which they belong." He then posited a contrast: "In our contemporary world we can see the power of personality, for good and for evil, in Roosevelt and Churchill on the one hand, and in Hitler and Mussolini on the other."[25]

Throughout the year, Rushbrooke's updates on Baptist movements across Europe were decidedly dark. Baptists in lands conquered by both the Soviet Union and Germany were suffering. Communication with Baptists across Europe had been cut, and Rushbrooke's concern was evident.[26] He was quiet about the activities of German Baptists, emphasizing the need for Baptists to consider one another as brothers and sisters in Christ, transcending politics and nationalism.

However, when Rushbrooke spoke before the West Midland Baptist Association meeting in Birmingham on May 27, 1941, he was uncharacteristically critical of the German Baptists: "The

Baptists in Germany . . . have always had two weaknesses—a singular dullness regarding the social application of the Gospel (because they wish to avoid politics) and a perverted racial feeling." Throughout the Nazi era, German Baptists defended the correctness of an apolitical approach, claiming that it permitted them to remain religiously active under Nazi rule.

Rushbrooke's charge that German Baptists had exhibited a "perverted racial feeling" was a remarkable admission from the BWA president! It was not a thoughtless criticism; Rushbrooke offered two examples of German Baptist racism: "With all their evangelistic zeal, they never regard converts of other races as equal with themselves and have never set up native preachers' schools. Preachers must be trained in Hamburg." He promised to hold the German Baptists accountable, when the war was won, for their refusal to oppose Hitler and racism, and then added his standard unity message: "Despite my strictures on my German brethren—strictures which I shall make to their face when the time comes—we must affirm our solidarity with them as fellow-Christians."[27]

On June 10, 1941, Rushbrooke spoke at the East Midland Baptist Association annual meeting, and once again addressed the position of German Baptists under Nazism. Rushbrooke estimated that "at least 97 per cent" of older teenagers and German young adults (forties and under) "would vote for Hitler." This extraordinary level of allegiance to Hitler played a significant role in making German Baptist leaders reticent to come to the aid of their Jewish neighbors. Rushbrooke revealed that "German Baptist preachers told him some years ago that they dared not denounce Hitler's anti-Semitism, as their young people would have made a riot. And these were young German Baptists." Most interesting was Rushbrooke's observation that the dynamics underlying the German Baptist support for Hitler was due to the power and influence of *personality*: "What captured the youthful followers of Hitler, Mussolini, Stalin and Lenin was personality." He observed that "strong personalities like those of the dictators could make youth a force for evil." In contrast, "Christianity was truth presented in a tremendous personality."[28] That "tremendous personality" was Jesus, whose message of a kingdom of justice and peace was intended to serve as a force for individual spiritual renewal and societal good.

Sacred Fires of Sympathy

Gazing toward the troubled European continent in November 1942, M. E. Aubrey addressed the question that Baptists across Great Britain were asking: "What is happening to our Baptist brothers and sisters living under Nazi rule?" Aubrey voiced his hope that verifiable reports of Lutheran, Reformed and Catholic resistance would "be reflected in the life and work of our Baptist people"—a wish that turned out to be applicable to Baptists in occupied territories but not in the German fatherland. At the very least, Aubrey hoped that European Baptists would not forsake their "traditional witness to freedom" and "the liberty of the Churches within their own sphere and the right to freedom of worship for all, even for the Jews." Citing reports of heroism in Norway, Holland, Belgium, and France, Aubrey declared that Christians had "boldly resisted the ill-treatment of the Jews" by the Nazis.[29] In a companion column, J. W. Ewing saw "points of light" in the midst of France's dark night, for "in spite of Hitler and Vichy, the Christian conscience is asserting itself in protests against the cruelties inflicted on the Jews; a secret but widely-distributed journal bravely declaring Anti-Semitism to be incompatible with Christianity."[30]

On November 24, 1942, Rabbi Stephen Wise, president of the World Jewish Congress, held a landmark press conference in which he revealed that Hitler's extermination of Jews across Europe was well underway. During a session of the House of Commons on December 17, 1942, Foreign Secretary Anthony Eden read from the *Joint Declaration by Members of the United Nations*, which was composed by the American and British governments on behalf of other Allied countries.[31] This was the first official Allied condemnation of Hitler's Final Solution, by which "German authorities, not content with denying to persons of Jewish race in all the territories over which their barbarous rule has been extended, the most elementary human rights, are now carrying into effect Hitler's oft-repeated intention to exterminate the Jewish people in Europe." The plight of Europe's Jewish population was dire: "From all the occupied countries Jews are being transported in conditions of appalling horror and brutality to Eastern Europe. In Poland, which has been made the principal Nazi slaughterhouse, the ghettos established by the German invader are being systematically emptied of all Jews. . . . The number of victims of these bloody cruelties is reckoned in many hundreds of thousands of entirely innocent men, women and children."[32]

Baptists throughout Great Britain expressed their revulsion to the mass extermination of the Jewish people. Arthur Porritt praised Eden's speech, in which Eden denounced "the barbarous and inhuman treatment to which Jews are being subjected in German-occupied Europe."[33] In March 1943 the *Baptist Times* shared that it had "received copies of resolutions passed by several of our churches in regard to Jewish refugees and also the scandalous persecution of Jews abroad," and advised that such statements be "sent to members of Parliament and Cabinet Ministers." The paper was gratified that Baptist churches were "alive to this most pressing problem and are exerting themselves on behalf of our Jewish brethren."[34]

One such resolution came from the Leeds and District Baptist Ministers' Fraternal. Responding to reports of "mass murders and loathsome cruelties suffered by the Jewish people in Eastern Europe, and through which upwards of two millions of Jews have perished," the fellowship sent a public message to the Jewish community: "We assure all Jews of our deep-seated sympathy and declare that as ministers of Christ, as citizens, and as members of the human family we will do our utmost to help the tortured and starving members of their race still in enemy hands." They committed themselves to pray that "the sacred fires of sympathy may burn, and the soul of the United Nations may be so stirred that the Powers that be may deal speedily with this matter of life and death."[35]

Individual congregations also reacted to the revelations about the killing of Jews by the Nazis. The Courtney Street Baptist Church in Hull requested that the British government locate "an immediate refuge in territories within the British Empire, as well as elsewhere, for all Jews who can escape from Axis hands, or for those who have already escaped to neighbouring neutral countries and can make room for other fugitives to take their places."[36] They passed this resolution on to their political representatives. The church's action was preceded by a public appeal from Hull's Roman Catholic and Protestant clergy, with T. J. Johnson representing the Baptists. They asked the government to "offer generous refuge . . . to Jews from the Continent," to make it easier for the "entry of Jews into

Palestine," and to facilitate the passage of Jewish refugees "into neutral countries."[37] Similarly, the Baptist church in Bugbrooke, near Northampton, joined with other churches in the town to sign a resolution concerning "the massacres and starvation of Jews and others." They supported "providing help and temporary asylum to persons in danger of massacre, who are able to leave enemy and enemy-occupied territory."[38]

Standing at the Bar of History

The 1943 Baptist Union Annual Assembly convened in London just after the American-British Bermuda Conference, which failed to resolve any of the issues facing desperate Jews. Delegates passed a significant resolution on "the plight of the Jews." The assembly sent a clear message to the governments of Great Britain and the United States, which served as a rebuke to their inaction. It requested that the Allied governments devise "effective measures for enabling Jews and other victims of German brutality to escape and find refuge." Noting that merely voicing "strong abhorrence and detestation of the persecutors . . . and of their purpose of exterminating the Jews" was insufficient, the assembly called for "energetic action, not only to bring justice in due course to the instigators and perpetrators of the massacres, but to give immediate aid, welcome and asylum in this and other free countries to those in peril." The resolution further called for Baptist churches to "show and inculcate a friendly and helpful attitude to such refugees, to pray for the deliverance of those who cannot escape beyond the reach of their barbarous enemies, and to resist as un-Christian all tendencies to anti-Semitism."[39]

Members of the Wiltshire and East Somerset Baptist Association, in southwest England, passed two resolutions that were inspired by the Union's action. The first recommended that the government take "more energetic action in enabling Jews and other victims of German brutality to escape and find refuge in this and other lands." The resolution also called for "churches to resist all tendencies to anti-Semitism."[40] The Suffolk Baptist Union forwarded a similar resolution to a committee to rework before sending it to the authorities, but the newspaper report did not indicate if their resolution contained the clause about homeland anti-Semitism.[41]

The protests of Baptist Union delegates and churches did not achieve their aim of compassionate care for Jewish refugees during this stage of the war effort. This convinced an anonymous lawyer to pen a remarkable protest for the *Baptist Times* in November 1943. Lamenting that the "apparent insensibility to Nazi persecution suggests that the gravity and enormity of the [Jewish refugee] problem and the recognition and acceptance of our responsibilities alike need emphasis," he asserted that aiding Jews was "a moral problem" and a "spiritual obligation" for Christians. "Pious sympathy" was an inadequate response to an "immediate problem demanding immediate action" to save Jews "from torture and death."[42]

Addressing the heart of the matter, the barrister declared that "anti-Semitism is fundamental to Fascism and has presented a grave problem for the past ten years which morally unconscious governments have failed to face." This was a remarkable criticism to wage against the Allies in wartime! He also observed that in the past year, a new level of Nazi-initiated evil had been unveiled: "The story of this persecution up to the beginning of 1942 was hideous enough, but a year or so ago the Nazi chiefs, dissatisfied with their previous brutality, determined upon a plan for the utter extermination of Jews in Europe."[43] After citing the horrific number of Jewish people killed, the barrister charged that the British government had not fulfilled its responsibility to accept refugees despite government pledges.

In his closing argument, the barrister proposed four responses to the plight of Jewish refugees. First, Baptists should strive to "arouse" British "moral passion" through sermons, resolutions, and articles in the press. Second, Germans should be advised that "we will not tolerate their condoning of and still less their participation in these barbarities." Third, Baptists should lobby for the right of Jews to enter Great Britain, the Middle East, and other countries. Fourth, "we should exert our influence by all the means open to us to impress our will upon the Government and compel it to action." Citing the parable of the Good Samaritan, the barrister suggested that "protest, indignation, and threats, unaccompanied by real help, are a mockery to victims and human alike." And then in conclusion, he urged his readers, "Let us not make the same error. We stand at the bar of history, of humanity, and of God."[44]

The Post-War Future

As Allied forces methodically advanced ever closer to the German border, British Baptists began imagining what a victorious postwar Europe might look like. In early 1944 the Anglican Church, the Free Church Federal Council (to which Baptists belonged), and the Church of Scotland issued a joint statement regarding the churches' "attitude toward Germany." While eschewing "vengefulness," it called for securing "full atonement for the appalling sufferings inflicted by Nazi Germany upon the peoples of Europe." To secure a peaceful and united Europe, the Allies would need to reintegrate Germany into "the European family of nations."[45]

British Baptist minister and author Hugh Martin, speaking at a meeting of the Baptist Union's board, focused on the "religious background of post-war Europe." Regarding the church in occupied countries, he claimed that "the Church had witnessed for human rights and not simply for its own ecclesiastical advantages and—a specially dangerous thing—it had protested against the indescribable cruelties inflicted upon the Jews."[46] Martin would later serve in leadership for the Christian reconstruction of Europe.[47]

English Baptists speculated about the wartime experience of their German Baptist counterparts. Dewsbury's Rev. E. J. E. Briggs, in his presidential speech to the Yorkshire Association of Baptist Churches in Leeds, judged that German Baptists "were not markedly successful in resisting the authority of the State." Their pietism and simplistic (literal) reading of the Bible made them "content to look after the next life" while Hitler accumulated absolute power. Briggs argued that although Baptists were not wedded to any one political order, they should reject any future trends toward the concentration of political power and totalitarianism.[48]

Rushbrooke reminded British Baptists that "there are groups of our brethren on both sides in the present conflict. On the side of the Axis—happily—they are very few." He sought to minimize the extent to which German Baptists were complicit in supporting Nazism while asserting that Baptist unity trumped politics: "We have never allowed political differences, even when they involved the terrible collision of war, to destroy our sense that the opponents may both be Christian." Alluding to the possibility that some German

Baptists accepted Hitler's anti-Semitism, Rushbrooke shared how the BWA would confront German Baptists following the war: "Our brethren will never be misjudged by us. We shall question them frankly about attitudes—and silences—that have puzzled us; but we shall not start with the presupposition that they have betrayed the faith or are unworthy of our confidence."[49]

The June 24, 1944, edition of the *Baptist Times* contains a remarkable letter from nineteen British evangelical leaders, including Rushbrooke and Martin Lloyd-Jones. The letter encourages Christians to care about the Jewish people, dedicating September 30 as a "day of special prayer for Israel." Two themes called for attention. First, a Christian vision for postwar Europe had to take into consideration the plight of the Jewish people on that continent. Their "physical sufferings under the Nazis are well known, and have evoked much sympathy; but their mental and spiritual needs are greater still. The situation is a challenge to the Church, for are they not God's ancient people through whom the Word of God came, and of whom was born our Saviour Jesus Christ?" Second, Christians were obligated to evangelize Jewish people after the war: "An adequate presentation of the Gospel to the Jews of Europe should have priority in our post-war missionary planning." The persecution of the Jewish community should not stifle missionary outreach, but rather encourage an evangelistic response: "No people have suffered as they; they need the Gospel the same as all mankind; and their spiritual condition presents a challenge to our belief in the efficacy of the Christian faith."[50]

Some Baptists looked to history for wisdom about the future. Rev. E. F. Sutton, speaking at the September 1944 meeting of the Maidstone District of the Kent and Sussex Baptist Association, recalled that the Nazi anti-Semitism did not arise out of thin air: "The watchword 'Blood, race and soil' was not the invention of the Nazi Party. It had been preached by German teacher after teacher in the nineteenth century."[51]

As devastating as the Nazi period was for Jews, British Baptists, like their counterparts all over the world, tended to focus on preparing for a postwar era in which the European Baptist movement, including German Baptists, could be resurrected. Unfortunately, a marginalization of the Jewish survivors coincided with the reestablishment of communication with European Baptist conventions and leaders. As British Baptists discovered the extent of their need, they concentrated their humanitarian efforts toward Baptist displaced persons as well as the reconstruction of Baptist churches and ministries throughout Europe.

British Baptists were excited to hear from their Italian Baptist counterparts in July 1944. A letter from Italian Baptist leader Manfredi Ronchi was delivered by Sergeant Denis Lupson, a Baptist in England's Eighth Army, which helped liberate Rome. Ronchi was delighted to "express my brotherly feelings for the Baptists of Great Britain without being considered a betrayer of my country as it was before the Allied troops entered Rome."[52] In November 1944 Rushbrooke shared an update indicating that communication was flowing through BWA-related channels to leaders in the Scandinavian countries, France, and even Romania. In all of these instances, reconstruction needs were part of the discussion.[53]

German reintegration into Europe was addressed in a speech by Sir Stafford Cripps to the board of the Baptist Union on January 3, 1945. Germans were "human beings like ourselves—equally brothers in the human family and sharing the Fatherhood of God." Cripps ignored Jews when he listed victims of the Nazi aggression by nationality. These "wronged people were as much or more entitled to our friendship, sympathy and support than our defeated enemies," he said.[54]

With victory over Hitler in hand, Rushbrooke assured the 1945 Baptist Union General Assembly that "Baptists in Europe had been faithful under intense suffering." Baptists throughout the continent—including German Baptists—had exhibited "no hypocrisy amongst them, and we might look to them as people who had kept the faith." He called for raising £150,000 for "post-war church reconstruction."[55]

Speaking to the East Midland Baptist Association in June 1945, Rev. V. F. Smithers shared an illustration about reconstruction that he hoped would be inspirational: "To-day German prisoners of war were helping to rebuild our homes and we were helping to rebuild Germany." For this Baptist preacher, these efforts symbolized "the only way to build up a new order" in which all nations "stand together and co-operate."[56]

NOTES

1. Gwilym Davies, "Enter 1939!," *Baptist Times*, January 5, 1939, 9.

2. "Threat to Peace: Germany's Suppression of the Individual—Baptist Views," *Birmingham Mail*, May 2, 1939, 10.

3. "Dignity and Worth of the Individual," *Birmingham Post*, May 2, 1939, 5.

4. 1939 Assembly—May 1–4, 1939, in Birmingham, *The Baptist Handbook for 1940* (London: Baptist Union Publication Department, 1940), 213–15.

5. M. E. Aubrey, "Somewhere in America: Some Further Considerations," *Baptist Times*, July 27, 1939, 583.

6. M. E. Aubrey, "Christianity and the Totalitarian State, Part 1," *Baptist Times*, August 3, 1939, 606.

7. "What the German People Say," *Lincolnshire Standard*, August 26, 1939, 10.

8. F. C. Bryan, "My Conversations in Central Europe," *Bristol Evening Post*, August 25, 1939, 6.

9. "Longing for Peace," *Lincolnshire, Boston and Spalding Free Press*, August 21, 1939, 8.

10. *Scunthorpe Evening Telegraph*, August 28, 1939, 8.

11. "Dr. Rushbrooke's Message to America," *Baptist Times*, September 7, 1939, 680.

12. M. E. Aubrey, "Baptists and This War," *Baptist Times*, October 5, 1939, 739.

13. "Found Haven at Torquay: Fled from Nazi Terror," *Western Morning News*, December 29, 1939, 7.

14. Sir John Harris, "Racial War and the Christian Church," *Baptist Times*, April 11, 1940, 233.

15. *Minutes of the 1940 Annual Session of the National Baptist Convention, U.S.A.*, President's Address, 72; quoted in Lee B. Spitzer, *Baptists, Jews, and the Holocaust: The Hand of Sincere Friendship* (Valley Forge, PA: Judson, 2017), 361.

16. *The Baptist Handbook for 1941* (London: Baptist Union Publication Department, 1941), 212.

17. Percy W. Evans, "Allegiance," in *The Baptist Union Presidents' and Other Addresses 1937–1942* (London: Baptist Union Publication Department, 1942), 13.

18. "Christianity at Stake: Yorkshire Baptists and the War," *Yorkshire Post and Leeds Mercury*, May 15, 1940, 8.

19. "Northern Baptist Convention, U.S.A.," *Baptist Times*, June 27, 1940, 412.

20. "Northern Baptist Convention, U.S.A."; see also editorial, "The British Viewpoint," *Watchman-Examiner*, July 4, 1940, 735.

21. J. H. Rushbrooke, "The Shrinkage of Religious Freedom," *Baptist Times*, October 10, 1940, 595.

22. J. H. Rushbrooke Christmas Letter to Unnamed Friends, December 5, 1940, 3.

23. "Hitlerism Will Be Defeated," *Gloucester Citizen*, March 3, 1941, 4.

24. The westernmost shoreline in Cornwall, England, featuring a magnificent view of the ocean, Land's End is a famous Cornish destination. https://www.visitcornwall.com/things-to-do/attractions/west-cornwall/lands-end/lands-end-landmark.

25. H. Wheeler Robinson, "Judaism and Christianity," *Baptist Times*, June 19, 1941, 300.

26. J. H. Rushbrooke, "European Baptists: Their Difficulties and Dangers," *Baptist Times*, June 19, 1941, 303; "Stand for Religious Freedom!", *Baptist Times*, November 20, 1941, 567; and "Russia: A Debt and a Duty," *Baptist Times*, November 19, 1942, 571.

27. "Position of Baptists in Europe," *Birmingham Post*, May 28, 1941, 2; and *Staffordshire Advertiser*, May 31, 1941, 3.

28. "Religious Liberty," *Nottingham Journal*, June 11, 1941, 4.

29. M. E. Aubrey, "Baptists on the Continent: What Is Happening?", *Baptist Times*, November 19, 1942, 571.

30. J. W. Ewing, "Baptists on the Continent: Watchman, What of the Night?", *Baptist Times*, November 19, 1942, 571.

31. Richard Breitman and Allan J. Lichtman, *FDR and the Jews* (London: Belknap Press of Harvard University Press, 2013), 211–12.

32. "Joint Declaration by Members of the United Nations," Wikipedia, https://en.wikipedia.org/wiki/Joint_Declaration_by_Members_of_the_United_Nations, accessed May 29, 2020. See also "11 Allies Condemn Nazi War on Jews," *New York Times*, December 18, 1942, 1.

33. Arthur Porritt, "Nazi Barbarities upon the Jews," *Baptist Times*, December 24, 1942, 638.

34. "Jewish Refugees," *Baptist Times*, March 11, 1943, 5.

35. "Tortured Jews," *Yorkshire Post and Leeds Mercury*, February 17, 1943, 2.

36. "Hull Baptists and Escaped Jews," *Hull Daily Mail*, February 19, 1943, 3.

37. "Persecution of Jews: Appeal by Hull Clergy and Ministers," *Hull Daily Mail*, February 12, 1943, 3.

38. "Aid Nazi Victims—Bugbrooke Plea," *Northampton Mercury and Herald*, March 12, 1943, 6.

39. 1943 Baptist Assembly "Resolutions on Public Questions: The Plight of the Jews," *The Baptist Handbook for 1944–45–46* (London: Baptist Union Publication Department, 1946), 170. The resolution was also printed in "Assembly Resolution," *Baptist Times*, May 27, 1943, 6.

40. "Baptists Meet at Frome," *Western Daily Press and Bristol Mirror*, May 28, 1943, 2.

41. "Suffolk Baptist Union," *Suffolk and Essex Free Press*, June 3, 1943, 11.

42. "The Refugee Problem by a Barrister-at-Law," *Baptist Times*, November 18, 1943, 7.

43. "Refugee Problem by a Barrister-at-Law," 7.

44. "Refugee Problem by a Barrister-at-Law," 7.

45. "Our Attitude toward Germany," *Baptist Times*, March 30, 1944, 5.

46. "The Religious Background of Post-War Europe," *Baptist Times*, April 13, 1944, 4.

47. Anthony R. Cross, "Revd Dr Hugh Martin—Publisher and Writer," *Baptist Quarterly* 37, no. 1 (1997): 38.

48. "Too Aloof from Life: An English View of German Baptists," *Yorkshire Evening Post*, May 30, 1944, 5; "Baptist Views on Social Order," *Yorkshire Post*, May 31, 1944, 8.

49. J. H. Rushbrooke, "Baptists on the Continent: 'Lift Up Your Hearts,'" *Baptist Times*, June 29, 1944, 9.

50. Editor's Letter Box, "Day of Prayer for Israel," *Baptist Times*, June 29, 1944, 8.

51. "Kent Baptists: Europe's Challenge," *Chronicle and Courier*, September 15, 1944, 3.

52. "A Message from Italian Baptists," *Baptist Times*, July 13, 1944, 6; see also "The Baptists in Italy," *Baptist Times*, November 16, 1944, 7.

53. J. H. Rushbrooke, "Renewal of Brotherly Fellowship," *Baptist Times*, November 16, 1944, 8–9.

54. "Post-War Treatment of Germany," *Gloucester Citizen*, January 3, 1945, 5; "Banish Spirit of Revenge," *Gloucestershire Echo*, January 3, 1945, 1.

55. "German Baptists 'Keep the Faith,'" *Liverpool Daily Post*, May 2, 1945, 4; "They Kept the Faith," *Birmingham Gazette*, May 2, 1945, 2.

56. "Only Way to Rebuild World—Baptist View," *Nottingham Evening Post*, June 6, 1945, 4.

CHAPTER 4

The Scottish Baptist Union's Indignation and Sympathy

The Man of Sin

A. Campbell Dovey pastored the Baptist church in Cupar, a small Scottish town situated approximately ten miles west of St. Andrews, from 1940 through 1944.[1] On Sunday evening, September 7, 1941, Dovey based his message on a controversial subject: "Is Hitler the Man of Sin?" Few members would have disputed the necessity of fighting against Hitler and Nazi Germany, especially after two years of attacks by German aircraft throughout the British homeland. But was Hitler really the Antichrist?

Whether Dovey really intended to literally identify the Nazi führer with the biblical Antichrist may be debatable, but he clearly asserted that Hitler embodied the significant attributes of that infamous eschatological figure. Hitler was a liar, a murderer, and a politician who sought power and glory in opposition to God (and the Christian church). Hitler's hatred of the Jews was an obvious example of evil. "Think of the Jews and the blood that lie at Hitler's hands," he declared. "The man of sin is to be the most bitter persecutor of the Jews. How does that apply to Hitler? Could there be found a more cruel, a more heartless, and a more bitter persecutor of the Jews than Hitler?"[2]

Although others within the Baptist Union of Scotland might not have been comfortable with taking an end-times approach to castigate Hitler for his anti-Semitism, it is fair to say that from the very beginning of the Third Reich, Scottish Baptists voiced their opposition and indignation in a clear and consistent manner.[3]

The First Wave of Persecution

In the February 1933 issue of the *Scottish Baptist Magazine*, J. T. Forbes,[4] principal of the Scottish Baptist College, imagined a Christian world order where all races were unified. He hoped that "the small matters and petty irritations which breed race hatred [shall] disappear in view of the majestic uniting powers." Despite the emerging threat of Nazi racial discrimination in Germany, Forbes denounced the ancient Jewish understanding of their relationship to Gentile nations, which was replaced by Christianity's doctrine of humanity as "one family" where no one race would reign supreme. In contrast, the contemporary Jewish dream of a homeland was less noble: "Christ had no territory to give men, like the patrons of the Zionists who wished to settle them in Palestine or British East India."[5]

Despite Forbes's criticisms of Zionism, the Baptist Union of Scotland, on behalf of its 151 churches and 22,900 members,[6] was among the first Baptist national conventions to express concern that Jews were suffering persecution in Germany. On May 31, 1933, Rev. James Hair, on behalf of the Social Service Committee, presented a resolution to the eighty-four delegates assembled in Edinburgh. Passing without dissent, it declared "their indignation at the persecution of the Jews in Germany, their dismay at the action of governments in denying freedom and the full rights of citizenship to well-disposed subjects on the grounds of race or of religious or political beliefs, and their abhorrence of all methods of repression and persecution."[7]

The Social Service Committee was "deeply concerned at the menace to religious liberty involved in the persecution of the Jews in Germany under the Hitler regime." It had sent the resolution to "the official heads of the Baptist Denomination in Germany" in response to the apparent lack of a similar protest by their German brethren. Most interestingly, the committee made excuses for the German Baptists: "What was done by these brethren in the matter we do not know, but we can make a shrewd guess. Comments made by German Baptists . . . point to the fact that the German Baptists are in ignorance of the excesses that we believe to have occurred, and share the belief of many good people in Germany that Hitlerism is the only alternative to Communism."[8]

As in England and the United States, Scottish Baptists were interested in the plight of the Jewish people and opened their doors to mission agencies that focused on Jewish evangelism. These organizations often dubiously interpreted contemporary struggles in conformity with their missional purpose. For example, Rev. D. J. Newgewertz, representing Mission to the Jews, informed the members of the Ward Road Baptist Church in Dundee that German attacks against the Jews were encouraging some Jews to "realise that they had made a mistake in rejecting Christ."[9]

In September 1934 the *Scottish Baptist Magazine* provided a brief but positive initial assessment of the Fifth Baptist World Congress and its German hosts. While the secular paper, the *Scotsman*, quoted the racialism resolution, the Baptist newspaper was satisfied merely to note, "Resolutions and speeches were characterised by that liberty of utterance which is the pride and the heritage of Baptists the world over."[10] A more detailed review followed in the October issue. Written by Baptist Union President James Macindoe and James Scott, the Jewish question received much-deserved attention: "Regarding the Racial question, the Congress deplored and condemned as a violation of the law of God all racial animosity, and every form of oppression or unfair discrimination toward the Jews, toward coloured people, or toward subject races in any part of the world."[11]

The Quiet Period

In his review of the congress in the *Scottish Baptist Magazine* in June 1935, Rushbrooke noted the world's press reported that "in the capital city of Adolf Hitler the world parliament of a great religious communion representing all parts of the earth unanimously adopted a resolution condemning racial pride, not in general terms but with express reference to 'oppression or unfair discrimination toward the Jews.'" He also was pleased that the "the Jews have expressed their gratitude in the highest terms."[12]

Published almost a year after the congress, Rushbrooke's remarks contained curious omissions. He did not admit that the plight of the German Jews continued to deteriorate following the congress, indicating that the resolution did not influence Hitler's anti-Semitic agenda. Second, Rushbrooke refrained from criticizing the German Baptists. Third, he excused German press censorship (specifically about the racialism resolution), rhetorically asking, "Is a religious conference ever fully reported in the secular press?"[13]

Quite startling was Rushbrooke's view that the resolutions passed did "not represent the largest and lasting significance of Berlin." Of greater significance were the congress's "theological, devotional and missionary themes." Rushbrooke stated, "Where we touched political and social issues—and we did not shirk them—it was not in the spirit of mere politicians. . . . We had not met to discuss public issues with an occasional and incidental reference to religion. We were there to testify to the faith that makes us Baptists." Nevertheless, he expressed thanks that the congress spoke "to the conscience of the world."[14]

On the associational level, the Berlin congress continued to receive attention. Robert Gibson, a layperson, addressed the Yorkshire Association of Baptist Churches in June 1935 and argued that Baptists acted "courageously" by passing the racialism resolution. Looking to the future, he argued that it was the "responsibility" of Baptists to impact the course of global politics in order to keep the world "safe from the modern menaces of an atheistic Russia and an anti-Christian Germany and an imperialistic Japan."[15]

Between 1935 and 1937 the *Scottish Baptist Magazine* and the Scottish Baptist annual meetings did not pay significant attention to the Nazi persecution of the Jews. In April 1935 James Hair published an article opposing the totalitarian nature of the Nazi government in light of the ongoing church struggle.[16] The annual assembly in October 1936 also featured a discussion on this topic during the Social Service conference. Dunblane Cathedral's minister, Rev. John Hutchinson Cockburn, was a guest speaker, and the Church of Scotland pastor told the Baptists that Nazi totalitarianism was opposed by a courageous church that refused to "bow the knee to Hitler." He criticized Hitler's "theory of race that no reputable scholar would subscribe to. From that had sprung the degrading and disgraceful persecution of the Jews."[17] Scottish Baptists did agree to participate in an ecumenical effort, the National Committee for Relief of Christian Refugees from Germany, at the end of 1936. Many of these refugees were Christians with a Jewish familial heritage (non-Aryans).[18]

Southern Baptist pastor and BWA president George Truett joined Rushbrooke at the Angus and Perthshire Baptist Association annual meeting at Ward Road Baptist Church in Dundee on July 7, 1937. According to the local newspaper, Rushbrooke focused on how Baptists differed from Lutherans concerning the relationship between church and state; the report did not indicate if he addressed the ongoing plight of German Jews.[19]

Indignation over Kristallnacht

The March 1938 German annexation of Austria elicited "a shock of horror" from Scottish Baptists. The *Scottish Baptist Magazine* noted the impotence of "the great democratic nations" who did "nothing to arrest the onslaught of dictatorial might." Germany's aggression foretold the imminent "eclipse of Christianity" in Europe, with "the bitter persecution of the Jews" as but one example.[20]

The Scottish Baptist Council, at its September 21, 1938, meeting in Glasgow, passed a resolution expressing opposition to Romanian persecution of Baptists.[21] A month later the Scottish Baptist Assembly approved a resolution opposing "the claim of the Totalitarian and Communistic Governments to set the State and its enactments above the citizens' loyalty to God"; it also criticized "the persecution of earnest Christians, pastors and laymen, in Germany, Russia, and elsewhere." The Nazi persecution of its Jewish population was not addressed. Another resolution supported appeasement and expressed the naive hope that in the aftermath of the German takeover of Czechoslovakia, "that harsh and oppressive measures will be excluded." They also dreamed that "in the struggle of ideologies in Europe, the rights and liberties of minorities and individuals must be upheld and defended at all costs."[22]

The next day the Social Service Committee praised Chamberlain and thanked God "that war [had] been averted." It repeated the need to protect the "rights and liberties of minorities and individuals" and added, "The only security against war and all of its horrors lies in the growth of unity between Christians in all lands, and a desire to live together by the grace of God, in increasing friendship." Copies of the statement were sent to the press, government officials, and Rushbrooke, so that through the BWA, "it may be circulated, if possible, among Baptists in other lands."[23] The sharing of such statements helped keep Baptists informed regarding how their peers were responding to key issues and sometimes influenced their own statements and resolutions.

It did not take long for Scottish Baptists to reconsider their enthusiasm for appeasement. Responding to the violence of Kristallnacht, the *Scottish Baptist Magazine* expressed shock and dismay, reviving the sense of indignation first expressed by Scottish Baptists in 1933. The paper railed against the Nazi-inspired attacks against innocent German Jews and confessed a sense of helplessness at this undermining of the spirit of Munich:

> We had just begun to breathe freely after a crisis that almost precipitated another World Conflict, we were slowly becoming accustomed to the dismemberment of Czechoslovakia, we were still beset by apprehension as to when and where the next rude blow would be struck at our sense of security when we were confronted with the spoliation and oppression of the German Jews in circumstances of harshness and cruelty that can only be matched in the records of the dark ages.

Most tellingly, the paper confessed it had no answer to the challenge posed by Kristallnacht: "The confusion of our minds, the courage to our sense of right, and the harrowing of our feelings were accentuated by our inability, in any effective way, to intervene."[24] A military intervention option, for example, was never contemplated.

The editorial recounted and bemoaned the sad plight of European Jews: "Persecuted, despoiled, killed in their thousands, the remnant driven from country to country, century after century, the Jews have been the Ishmaels of history, every man's hand against them." Even in Scotland, Jews "remained a people apart, with whom we had little intercourse and less common understanding," that was due to "an aloofness on our part which made us heedless of any demand for interest and sympathy where they were concerned."[25] Nevertheless, this historical legacy could not prevent Scottish Baptists from expressing "pity and indignation" in response to Kristallnacht's unbridled violence and persecution:

> We cannot have quiet of mind and conscience, however, until everything possible is said and done to impress the perpetrators with the intensity of the horror their doings have aroused in the breasts of people who still cling to the primal decencies of international behaviour. Nor can we rest until some strong effort is made to mitigate the sufferings of so many innocent people. Shylock's words, "Hath not a Jew eyes? Hath not a Jew hands, organs, dimensions, senses, affections, passions? . . . If you prick us, do we not bleed? . . . If you poison us, do we not die?" must have been recalled by many as the story of outrage upon outrage came across the wires.[26]

Scottish Baptists could not save the German Jewish community, but their Council agreed to "be associated with the appeal being sent out by the Scottish churches on behalf of non-Aryan Christian refugees from Germany and Central Europe" on November 30, 1938.[27] Representatives of the Baptist Union attended a public meeting of the Scottish Council for Refugees on December 6, 1938, in Edinburgh. Rev. John Hutchinson Cockburn, who had spoken at the 1936 Baptist Assembly, asserted that Kristallnacht was not just an attack against Jews but also an "attack upon the soul of the German people" and an "insult to human personality." In response, Salis Daiches, chief rabbi of Edinburgh, praised the relationship between Jews and Christians in Scotland.[28]

On December 9 the town council of Glasgow, with the support of the churches, voted to welcome five pastors of the Confessional church from Germany. W. Holms Coats, principal of the Baptist Theological College of Scotland since 1935,[29] claimed that a majority of Germans did not support attacking their Jewish neighbors, revealing that "a German had told him recently that there were only 5 per cent of the Germans in favour of this persecution."[30]

Scottish Baptist indignation continued as 1939 dawned. The terror of Kristallnacht placed a spotlight on the needs of Jewish children. James Hair wrote of the "inhumanity of the pogrom" and of "child-refugees landing in this country and elsewhere, fatherless and motherless as the result of this insensate decree." But, he wondered, what about "others who are huddled in concentration camps in No-Man's Lands that are their only refuge, in the Arctic weather conditions of the past week?" Hair took comfort knowing that Baptists and other Christians stood in solidarity with the Jewish community in Edinburgh. Their meeting with a Jewish rabbi "revealed the widespread nature of the indignation and disgust which Hitler and his henchmen have aroused by this latest exhibition of the frenzied fury which is Nazism."[31]

A companion editorial placed Nazi anti-Semitism in a historical perspective: "Herr Hitler assumed power in February 1933, and between then and March 1936, about 100,000 Jews left Germany, about one-third of them going to Palestine." Immigration decreased beginning in 1936 due to "the fact that foreign countries are reaching the limit of their willingness to receive Jewish refugees." With the Austrian Anschluss, Nazi policy toward the Jews had entered a more sinister phase, characterized by a desire to achieve a "systematic destruction" of the Jewish populations under Nazi rule:

> In Vienna and Austria generally, for a time, neither decency nor humanity checked the will to destroy. There have been several orgies of Jew-baiting, such as Europe has not known since the darkest days of the Middle Ages; a community once outstanding in intellect and culture is in danger of being turned into a community of beggars. When the Nazis invaded Austria they at once forced masses of Jews and Jewesses to scrub streets and Nazi barracks, houses of wealthy Jews were ransacked. Jewish businesses were taken over arbitrarily by "Aryans." That period came to an end, the considered policy now is one of systematic destruction and the maintenance of panic for the whole Jewish population. Tens of thousands of Jews have been thrown out of employment; many important Jewish businesses have been confiscated or placed under an Aryan Commissar, under conditions which compel Jews to sign them away at any price.[32]

The conclusion left no doubt that Nazi anti-Semitism, if left unchecked, would culminate in the annihilation of the Jewish population in Europe. As proof, it quoted the notorious Jew hater Julius Streicher, who said, "The sun will not shine again for the peoples of the earth until the last Jew has died, that is, when the last bacillus of disease is gone."[33]

Pity, Sympathy, and Indignation

The *Scottish Baptist Magazine*'s coverage of the BWA's 1939 World Congress was similar to that of other Baptist newspapers. W. Holms Coats applauded the congress's admirable protest against segregation: "A special welcome was given to the negro delegates, whose presence on the platform along with their white brethren was something of a novelty in the Southern States." Rushbrooke recalled that "when war seemed imminent" in 1938, he issued a nonpolitical "call to prayer to renounce the spirit of hate, to hold fast to our unity in Christ whatever may happen in the earthly sphere," and he was happy to share that the "response was general and wonderful—and most significant was that of our German brethren."[34]

Nevertheless, it was not possible to deny the political divide between Baptists. Coats, though siding with Aubrey's pro-democracy and freedom position, observed that the German Baptists offered a "courageous protest against what they considered misrepresentation of their position in Germany. Baptists, they said, were perfectly free to carry on their work; indeed, the Church was not oppressed in Nazi Germany except when it meddled with politics."[35]

On September 10, 1939, Rev. Dr. R. J. Smithson, of Kirkcaldy, preached a sermon in support of Great Britain's entry into the war. He maintained that war was justifiable because of the "*implacable*" opposition "*between the fundamental principles of Hitlerism and the fundamental principles of Christianity.*"[36] He delineated three clear themes that pitted Christianity against Nazism. First, the Nazi racial doctrine of Nordic superiority rejected Christianity's emphasis on the unity of humanity: "Nazi-ism [*sic*] is based on its theory of blood superiority to all the rest of mankind. The Nordic race—which, we are informed, comprises all who are of pure German blood—is the race whose destiny is supremacy among all races." Second, Smithson claimed that the "extermination of the Jews" was an essential feature of Nazi racial doctrine, whereas Christianity was inclusive, "elevating and educating the backward races"[37] for citizenship in God's kingdom. Third, totalitarianism was at odds with the Baptist understanding of *personality*:

> In Nazi-ism man's worth is determined by his value to the State. Human personality is no more than a means to the State's ends.

> In Christianity the determining factor is what a man is worth to
> God. In the Nazi State the power of the State is absolute over
> the citizen's entire life. The only test for what a man may do,
> say, or think is, "Does it promote the welfare of the State?" In
> Christianity the will of the Living God is supreme over both the
> individual and the State. Men are to know that will and to do it.
> Out of that demand there spring the sacred right of conscience
> and the abiding imperatives of civil and religious liberty.[38]

On September 20, 1939, the Scottish Baptist Council unanimously
accepted a resolution from the Social Service Committee, expressing
"its profound sorrow at the outbreak of war between this country,
Poland and France on the one hand, and Germany on the other. . . .
It expresses deep sympathy with the Polish nation in its heroic stand
against Nazi ill-faith, aggression and violence."[39] The full assembly
passed the same resolution on October 25, 1939.[40]

Following attacks on London in which the Baptist Church House
was damaged, President Alexander Clark lamented during the 1940
assembly that "Hitler is hailed as a Messiah sent for deliverance of
the German people from dishonour, slavery, misery. . . . The spiritual foundations of Western civilization have been undermined."
In contrast, Jesus, the "King of the Jews," promoted "a realised
brotherhood. . . . Where He holds sway, racial, national and class
barriers fall." Against all forms of totalitarianism, God's kingdom
forges "new courses in the sphere of human relationships—social,
international, inter-racial." Communism, fascism, and Nazism
constituted a triune assault against Christianity. In particular, "In
Germany the nation is god, and Hitler is his prophet." Hitler was
at war with the church; Christians, including Baptists, "have been
banished into exile with its terrible hardships; others languish in
concentration camps amid unspeakable horrors; the new pro-Nazi
Government in Rumania has suppressed Baptists and other dissent-
ers, and confiscated their church property."[41]

After the release of the *Joint Declaration by Members of the
United Nations* on December 17, 1942, calling for the "prosecution
of those responsible for Nazi crimes against the Jews in Europe,"[42]
W. Holms Coats wrote that the minute of silence observed by the
House of Commons, "as a symbol of pity, sympathy and indigna-
tion, was one that will never be forgotten." He spoke for many

Scots in combining moral outrage with a sense of helplessness in the face of an unprecedented atrocity:

> Hitler's threat to exterminate the Jews, which the world received with incredulity, seems to be in process of cold-blooded and inhuman execution. It is right that solemn expression should be given to the determination of the United Nations that its perpetrators shall not escape condign retribution; but that alone brings no respite or comfort to the victims. The dreadful fact seems inescapable that there is little we can do about it just now: yet no effort should be spared to devise some means of bringing at least a measure of relief.[43]

On January 27, 1943, Baptist Union delegates participated in an ecumenical conference focused on assisting Jewish survivors of the Holocaust during the postwar period. The conference denounced "any denial to persons of Jewish descent of the right of equal treatment before the law and of other rights due to their status as ordinary citizens" and demanded that governments "restore to the full status of human dignity such Jewish people as had been deprived of it." They called for the Allies to "ensure that those responsible for these crimes should not escape retribution." Furthermore, the conference was united in asserting that "both Jewry and the Christian Churches had a definite and urgent duty in combatting anti-Semitism," and so they agreed to create a "Continuation Committee" of both Jews and Christians for the "consideration of ways and means whereby anti-Semitism could be effectively met and overcome."[44]

From Indignation about Jewish Suffering to Hope for German Baptists

Following the liberation of the concentration camps by Allied forces in the spring of 1945, the *Scottish Baptist Magazine* described the full extent of the horrors endured by Jewish victims under Hitler's Final Solution:

> The indisputable evidence of Nazi brutality revealed by the capture of German concentration camps has filled the Allied armies with cold fury and the whole world with nausea. Any secret

hopes that accounts of German barbarity had been exaggerated are thereby blown to the winds, for the reality is infinitely worse than any rumours. Torture, starvation, sadistic inhumanity to men, women and little children, carried out with fiendish ingenuity and cold-blooded callousness, now lie open before the horrified eyes of mankind. The prompt action of Parliament in sending out a delegation of M.P.s to see for themselves has forestalled any denial: and though the worst traces of bestiality had perforce been removed before their arrival, accounts already published of their reactions prepare us for a document that will make the worst stories of mediaeval cruelty and the Spanish Inquisition pale into insignificance.[45]

The Holocaust raised troubling existential and practical questions for Scottish Baptists. Justice needed to be dealt out to perpetrators, but what about German Baptists who did not protest against Nazi anti-Semitism? A *Scottish Baptist Magazine* editorial stated that restoration of fellowship with German Baptists depended on certain assurances: "We cannot yet enter into full Christian fellowship with pastors who have actively supported or defended the Nazi regime."[46] Nevertheless, by the end of 1945, attitudes toward German Baptists were beginning to soften. The European Committee of the Scottish Baptist Union "hoped that soon effective contacts will be established" with Baptists on the Continent.[47] A report on Aubrey's visit to Germany stated, "Berlin Baptists are anxious to re-establish relations with British and American Baptists. The churches are now the great hope of Germany; but they need wise, strong leadership and encouragement, for their hardships are great, and the way will be difficult. They have brought on themselves the judgment of despair; but despair cannot be the last word."[48]

Throughout the Nazi era, Scottish Baptists periodically expressed their indignation over Hitler's persecution of the Jewish population of Germany and occupied Europe. Scottish Baptists had a sound grasp of the theological challenges Nazism posed for Christianity and responded according to historical Baptist core convictions. Additionally, they acted as loyal British subjects, supporting appeasement prior to the war and the entry of Great Britain into conflict against the Axis powers following the invasion of Poland.

As the Third Reich succumbed to Allied military might, Scottish Baptists confessed impotence regarding offering an effective response that might materially alleviate the suffering of Jewish victims. Like other Baptist national bodies, Scottish Baptists prematurely welcomed German and Italian Baptists back into fellowship, supported humanitarian assistance to continental Baptists, but provided little practical aid for Jewish concentration camp survivors. In the Scottish Baptist transition from indignation about Jewish persecution to hope for a restored relationship with estranged Baptists, Jewish survivors of the Holocaust were not a significant priority. Scottish Baptists were by no means unique in this regard but rather representative of how the wider Baptist family reacted during the postwar period.

NOTES

1. See https://www.cuparbaptist.org.uk/index.html.

2. "Is Hitler the Man of Sin?", *St. Andrews Citizen*, September 13, 1941, 4.

3. An earlier version of the rest of this chapter was published as Lee B. Spitzer, "Nazi Persecution of the Jews and Scottish Baptist Indignation," *Baptist Theologies* 9, no. 2 (Autumn 2017), 68–84. Permission to reuse this material was granted by journal coeditor Toivo Pilli.

4. Brian R. Talbot, ed., *A Distinctive People: A Thematic Study of Aspects of the Witness of Baptists in Scotland in the Twentieth Century* (Eugene, OR: Wipf and Stock, 2014), 58; and Thomas Stewart, "Our Theological Colleges (II) in Scotland," *Baptist Quarterly* 1, no. 2 (1922): 67.

5. J. T. Forbes, "The Christian World State," *Scottish Baptist Magazine*, February 1933, 3–4.

6. *The Scottish Baptist Yearbook for 1934* [covering 1933] (Glasgow: Baptist Union of Scotland, 1934), 61. For an overview of the Scottish Baptist Union, see Talbot, *A Distinctive People*, 80–98; and Brian R. Talbot, *Building on a Common Foundation: The Baptist Union of Scotland 1869–2019* (Eugene, OR: Pickwick, 2021), 117–210.

7. "Baptist Union of Scotland Quarterly Meetings," *Scottish Baptist Magazine*, July 1933, 14; *Scottish Baptist Yearbook for 1934*, 107–8; and "Baptists and the Jews in Germany," *Scotsman*, June 5, 1933, 7.

8. *Scottish Baptist Yearbook for 1934*, Social Service Committee, 173.

9. "Jewish Sidelights in Dundee Lecture," *Dundee Courier and Advertiser*, February 7, 1934, 3.

10. "Baptist World Congress," *Scottish Baptist Magazine*, September 1934, 1. The resolution was quoted in "Free Speech in Berlin," *Scotsman*, August 1934, 11.

11. James Macindoe and James Scott, "Fifth Baptist World Congress," *Scottish Baptist Magazine*, October 1934, 2. In an addendum to the main article, D. Merrick Walker, who organized the Scottish delegation, had only praise for the German hosts, both secular and Baptist.

12. J. H. Rushbrooke, "The Fifth Baptist World Congress," *Scottish Baptist Magazine*, June 1935, 5.

13. Rushbrooke, 5.

14. Rushbrooke, 5.

15. "Baptist Association," *Scotsman*, June 25, 1935, 14.

16. James Hair, "The Fight for Religious Liberty," *Scottish Baptist Magazine*, April 1935, 6.

17. "Church Menaced by Modern State," *Dundee Evening Telegraph*, October 20, 1936, 4; "German Church," *Scotsman*, October 21, 1936, 17.

18. "Christian Refugees from Germany," *Aberdeen Press and Journal*, December 19, 1936, 7; Letters from Readers, "Christian Refugees from Germany," *Scotsman*, December 19, 1936, 15.

19. "German Church Strife Too Late: Baptist View at Dundee Meeting," *Dundee Courier and Advertiser*, July 8, 1937, 3.

20. "The Rape of Austria" *Scottish Baptist Magazine*, April 1938, 1.

21. *The Scottish Baptist Yearbook for 1939* [covering 1938] (Glasgow: Baptist Union of Scotland, 1939), Council Report—September 21, 1938—at Glasgow, 127–29.

22. *Scottish Baptist Yearbook for 1939*, Assembly Report—October 26, 1938, 158–61.

23. *Scottish Baptist Yearbook for 1939*, Social Service Committee Report—October 27, 1938, 165–66.

24. "The Mailed Fist," *Scottish Baptist Magazine* (December 1938), 1.

25. "The Mailed Fist," 1.

26. "The Mailed Fist," 1.

27. *The Scottish Baptist Yearbook for 1940* [covering 1939] (Glasgow: Baptist Union of Scotland, 1940), Digest of Minutes for the Council—November 30, 1938, 122; see also The Finance Committee Report—November 22, 1938, 130.

28. "Nazi Persecution," *Scotsman*, December 7, 1938, 8.

29. David W. Bebbington and David Ceri Jones, eds., *Evangelicalism and Fundamentalism in the United Kingdom during the Twentieth Century* (Oxford: Oxford University Press, 2013), 281.

30. "Refugee Problem—Glasgow Protest against Persecution in Germany," *Scotsman*, December 10, 1938, 18.

31. James Hair, "Spread of Religious Persecution," *Scottish Baptist Magazine*, January 1939, 5.

32. "The Crime of Being a Jew in Germany," *Scottish Baptist Magazine*, January 1939, 16.

33. "Crime of Being a Jew in Germany," 16.

34. W. Holms Coats, "Atlanta," *Scottish Baptist Magazine*, September 1939, 1–3.

35. Coats, 1–3.

36. R. J. Smithson, "The Battle Is Not Yours, but God's," *Scottish Baptist Magazine*, October 1939, 4 (italics in original).

37. Smithson's use of "backward races" revealed his own prejudice.

38. Smithson, "Battle Is Not Yours," 4–5.

39. *The Scottish Baptist Yearbook for 1940,* Digest of Minutes for the Council—September 20, 1939, 126; see also The Social Service Report—September 20, 1939, 141.

40. *Scottish Baptist Yearbook for 1940*, Minutes for the Assembly—October 25, 1939, 159.

41. *The Scottish Baptist Yearbook for 1941* [covering 1940] (Glasgow: Baptist Union of Scotland, 1941), Presidential Address, 154–64. See also "A Spiritual Struggle," *Scotsman* (October 29, 1940), 3.

42. John P. Fox, "The Jewish Factor in British War Crimes Policy in 1942," *English Historical Review* 92, no. 362 (January 1977): 82. See also David S. Wyman, *The Abandonment of the Jews: America and the Holocaust, 1941–1945* (New York: New Press, 1984, rev. 2007), 104.

43. W. Holms Coats, "The Jewish Horror," *Scottish Baptist Magazine*, January 1943, 2.

44. "Post-War Jewry: Scottish Churches' Conference," *Scotsman*, January 28, 1943, 3.

45. "The Concentration Camp Horror," *Scottish Baptist Magazine*, May 1945, 1–2.

46. "Fraternising with the Enemy," *Scottish Baptist Magazine*, July 1945, 1–2.

47. *The Scottish Baptist Yearbook for 1946* [covering 1945] (Glasgow: Baptist Union of Scotland, 1946), European Committee Report and Resolution, 76.

48. W. Holms Coats, "Rev. M. E. Aubrey in Germany," *Scottish Baptist Magazine* (January 1946), 2.

PART TWO

The Solidarity of Baptists with
Jews in France

CHAPTER 5

The Compassion of L'Église Évangélique Baptiste de l'avenue du Maine

French Baptist Philo-Semitism

Ties between Baptists in the United States, England, and France existed from the very beginning of the French Baptist movement in the nineteenth century. The American Baptist Foreign Mission Society supported more than a dozen French workers by midcentury, while London's Spurgeon's College trained leaders. Emerging differences in theology and polity led to a threefold division within the movement by 1930: La Fédération des Églises Évangéliques Baptistes de France (FEEB), L'Association Évangélique des Eglises Baptistes de Langue Francaise, and independent Baptist churches, such as The Tabernacle in Paris.[1]

Several formative French Baptist leaders expressed philo-Semitic views about the Jewish people. Ruben Saillens (1855–1942) defended the Jewish people in a prophetic manner. He linked the infamous Dreyfus trial to Jesus' sufferings, with both innocent figures "caught in the same spiral of injustice."[2] As a Protestant evangelical, Saillens believed that it was not anti-Semitic to offer the possibility of following Jesus to Jewish people.[3]

Samuel Vincent discerned a spiritual principle behind the continued existence of the Jewish people despite millennia of persecution. In an article for the journal *La Pioche et la Truelle* (The Pick-Axe and the Trowel), edited by his brother Philémon Vincent,[4] he argued that only the existence of God could explain the extraordinary ability of the Jews to maintain their collective identity in exile. The "Jewish race" was in actuality a "witness of God." Since each individual Jew shared in that vocation, Vincent declared that there were nine million such witnesses validating God's existence and covenant fidelity, for all to see: "Friendly reader, be careful when you see a Jew pass: God is there behind (them)."[5]

French Baptist philo-Semitism, whether based on justice concerns (Saillens) or religious respect (Vincent), were subjected to a supreme test when the Nazis assumed power in 1933. French Baptists in general maintained the respect for Jews promoted by Saillens and Vincent. Following in Saillens's footsteps, Joël Carlier wrote in September 1934, "In the face of the savage explosion of anti-Semitism which Germany has given the sad example to the civilized world, in front of the new dangers which threaten them there and elsewhere, it is only natural that Jews everywhere feel the need to get closer and to coordinate the defense of their just cause."[6] French Baptists were predisposed to affirming their "elective affinities" (such as love for the Jewish Scriptures and experiences of historical victimhood) with Jews and Judaism.[7]

A Poem to Hitler

Ruben Saillens's love for the Jewish people was illustrated by an unpublished poem he crafted in response to reading "A Jew to Hitler," composed by Jewish poet Phillip Raskin in early 1933.[8] Raskin's defiant challenge to Hitler's hubris was published in newspapers around the world. The poem compared Hitler with Haman, Titus, Nero, Torquemada, and Pharaoh, and in the final stanza declared that Hitler would fail just like his predecessors:

> Hitler, we shall outlive you,
> However our flesh you harrow;
> Our wondrous epic shall only add
> The tale of another Pharaoh.[9]

Saillens's French "translation" reworked Raskin's poem. The first and last stanzas of Saillens's version powerfully expressed his solidarity with the Jewish people in their present time of suffering:

Les Juifs te survivront, Hitler, (The Jews will survive you, Hitler.)
Toi qu'un peuple de fous adore! (You whom a mad people adore!)
Comme autrefois Haman tomba devant Esther, (As in the old days
    Haman fell before Esther,)
Tu mourras,—nous vivrons encore! (You will die—we will still
    live!) . . .

Hitler, les Juifs te survivront! (Hitler, the Jews will outlive you!)
Malgré ta puissance usurpée, (Despite your usurped power,)
Ton destin sera d'être un autre Pharaon (Your destiny will be to be
    another pharaoh,)
S'ajoutant à notre Epopée![10] (Adding to our epic!)

In the original poem, Raskin provocatively called the Jewish people the race of the "eternal martyr." For Saillens, martyrs from the past are transformed into heroes of the faith. Both Raskin and Saillens, with utter confidence, predicted Hitler's demise. Although it apparently was never published during the Nazi era, Saillens's poetry clearly demonstrated his profound and deeply rooted opposition to the German Nazi revolution and its anti-Semitic agenda.

The American-French Missions Connection

Following a decade of partnership with the American Baptist Home Mission Society, Leopold Cohn, missionary to the Jewish community in Brooklyn, established an independent ministry in 1907—the American Board of Missions to the Jews (ABMJ).[11] In 1935 Cohn's son and ministry successor, Joseph Hoffman Cohn, recalled his seminary friendship with a French Baptist, Paul Vincent. Eager to establish a beachhead for ABMJ in Europe, he sought him out while in Paris, only to discover from Paul's older brother that he had died in the Great War. That older brother was Rev. Henri Vincent, pastor of L'Église Évangélique Baptiste de l'avenue du Maine. They corresponded over their common concern for German Jewish refugees. On March 1, 1936, the church, with support from ABMJ, launched its ministry to the Jewish community, including those fleeing from Germany.[12] This partnership lasted throughout the Nazi era.

Vincent relied on volunteers and staff to help him serve the Jewish refugee community around his church. Miss Elsie Tilney, an English missionary, joined the church's outreach efforts in 1936.

She felt "privileged to help and witness to the suffering German Jewish refugees," which by 1937 included many Austrian Jews. She was impressed by Vincent's pastoral leadership and passion, as she observed the Baptist minister "throwing open his Church—and heart—to Jewish people." She continued working at the church until sometime in 1939 and subsequently in other situations saved several Jews. In 2013 Tilney was given the honor of being recognized as a "Righteous among the Nations" by Yad Vashem for her sacrificial service on behalf of Jews.[13]

With ABMJ's support, Vincent recruited two other key mission workers for this cutting-edge ministry. Mlle Marie Salomon was a Jewish-Christian woman and a "devout" member of the congregation. She assisted Vincent on many projects. Rev. André Frankel, a Baptist Jewish-Christian, became ABMJ's missionary "under the guidance" of Vincent.[14]

From the outset, the joint Baptist/ABMJ outreach faced a tremendous challenge—the German Jewish refugee population in Paris was exceptionally large. The city hosted about twenty-five thousand German Jewish refugees, including many teachers, entertainment professionals, lawyers, and doctors, representing "the very finest stratum of social life." Cohn, Vincent, and Frankel developed a strategy to "bring immediate relief to substantial numbers of these destitute families." Families received tickets for "one meal in a restaurant in the Jewish ghetto district. . . . We will also provide, whenever we can, clothing, either by purchases or from gifts, which Pastor Vincent will receive from friends in France."[15]

With Frankel performing both evangelistic and social assistance ministries, the church continued throughout 1937 to provide targeted financial support, including "meal tickets, tickets for lodgings at the Salvation Army houses, tickets to buy shoes. When help is necessary for the rent, we have paid it directly to the landlord." They also provided assistance with medical care.[16]

Visiting the Jewish refugee community in Paris in October 1937, Cohn observed "the problem of stark poverty, of human despair such as is not possible to describe unless one had the gift of a master writer." He affirmed the church and the leadership of Vincent and Frankel. Cohn was especially taken by Salomon, "a devoted little Jewish woman, who loves the Lord Jesus Christ with all her heart, and who is a companion in manifold labors together with the two brethren just mentioned. . . . She not only spends and is being spent in her daily errands of mercy and love in these unspeakably miserable tenement rooms, but she also does the editorial work on the French edition of our Yiddish Gospel paper, *The Shepherd of Israel*," which was in high demand. The church was now serving as an ABMJ headquarters, and its Jewish refugee ministry had a profound impact on the membership. Vincent shared that members "would come to meet some of these refugees and they too would cry." This difficult ministry promoted "a new awakening of power in the church, a new life of sacrifice, and a new devotion to the Lord Jesus Christ."[17]

Germaine Melon-Holland, a Quaker relief worker, joined the team in 1937 and, working closely with Frankel, counseled streams of Jewish refugees every Tuesday: "Very often they are in so great distress, and are crying. Then, it is to us to find the right words for those poor people. . . . New refugees continue to come, especially from Germany, and this refugee problem seems to be a permanent one." She reported to ABMJ that about 120 Jewish refugees came to the church's Christmas dinner.[18]

In July 1938 Cohn attended the wedding of Germaine Melon-Holland and André Frankel and noticed that about one-third of the congregation "was made up of our own Jewish refugees, the larger part of them Jewish Christians." They were "a cross-section of human life, sorrow, and joy." Cohn and Frankel "distributed several thousand francs in just a few hours of time. In every case our effort was directed towards the helping of the individual to a footing whereby he might help himself, that is, to earn his own living." The ministry was a team effort: "In every case, our missionaries . . . had made thorough investigation and this investigation had been checked upon by Pastor Henry Vincent, and so we knew each case to be genuine."[19]

Following Kristallnacht, Paris had become "the vortex of the German Jewish suffering" from Cohn's perspective: "The city swarms with new refugees." Germaine Frankel-Melon, in a very personal report, expressed her fear that the "future will be more and more terrible" for Jewish refugees from Germany and other Central European nations. More positively, she documented the Baptist church's effective ministry. Her husband's Friday evening service had some sixty refugee attendees, while the Monday Bible study was averaging about twenty participants. She also expressed her appreciation for Pastor Vincent's willingness to share "so much of his life and thought to the Mission, in spite of all the other work he has to do, and his advice and inspiration are a permanent comfort for us," and for the Baptist congregation's involvement in the Jewish work—"many members do something for it, and are always ready to help in a way or another."[20]

Pastor Vincent modeled how to integrate outreach and compassion in a manner that spoke to ABMJ's supporters. In his 1938 year-end review of the church's Jewish ministry, Vincent shared that he personally baptized eight Jews (four each on July 24 and October 16). Jewish attendance at church events was high; at one Sunday afternoon meal, seventy Jewish people participated. Vincent noted that Jewish refugees were flowing into Paris from Austria and Czechoslovakia. At the same time, the French government was far less open to this humanitarian need, and some refugees were forced out of the city and into the countryside. The church attempted to keep in touch with such families and offer ongoing assistance. Vincent stated, "The misery of the people makes it pretty hard to keep within the limits of material help we try to fix to ourselves. . . . May God help us in His work among His children."[21]

In April 1939 Frankel-Melon resumed her practice of updating ABMJ's supporters on ministry provided to specific Jewish refugee individuals and families. The church ministered to both Jews and Jewish-Christians without discrimination, continued to balance evangelism with practical and financial assistance, and maintained an interest in the refugees over time and regardless of whether they remained in Paris. The team routinely took risks. At the request of Cohn, the ministry team even attempted to reach out to and visit Herschel Grynszpan, the young Jewish man whose assassination of German diplomat Ernst vom Rath served as the excuse to perpetrate the horrors of Kristallnacht. Their efforts were thwarted by French prison regulations, but they were able to "send directly [via mail] Gospels" to the prisoner.[22]

The Occupation of Paris and the Silent Years

Along with other Baptist leaders at the 1939 BWA Congress in Atlanta, Henri Vincent "did not believe war was possible." He continued, "But I am obliged to acknowledge I was mistaken. I could not believe Hitler was quite as mad as he really is." Most surprisingly, he found himself drafted into the French army. The church's Jewish ministry was naturally left in the hands of his colleagues, and an English-speaking member, Jean Tanguy, was added to the leadership.[23]

The refugee ministry was disrupted by the loss of men who joined the French army. Public meetings were suspended by order of French authorities, but private visits in refugee homes and at the church continued. As a Hungarian, Frankl (the ABMJ paper changed the spelling from Frankel to Frankl in this edition) was able to remain in Paris, and he sought official documents confirming his appointment from ABMJ, an organization from a neutral country, to gain "permission to visit the foreigners who are in France in camps because of the war."[24]

In mid-September 1939 Vincent reported to the military in Fontainebleau, but his future assignment was unclear. The Frankls were living in "a small village, 70 kilometres" outside Paris, and they commuted to the city to work. Salomon lived in Veneux les Sablons and edited *Le Berger d'Israel* from home. The church continued to serve refugee individuals and families, including an elderly rabbi and his daughter. Two Jewish refugee families had been successfully relocated to new countries before hostilities commenced.[25]

ABMJ decided to fund the start-up of a soup kitchen for Jewish refugees, and Tanguy agreed to organize the project in cooperation with Salomon and Germaine Melon-Frankl. Recognizing that the soup kitchen required more space than could be provided at 123 avenue du Main, Melon-Frankl suggested an alternate site be secured. Several church women were willing to volunteer time to staff the project.[26] In the first quarter of 1940, the food kitchen was feeding between 150 to 200 "of the most destitute of these Jewish refugees, many of them Jewish Christians, men, women and children."[27] Tanguy claimed, "We are giving more than 100 meals each day, and we shall attain easily 3,000 meals" per month throughout the spring. Bible studies and French lessons had been resumed at the church, while Salomon continued to work on the outreach newsletter with "the assistance of our Baptist pastors."[28]

On May 10, 1940, Germany invaded France and swiftly brought the French military to its knees. The bombing of Paris commenced on June 3, and eleven days later German troops entered the city. An armistice agreement was signed on June 22, and Hitler triumphantly toured the streets of Paris on June 23, 1940.

As the Nazi armies overwhelmed the capital, thousands of Parisians fled toward the southern part of the country. Many refugees associated with the Jewish mission took part in this mass migration. One such refugee, a Mr. Singer, had come to faith through Frankl's ministry. He and his wife made it to Portugal, where he longed to correspond with ABMJ in the United States, but he had lost the ministry's address. He discovered a copy of the *Watchman-Examiner*, which noted that ABMJ had conducted meetings in the Greenwood Baptist Church of Brooklyn. He wrote a letter to the pastor who passed it on to ABMJ. He shared that Frankl gave him 5,000 francs, and with the remaining funds in his possession when he had to flee, he and his wife were able to escape.[29]

Frankl continued working in Paris while his wife remained outside the city. It became increasingly difficult to meet refugee needs during the Nazi occupation: "In July, Andre wrote me that 30 to 35 of our people stayed in Paris, but in desperate distress, living in misery—Andre not able to give some financial relief, because of lack of money." Their own security was in doubt; Germaine confessed that "about Andre's liberty, all is actually very dark in my soul and my heart. I do not see any possible future in the actual state in Europe."[30]

The darkness of occupation grew deeper in 1941. The February issue of the *Chosen People* offered a bleak assessment of the situation, admitting that "there is no way for us to get money into Paris or for our beloved workers there to write letters to us." An American woman "wrote us of the terrible suffering through which our workers are going, and she bemoaned that there is no way for us to get help to them." There was some encouraging news—Vincent had returned to Paris and resumed his pastoral ministry. ABMJ urged its supporters to "pray for Andre Frankl and for his good wife, Germaine . . . and we must not forget to pray also for Pastor Vincent."[31]

Correspondence between the Paris team and ABMJ in New York was cut off for most of 1943–44. However, following the liberation of Paris (August 25, 1944), a postcard mysteriously arrived, written by Germaine Melon-Frankl. In part, it said,

Here in Paris, we are safe. Pastor Vincent is well, as my husband, our little girl, myself, and all the staff. . . . Our work among Jews was never stopped, but we saw our people secretly, and André did not live at home, but went to hide himself in three different places in friends' homes. During this time the police came twice at home to arrest him, but he was not here—and all was well. And now it is the splendid liberation! André is at home again, and all the work begins again.[32]

The Philo-Semitic Legacy of Rev. Henri Vincent

After the war, Joseph Cohn would reveal details from conversations he had with Henri Vincent concerning the silent period. These stories focused on the impact of Vincent's pastoral ministry to Jewish refugees, many of whom had embraced Christianity despite trying circumstances. From these and other stories, it is evident that the compassionate ministry to Jews conducted at l'Église Évangélique Baptiste de l'avenue du Maine in Paris could not have thrived without the unceasing support of its senior pastor.

Descriptions of Vincent's ministry reflected ABMJ's primary focus—evangelistic activities. Vincent spoke of a seventy-six-year-old Jewish woman "whom he had had the privilege of baptizing in the church in Paris." Arrested by the Nazis and transported to an unnamed concentration camp, she was able, "even under the most ubiquitous and vicious snooping of the Nazi soldiers, to write a little note, crumple it up and throw it out of the train window to some friend on the station platform." When Vincent received it, he read that "she was on the way to the extermination camp and that her faith in the Lord Jesus Christ was now stronger than ever before in all her life! In that strength she went to her death."[33]

Vincent did not denigrate social action. No doubt influenced by his seminary studies in Rochester, he grasped the teachings of Rauschenbusch's social gospel and applied it in his pastoral context in Paris.[34] Vincent's passion for improving the conditions of the Jewish refugee community led him to make a most fortuitous personnel appointment—the hiring of Marie Salomon as a social worker in January 1930. A Jewess, she became a follower of Jesus while studying at the Sorbonne, and at the church she immediately established herself as a dedicated and talented leader. She directed *La Fraternitié*, which served primarily women and children, from 1930 to 1945. In this capacity, she worked alongside André Frankl. After the war she continued to work closely with Vincent, serving as his secretary for his Jewish evangelism ministries.[35]

Vincent took many personal risks to protect Jews who came to the church. He was repeatedly called before the Gestapo, even while the church's baptistry was secretly being employed as a depot for hiding weapons presumably used by the resistance (apparently without the pastor's knowledge). The pressure of the occupiers did not deter Vincent's efforts to place Jewish refugee children in sheltering homes, not only in Paris, but all across the country (including Brittany, Savoy, and Poitou).[36]

The Nazi's deportation campaign decimated the community of Jewish Christians that Vincent and Frankl pastored. Cohn claimed that approximately three hundred Jewish converts were associated with L'Église Évangélique's outreaches in 1939, while when "the war ended we had only 20 left!"[37] Nevertheless, in a report Vincent prepared for the BWA just one month after the liberation of Paris, he expressed hope that ABMJ would resume funding the church's Jewish work.[38] He encouraged Cohn to see new possibilities for evangelism, outreach, service, and growth. Vincent wrote in February 1948, "This year has really seen a revival of the work in Paris. After the liberation, it is only slowly that it has begun again. All the Jews that used to come to our Mission have been scattered, or are dead. Slowly others have gathered. New contacts have been made."[39]

The BWA was also eager to resume cooperation with Vincent following the liberation of France. A "Provisional Schedule for Baptist Work in France" was prepared in 1944. Perhaps assuming ABMJ's resumption of support for Jewish evangelism, the proposal focused on ministerial training, personnel needs, literature, equipment, and repairs to damaged properties. Five-thousand dollars was designated for children's ministry, mostly in support of an orphanage in Brittany that Vincent supported, which during the war may have housed Jewish children.[40]

Vincent exhibited both modesty and reserve when speaking of the risks he and other French Baptists took on behalf of Jewish refugees. In a letter to Rushbrooke dated November 30, 1944, he simply reflected, "I myself, and several of my colleagues have been several times in great danger, but we have been wonderfully preserved. All of us tried to remain faithful to the mission we had been given by God Almighty during the critical period where we had the task of preaching the Gospel of salvation, and protect all the suffering people of our country."[41]

In 1946 the Federation of Jewish Societies in France graciously recognized the philo-Semitic actions of the leading French Baptist pastor. The Federation acknowledged that during the darkest period (between 1942 and 1944), Vincent's "activity for the benefit of Jewish adults and children were extremely varied" and so on behalf of "all Jewish Resistance organizations," they wished to express "respectful gratitude."[42] From a greater distance in time, American messianic leader, Joseph Cohn, noted that Vincent's unwillingness to betray his Jewish friends to the Gestapo was extraordinary and that Vincent had confided his belief that "just as God delivered Daniel from the jaws of the lions, so too he delivered Vincent from the Nazi beast and his destruction."[43]

NOTES

1. "France, Baptist History in," in *A Dictionary of European Baptist Life and Thought*, ed. John H. Y. Briggs (Milton Keynes, UK: Paternoster, 2009), 208–9; see also *Histoires D'Une Famille* 1, 2007 (Paris: La Société d'Histoire et de Documentation Baptistes de France, 2007).

2. Sébastien Fath, "Le pasteur évangélique Ruben Saillens et le judaïsme," *Archives Juives* 1 (2007): 48. For more on Protestant responses to the Dreyfus Affair, see Patrick Cabanel, *Juifs et protestants en France, les affinités Electives XVIᵉ–XXIᵉ siècle* (Paris: Fayard Histoire, 2004), 155–80.

3. Fath, 49–50.

4. Philémon Vincent was the founding pastor of l'Église Évangélique Baptiste de l'avenue du Maine; see a brief biography in André Thobois, *Cent ans de l'Église baptiste de L'avenue du Maine à Paris* 1899–1999 (Paris: Croire et Servir, 1999), 87–88.

5. Samuel Vincent, "Neuf millions de preuves de existence de dieu," *La Pioche et la Truelle*, June 1, 1907, 1. The original full journal page with the article can be found at https://gallica. bnf.fr/ark:/12148/bpt6k95433552/f1.image#. I am grateful to Sébastien Fath for pointing me to this article; see "Le pasteur évangélique Ruben Saillens et le judaïsme," 50; and *Les baptistes en France (1810–1950): Faits, dates et documents* (Cléon d'andean, France: Éditions Excelsis, 2002), 78.

6. Joël Carlier, "Le legs d'Israël," *Solidarité Sociale* 674 (September 22, 1934): 2, quoted in Fath, "Le pasteur évangélique Ruben Saillens et le judaïsme," 56n30.

7. Fath, "Le pasteur évangélique Ruben Saillens et le judaïsme," 51–54.

8. "A Jew to Hitler," *Jewish Western Bulletin*, May 4, 1933, 2; "A Jew to Hitler," *Sentinel*, June 1, 1933, cited in D. Rosenfeld, "Who Was 'Hitler' before Hitler? Historical Analogies and the Struggle to Understand Nazism, 1930–1945," *Central European History* 51, no. 2 (2018): 264n96.

9. Raskin composed a much more sophisticated and lengthy poem following Kristallnacht, "The Jew's Answer to Hitler"; contained in *The Collected Poems of Philip M. Raskin 1878– 1944* (New York: Bloch, 1951), 16–26.

10. For the complete poem in French, see http://rubensaillens.over-blog.org/article-6394831. html. The English translation is mine.

11. Lee B. Spitzer, *Baptists, Jews, and the Holocaust: The Hand of Sincere Friendship* (Valley Forge, PA: Judson, 2017), 31–34. Cohn retained his membership in the Marcy Avenue Baptist Church in Brooklyn and the Long Island Baptist Ministers' Association; see "In Memoriam," *Chosen People*, February 1938, 5–6.

12. Joseph Hoffman Cohn, "And Now, a Branch in Paris," *Chosen People*, April 1936, 7. For a thorough account of the work of ABMS in France, see Mitchell Leslie Glaser, "A Survey of Missions to the Jews in Continental Europe 1900–1950" (PhD diss., Fuller Theological Seminary, 1998): 283–93. I am indebted to Glaser for granting me access to the *Chosen People* collection. See also André Thobois, *Henri Vincent: infatigable serviteur du Christ, passionné d'évangélisation* (Paris: Croire et Servir, 2001), 65.

13. Philippe Sands, *East West Street* (New York: Vintage Books, 2017), 121–32, 365.

14. Cohn, "And Now, a Branch in Paris," *Chosen People*, April 1936, 7–10.

15. Joseph Hoffman Cohn, "Salutation," *Chosen People*, November 1936, 4–6.

16. Henri Vincent, "Helping Refugee Jews in Paris," *Chosen People*, February 1937, 11.

17. Joseph Hoffman Cohn, "Salutation," *Chosen People*, October 1937, 6–8.

18. Germaine Melon-Holland, "Christmas in Paris" and "Food and Gospels Together," *Chosen People*, February 1938, 14. See also "Portraits of Delegates to the Friends' World Conference," *Bulletin of Friends' Historical Association* 26, no. 1 (Spring 1937): 2a–2b.

19. Joseph Hoffman Cohn, "Salutation," *Chosen People*, November 1938, 5–7.

20. Hoffman Cohn, "Salutation," and Germaine Frankel-Melon, "Behind the Scenes in Paris," *Chosen People*, January 1939, 3, 10–12.

21. Henri Vincent, "When War Threatens Paris," *Chosen People*, January 1939, 12–13.

22. Germaine Frankel-Melon, "Statenlos! Where Shall I Go?", *Chosen People*, April 1939, 9–11.

23. Henri Vincent, "Paris behind the War Smoke," *Chosen People*, November 1939, 6. Vincent also visited the ABMJ's Brooklyn headquarters.

24. André Frankl, "From André Frankl," *Chosen People*, November 1939, 7.

25. Germaine Melon-Frankl, "Out of a Woman's Heart," *Chosen People*, November 1939, 7–8.

26. "Soup Kitchens in Europe" and "The Woman's Angle," *Chosen People*, January 1940, 10–11.

27. "We Pioneer in Soup Kitchens," *Chosen People*, May 1940, 5.

28. "Thank You for the Soup Kitchens," *Chosen People*, May 1940, 9.

29. "In the Nazi Infernos," *Chosen People*, October 1940, 11.

30. Germaine Melon-Frankl, "A Picture of Unoccupied France," *Chosen People*, October 1940, 13.

31. Joseph Hoffman Cohn, "Salutation," *Chosen People*, February 1941, 14.

32. Germaine Melon-Frankl, "More Word from Paris," *Chosen People*, December 1944, 13.

33. Joseph Hoffman Cohn, "Salutation," *Chosen People*, October 1947, 6.

34. Thobois, *Henri Vincent*, 16–19, 54–55, 58–64.

35. Thobois, *Henri Vincent*, 29–31, 57. See esp. 31n19. See also André Thobois, *Cent ans de l'Église baptiste de l'avenue du Maine* à *Paris 1899–1999*, 39–40.

36. Thobois, *Henri Vincent*, 40–41.

37. Joseph Hoffman Cohn, "Salutation," *Chosen People*, October 1947, 7.

38. Henri Vincent, *Study of Possible Developments for Baptist Work in France*, September 1944, 7, Angus Library and Archive.

39. Joseph Hoffman Cohn, "Salutation," *Chosen People*, February 1948, 4–5.

40. "Provisional Schedule for Baptist Work in France," 1944, 1–3, Angus Library and Archive.

41. Henri Vincent to J. H. Rushbrooke, November 30, 1944, 1, Angus Library and Archive.

42. Thobois, *Henri Vincent*, 89.

43. Quoted in Glaser, "A Survey of Missions to the Jews in Continental Europe 1900–1950," 288.

CHAPTER 6

The Heroism of French Baptist Resisters and Rescuers

French Baptist Resisters and Rescuers

From Paris to Nice, French Baptist clergy and laypeople came alongside Jews who were fleeing German persecution. Sébastien Fath has observed that, generally speaking, French Baptists were "not indifferent to the events of the war." Even though Baptists in France constituted a very small minority of the population, certain individuals did embrace the spirit of resistance, even at the cost of their own lives. The "first Protestant resistance fighter shot" in the war was a Baptist—André Guéziec, whom the Nazis captured and then executed on May 12, 1941. Approximately twenty French Baptists were killed in combat roles.[1]

Other French Baptists specifically expressed resistance through nonviolent forms of rescue.[2] Several of their stories are the focus of this chapter. Hearing their narratives, several considerations should be kept in mind. Jacques Semelin speaks of "civilian resistance," which involves "the spontaneous process by civilian society using unarmed means, and mobilizing either its principal institutions or its people—or both at the same time." For certain French Baptist leaders and churches, encountering Jewish people who were suffering persecution called forth a "moral and spiritual" response.[3] Their expressions of philo-Semitism, inherited from a prior generation of French Baptist leaders, encouraged them to respond sacrificially and courageously. Rescue efforts represented both a reaction to the needs of those fleeing Hitler's wrath and a simultaneous rejection of the anti-Semitism imposed by the Nazis and sometimes embraced by citizens of conquered territories.[4] Most importantly, French Baptist rescuers did not operate in isolation; they functioned as part of a larger "interwoven fabric of individuals and groups . . . that shielded Jews from arrest through networks of social solidarity."[5]

Approximately 75 percent of the Jewish population in France survived the Holocaust. Rescuers played their part, but persecuted Jews (whether they survived or not) were not passive or helpless. Jewish men, women, and children actively, courageously, and creatively searched for ways to escape arrest and deportation, and along the way they sought assistance from sympathetic neighbors, strangers, and organizations. These Jews were "agents of their own survival" who at times "discovered the existence in France of a supportive web of social relationships, even as there was a parallel social current of denunciation and anti-Semitism."[6] In various locations across France, Baptists were part of that supportive web of relationships.

Rachel Revoy and the Home for Jewish Christian Refugee Children in Nurieux

Prior to Germany's victory over France, ABMJ and its Parisian Baptist church partner became beneficiaries of a change in fortunes of one of the congregation's female members. According to *Chosen People* (December 1939), she inherited "a chateau some 300 miles south of Paris" and offered it to the ministry to serve as an orphanage for Jewish children: "If you can use the property as a Home for some of the dear children of your Jewish Christian refugees, you are welcome to it, and I will further devote my own time and strength to help in such a work."[7]

The article, perhaps intentionally to protect the generous Baptist "widow," did not reveal her name or family background. She was Rachel Revoy, the daughter of a Baptist father and a Jewish mother. She self-identified as a religious Baptist and for civil registration purposes, as a Jew. Rachel was born on March 1, 1892, and was not actually a widow (she married in 1946). That fiction probably was advanced to protect Rachel (and the ministry) from scandal, since she had adopted a boy, Fernand, in 1938. She had rented the farmhouse in Nurieux since 1934, and purchased it on

April 22, 1938, for 30,000 francs (approximately $450). Within a year after assuming ownership, she offered her home (La Maison) as a refuge for Jewish children.[8]

In just a few months, the Home for Jewish Christian Refugee Children in Nurieux (near Lyon) was providing a dozen children shelter, meals, clothing, and health care for $100 per month. The children were not necessarily orphans—their parents were in Paris or their fathers were in the military—and were probably referred by the church or one of the deaconess hospitals in Paris. With Revoy providing the house for free, ABMJ's initial grant for food, utilities, and supplies of $1,200 would last until the end of June 1940.[9]

As the Nazis consolidated control over additional parts of France, ABMJ found it difficult to get funds to the home: "It took us a long time before we were allowed by our own Government to cable funds to Nurieux; in the meantime Mme. Revoy had spent every franc she had, had borrowed wherever she could, and then like the widow of Zarephath, she was ready to eat her last morsel and die. It was at this crucial moment that our cabled funds reached her, and we have been able to get money to her regularly each month since."[10] Revoy described the difficult circumstances under which the home functioned throughout 1941: "Here with my children I have come across terrible moments, but now thanks to your help, things are much better. Our little ones are feeling well. For our nourishment we are lacking a great many things, but we are trying to sustain ourselves just the same, and we are trusting God to keep us in good health."[11]

However, the United States and Great Britain also made it increasingly difficult to transfer money to German-occupied countries. ABMJ became unable to continue funding the home,[12] and by spring 1942 Revoy could no longer pay its debts to food vendors. In deep distress, she reacted to the prospect of closing the home, sending its refugee children away, and suffering personal loss: "When Mr. C_____ brought me the money he also brought me some news which has troubled me greatly: the question whether to close the house or not! Not only that I shall miss the little children terribly which I love so much (because of the promises of the Bible on this subject); this would also be a catastrophe for me, since I shall be—from one day to the next—without job, without money, with a child to bring up, and a house in which I put everything that I possessed." One can easily hear Revoy's feelings of betrayal: "Why did not Paris tell me several months ago about her intentions (or Mr. C_____) instead of letting me wait and not providing me with the most necessary!" ABMJ could only respond: "And with saddened hearts, we say farewell. May the God of all mercies deal tenderly with this widow and the starving children. They are beyond human help for our government will no longer permit funds to be sent to France. Only God can intervene!"[13]

However, it appears that the home in Nurieux did continue operating for two more years. Even during the occupation (1943–44), the home served up to forty children, many of whom survived. Revoy cooperated with Protestant rescue organizations throughout southern France. She and others were in constant danger, for even though many in the Ain region were active in saving Jews, repressive actions were not uncommon. One hundred and two Jews were captured and sent to camps from this region, including forty-two children from a rescue home in Izieu.[14]

Amazingly, the children under Revoy's care did not share in this fate. In 1943 correspondence between Revoy and municipal authorities indicated that the home was serving up to twenty-five children, ranging in ages from eighteen months to thirteen years old. Some were of French nationality, but others had come from Belgium, Russia, Germany, and Poland. Revoy's home church referred some of the children,[15] while others came via relationships established with the Friends (Quakers) in southern France. A few came from the Rivesaltes and Gurs internment/transit camps located in southern France. In the spring of 1944, the children's safety could only be maintained by evacuating them temporarily to Lozère, some four hours away by automobile.[16]

Despite her heroic and sacrificial service, Rachel Revoy has not been acknowledged by Yad Vashem as belonging to the "Righteous among the Nations," due perhaps both to her Jewish background or her acceptance of financial support. She died at the age of eighty-nine in 1981.

The Vincents in Marseille

Henri Vincent was not the only member of his family to resist the Nazis. His two cousins, Gaston and Raymond Vincent, along with Gaston's oldest son, Michel, and Michel's future spouse, Suzanne

Jacquet, were heavily involved in resistance networks in southern France. Their stories have been preserved by Yad Vashem[17] and various websites dedicated to their legacy.[18]

Gaston Vincent (1891–1944) served as a radio operator and was injured during the First World War. He married Éliane Lucienne Amélie Cojonnex on May 5, 1923. Gaston participated in resistance networks and developed personal relationships with people sympathetic to his concerns. He started the Marseilles chapter of the ecumenical Amitié chrétienne (Christian Friends),[19] a movement Suzanne Jacquet soon joined. He also launched the Vert Plan shelter in Mazargues, in cooperation with OSE (Oeuvre de Secours aux Enfants—Society for Assistance to Children), a Jewish organization that "provided homes for Jewish refugee children from all over Europe."[20] The children OSE delivered to Vert Plan came from nearby detention camps.

In August 1942 a harrowing challenge confronted Vincent— a friendly policeman warned him that "the mass arrest of foreign Jews was imminent." He and Michel "warned many of the threatened families, who fled their homes before it was too late." When on November 11, 1942, the Vert Plan was taken over by the Germans, new quarters for its thirty Jewish boarders were needed, and "dressed in the uniforms of the Protestant scouts, the young refugees were taken to Vic sur Cère (Cantal). Vincent had organized the convoy and Michel . . . made the trip with the children, who were taken in and hidden in an improvised shelter directed by Suzanne Jacquet located in a building bearing the sign, 'Touring Hôtel.'"[21]

The Touring Hôtel was also related to OSE and served as "a transitory place of refuge from which every child was later taken either to a host family or spirited across the Swiss border." Two Jewish survivors, eighteen-year-old Hélène Turner (who "had been saved from the Rivesaltes camp and placed in Vic sur Cère") and seventeen-year-old Ryna Himmelfarb (who "narrowly escaped arrest in a roundup in Périgeux, arrived at the Touring Hôtel only in 1944"), provided the eyewitness testimony Yad Vashem requires to designate a person as a "Righteous among the Nations."

After the takeover of the Vert Plan shelter, Vincent Gaston continued his resistance work in North Africa. In cooperation with the Office of Strategic Service and along with his brother Raymond, Gaston utilized his radio operator skills. Raymond was active in various battlefields and was killed by the German Gestapo in

September 1943. According to Yad Vashem, Gaston was also captured and executed on June 25, 1944.[22]

After the war Suzanne married Michel Vincent. Yad Vashem officially recognized Gaston Vincent, Michel Vincent, and Suzanne Vincent-Jacquet as "Righteous among the Nations" on January 28, 1986.

Rev. Edmond Evrard and his Family in Nice

Yad Vashem[23] includes Rev. Edmond Evrard, his wife, Ida, and sons Daniel and Louis as "Righteous among the Nations," but this courageous family is virtually unknown in contemporary global Baptist circles. Their commitment to the Jewish people was caring, comprehensive, and sacrificial, and as a pastoral family they were an exceptional example of how to serve persecuted Jews under dangerous circumstances.

The Evrard family ministered to scores of Jewish people seeking freedom and safety in Nice. Their predicament was constantly in flux, as the Italian administration of that region of France gave way to increasing German influence. The Yad Vashem file reveals that "as early as 1940, Evrard explicitly denounced the anti-Jewish policies of the Vichy regime and the German authorities in his Sunday sermons, urging his congregants to help Jews who had lost their jobs, livelihoods, and property."[24]

The Baptist minister cooperated with Jewish resistance groups in Nice, including the Marcel Network, which through the leadership of Moussa Abadi and Odette Rosenstock, saved 527 Jewish children.[25] Decades later they wrote a recommendation letter to Yad Vashem declaring that Evrard "always responded, to the fullest extent possible, to our calls" for assistance for Jewish children. They also praised the church, calling it a "place of reception and refuge for the victims of racial persecution, who were chased by the Gestapo and the militia of Vichy."[26]

Evrard also worked with Russian-born Jewish rescuer Joseph Bass and his Service André, who saved thousands of Jews in Marseilles and beyond in collaboration with both Protestant and Catholic clerics.[27] Graciously, Bass wrote letters of recommendation out of gratitude for Evrard's resistance efforts, sharing that he had "a modest heart."[28]

Evrard's prewar experiences and relationships prepared him for this dangerous work. He was one of only two French Baptist delegates to the 1934 BWA World Congress in Berlin, and in that capacity, he personally witnessed the debate on racialism and voted in favor of the resolution against anti-Semitism.[29]

He came to that historic event with a social justice track record. In collaboration with André Trocmé, Evrard published "a small journal, *La bonne semance*." The paper aimed to discuss, in the words of Trocmé, "the social and international implications of the Christian faith."[30] Evrard's friendship and professional collaboration with Trocmé paved the way for their later partnership in serving Jewish people seeking safety and asylum. The Yad Vashem file documents Evrard's activities in Le Chambon-sur-Lignon, where Trocmé had established one of the greatest communitarian efforts to protect Jewish refugees:

> His wife and two sons, aged sixteen and eighteen, participated in his activities, notably by leading groups of Jewish children from Nice to the village of Le Chambon-sur-Lignon and from there to Switzerland. The pastor and his sons were counselors in a Salvation Army summer camp in Le Chambon, and in that capacity they escorted their Jewish wards, dressed as Swiss Scouts, to the border. In late 1943, in response to the difficult situation, Pastor Evrard intensified his action. He sheltered various fugitives, chiefly Jews without French citizenship, for short periods until they could be placed in more permanent hiding places. With the assistance of Jewish underground members, he provided forged papers.[31]

The Baptist congregation in Nice permitted their building to become "a gathering point and shelter for Jews and a center of unusual activities." In March 1944 Evrard was approached by three Jewish representatives seeking to conduct a Purim service in the church. Evrard believed it was "his duty before God" to authorize the service and facilitate its actualization. Jewish participants arrived by bicycle, while his two sons maintained a watch outside.[32]

Evrard also intervened on behalf of Jews in trouble, protecting them from local informants who betrayed them for money or other favors. On several occasions he urged the Gestapo to release Jewish women from prison:

> One woman, Vera Kogan, who had been arrested in the summer of 1944, tried to commit suicide in her cell to avoid deportation. Kogan was taken to the hospital, treated, and returned to jail. Evrard visited the prison three times and succeeded in persuading an officer there to release Kogan, saying that this would strengthen French-German relations. In the second case, at extreme risk, Evrard arranged the release of Mme Straussman, who had been arrested at the maternity hospital when she gave birth to her son, in early 1944. The local Gestapo commander, Strauss, was determined to send Straussman to Drancy. Right before Straussman was deported, Evrard convinced another officer to release her.[33]

During the wartime years, the Evrards also experienced personal suffering. Although limited amounts of news were seeping out of occupied Europe, W. O. Lewis attempted to stay in touch with as many European Baptist conventions as possible. In an April 1942 article, Lewis relayed sad news: "We sympathize with Pastor and Mrs. Edmond Evrard, of Nice, France, in the loss of their son 'Joe.' He had been an invalid for some time. His end was hastened by inability, on account of the war, to get the diet and medicine he needed."[34]

The French government awarded Evrard the bronze medal on June 27, 1947. Reflecting on his resistance years, Evrard said, "What we did was altogether natural. We, other Christians, Protestants, and especially those of the Baptist Church, are nourished by the Bible. The history of the Jewish people is our history as well. Palestine is our second homeland. We love the Jews and we hold them in esteem. They are brave people."[35]

On December 26, 1994, Yad Vashem recognized Edmond, Ida, Louis, and Daniel as "Righteous among the Nations." Louis responded to the announcement on behalf of his deceased parents, sharing that the whole family simply responded to the plight of the Jews they encountered with "gestures which, after all, were very natural in those dark years."[36]

The Pioneering Pastoral Ministry of Rev. Madeleine Blocher-Saillens in Paris

In *Les Parisiennes*, Anne Sebba surveys how French women, especially in the capital, responded to the German occupation of their country. Under German control, "Paris became a significantly feminized city, and the women had to negotiate on a daily basis with the male occupier." Jewish women in Paris, however, found life under the Germans and its "ever harsher exclusions . . . close to impossible." Seeking to survive and care for their families, French women chose various responses; they might collaborate, resist, or act as passive bystanders.[37] In French Baptist circles, Pastor Madeleine Blocher-Saillens provided an inspiring example of how to resist and serve the persecuted Jewish community around her church.

Madeleine Blocher-Saillens (1881–1971) was the daughter of Ruben Saillens and became the first French Baptist female congregational pastor. Following the death of her husband, Arthur Blocher, she assumed leadership in The Tabernacle, a doctrinally fundamental congregation in Paris.[38] She kept an enlightening wartime journal, documenting her compassion toward Jewish refugees and the choices she made in response to their struggles.[39]

As Hitler's appetite for territory grew, Blocher-Saillens expressed amazement that he enjoyed the support of Germans (September 17, 1938). She initially rejoiced that war had been avoided at Munich (September 30, 1938), but soon realized that the agreement betrayed Czechoslovakia (October 23, 1938). She mourned its demise and recognized that it would result in "Jews and Czechs arriving" in France. She wrote, "We are saturated with foreigners, all the unwanted people from Europe are coming to us" (March 16, 1939). She was particularly vexed by Hitler, who "tortures the Jews more than ever" (June 28, 1939), as well as by "the cruelty of the Germans to the Jews" (July 15, 1939). In May 1940 Blocher-Saillens noticed how many refugees were flooding into France and wondered about "the fate of the Jews if we succumb" (May 18, 1940). She also took notice of German anti-Semitic attacks, following Georges Mandel's appointment to be the French interior minister (May 29, 1940)—he was Jewish.

Blocher-Saillens admitted she was pained by German-controlled press and media offering "articles against the Jews" (August 12,

1940). She worried that Jews would be persecuted if German-style anti-Semitic occupational standards were to be applied in France (July 23, 1940). She did not have to wait long to see her fears realized: "The Nuremberg laws are applied. All Jewish traders have a yellow sign in the storefront. We decided to come in to extend our sympathy and offer a New Testament. The status of the Jews drives them out of government offices and most professions" (November 14, 1940). A year later she expressed disgust at anti-Semitic propaganda posters and commented, "Measures against the Jews are constantly increasing. They can do nothing more than the lower tasks. These are the laws of Nuremberg in all their rigor" (December 8, 1941).

Blocher-Saillens's first mention of mass deportation of Jews was recorded in her journal entry of December 22, 1941. She observed that "elite" Jews (doctors, lawyers, writers) were among the chosen to be deported, including one, now a Protestant, who committed suicide when the Gestapo came for him. The loss of Jewish doctors had diminished patient care, but worse still, a hundred "Jews and communists were deported to Germany and shot" (February 9, 1942). On April 30, 1942, she wondered, "1,000 Jews from Drancy Camp have just been sent to forced labor in Germany. How many will return?"

Surprisingly, Blocher-Saillens's journal entries rarely mention ecclesiastical matters or the functioning of her own church. In July 1941 a Baptist pastor informed her about a possible protest against a law invalidating baptisms by denominations not recognized before 1905 (July 15, 1941). Perhaps to prevent an arrest or deportation, she created a certificate of church membership for three children whose father was Jewish (March 13, 1942). Disturbed that Jews were required to wear yellow stars (June 2, 1942; June 6, 1942), she decided to read a Protestant Federation's message during the temple's worship service, defending Christians of Jewish descent who were suffering discrimination along with the Jewish community (June 14, 1942). She baptized "a young Jew with a Jewish star two weeks later and quoted from a newspaper article: "A number of non-Jews who wore the Jewish star or an imitation of this badge and who had thus expressed their sympathy for Judaism were sent to camps for Jews." She wrote, "A camp of Jews is often death. What terrible condemnation for having carried a star!" (June 27,

1942).[40] Henri Vincent warned Blocher-Saillens to exercise "caution" while preaching after he was interrogated by German authorities. She referred a Polish Jewish woman, whose father and brother were in a concentration camp, to La Cité de Refuge, a Salvation Army center (July 13, 1942).

The attacks against the Jews in Paris reached a climax on July 16–17, 1942, with the Vel' d'Hiv' Roundup. Over 13,000 Jews were arrested and penned in the stadium under horrendous conditions before being transferred to transition camps and then Auschwitz. Blocher-Saillens's journal focused especially on the difficulties of Jewish mothers and children. She relied on André Frankl's wisdom and pastoral expertise to help her deal with a distraught Jewish man who had abandoned his wife while attempting to escape imprisonment. Prohibitions against selling Jewish books made her wonder if the Nazis would target worship service attendance. She wrote that "to help a Jew escape is to share his fate" (July 16, 1942; July 18, 1942; July 19, 1942), as roundups of Jews continued (September 2, 1942).

Blocher-Saillens occasionally mentioned protests; one pastoral letter declared that "the Jews are men, the Jews are women. Not everything is allowed against them. They are part of the human race, they are our brothers. A Christian cannot forget it." She rejected ministering to German Baptists working in Paris on the grounds that to support them would be a form of unethical collaboration: "As long as they are our invaders we cannot collaborate" (October 4, 1942; see also February 15, 1943).

Blocher-Saillens journaled that the "persecutions against the Jews continue, odious and so cruel that one would not dare imagine such barbarism" (November 27, 1942). As the Nazis' extermination campaign became public knowledge, she wrote about mass deportations, Jews in concentration camps and the Warsaw ghetto (March 1, 1943; April 12, 1943; June 6, 1943). From the BBC, she learned that "two million Jews" had possibly died in Poland, "which is the European slaughterhouse of this martyred people" (July 31, 1943). While "a new roundup of Jews" was taking place in France, Blocher-Saillens risked taking in a Jewish family's children. Other children were facing deportation; she asked, "In which slaughterhouse are they going to succumb?" (August 9, 1943).

Not just children were in danger. Her journal spoke of a Mrs. Getting, a Jew who established a hospital's social work program.

She was deported to Drancy (October 8, 1943; December 21, 1943). A Jewish mother visited Blocher-Saillens and pleaded for shelter for her two children, who attended the church's school. She offered to provide for their expenses by selling her furniture. Blocher-Saillens responded, "We will see what we can do" (December 31, 1943).

Roughly a quarter of the journal covered the Allied advance and victory in 1944–45 and included examples of Nazi atrocities against the Jews in various parts of Europe (January 1, 1944; January 28, 1944; March 17, 1944; March 2, 1945). On January 29, 1944, Blocher-Saillens shared that André Frankl was under observation by the authorities in Paris,[41] and lamented the plight of Jews in the Gurs internment camp in southwest France: "The Jews die there like flies." In the margins, she wrote that she helped a French Jewish convert "escape the Gestapo."

Escape was never easy and often impossible. Blocher-Saillens hid an unspecified number of Jewish children in a Catholic orphanage near Fontainebleau, southeast of Paris. She later learned that the Gestapo tortured a Jewish child in the home, who died (April 11, 1944). By the middle of 1944, there were barely any Jews left in Paris (July 4, 1944). Referring to the discovery of the German death camps by the American army, Blocher-Saillens wrote, "Pits full of mutilated corpses, we visit the crematoria, the Americans finally believe in German atrocities . . . what they discover in horror persuades them that we have not exaggerated" (April 18, 1945). Her son Jacques subsequently told her about the "atrocities" committed at Bergen-Belsen (May 12, 1945).

In his report to the BWA, Rev. C. H. Jenkins shared his conversation with Blocher-Saillens that took place around April 30, 1945. He noted that The Tabernacle required significant repairs, and he gave a positive but understated assessment of her pastoral activities: "A good work is being done, and she has saved the lives of many Jewish children."[42]

NOTES

1. Sébastien Fath, *Les baptistes en France (1810–1950): Faits, dates et documents* (Cléon d'andean, France: Éditions Excelsis, 2002), 35. Fath cites his source in n. 19: Michel Thobois, "Encore des temps d'épreuve," série "Histoire des baptistes de France," *Le Rétroviseur*, supplément de *Croire et Servir*, no. 8 (April 1997), II.

2. On the qualities of rescuers, see Pearl M. Oliner, *Saving the Forsaken: Religious Culture and the Rescue of Jews in Nazi Europe* (New Haven, CT: Yale University Press, 2004; e-book, 2005); and Samuel P. and Pearl M. Oliner, *The Altruistic Personality: Rescuers of Jews in Nazi Europe* (New York: Free Press, 1988).

3. Jacques Semelin, *Unarmed against Hitler: Civilian Resistance in Europe, 1939–1943*. Trans. Susan Husserl-Kapit (Westport, CT: Praeger, 1993), 2, 25.

4. Semelin, 84, 132.

5. Semelin, 148.

6. Jacques Semelin, *The Survival of the Jews in France 1940–44*. Trans. Cynthia Schoch and Natasha Lehrer. (Oxford: Oxford University Press, 2018), 1–4.

7. "We Open a Children's Home in France," *Chosen People*, December 1939, 7. A picture of the building is on p. 6; see also "From Germany to Belgium," *Chosen People*, February 1940, 9.

8. Yves-Emmanuel Dulauroy and François Recamier, "'La Maison'—la pouponnière de Nurieux," *Histhoíría* 8 (2015), 22.

9. "Incidents in the Work," *Chosen People*, May 1940, 9.

10. Joseph Hoffman Cohn, "Salutation," *Chosen People*, February 1941, 14.

11. "Our News Budget from Across the Waters," *Chosen People*, May 1941, 16.

12. Joseph Hoffman Cohn, "Salutation," *Chosen People*, February 1943, 5.

13. "Farewell, Our Home for the Little Ones, in France!" *Chosen People*, May 1942, 13.

14. "Répressions et déportations en France et en Europe 1939–1945, Dossier 2018–2019," Musée de la Résistance et de la Déportation de l'Ain, 31.

15. André Thobois, *Henri Vincent: infatigable serviteur du Christ, passionné d'évangélisation* (Paris: Croire et Servir, 2001), 68, 87.

16. Dulauroy and Recamier, "'La Maison'—la pouponnière de Nurieux," 22–26.

17. Mordecai Paldiel, ed., *The Righteous among the Nations: Rescuers of Jews during the Holocaust: France* (New York: HarperCollins, 2007), 543–44, which are summaries from Yad Vashem's rescuer case file 3338. See https://www.yadvashem.org/righteous.html and le comité français pour Yad Vashem's website: https://yadvashem-france.org/dossier/nom/3338/.

18. This account is based on the following sources: Frédéric Stévenot, "Vincent Gaston, Arthur [alias Commander Azur]," June 6, 2019, last modification on April 16, 2021, https://maitron.fr/spip.php?article216151; "Gaston Vincent," ajpn.org, accessed March 17, 2022, http://www.ajpn.org/juste-Gaston-Vincent-2795.html; and "Suzanne Jacquet Vincent," ajpn.org, accessed March 17, 2022, http://www.ajpn.org/juste-Suzanne-Jacquet-Vincent-2798.html.

19. See Michael Sutton, "Jews and Christians in Vichy France," *French Politics, Culture & Society* 35, no. 3 (Winter 2017): 105–28.

20. See https://encyclopedia.ushmm.org/content/en/article/childrens-aid-society-oeuvre-de-secours-aux-enfants.

21. Yad Vashem's rescuer case file 3338. See https://www.yadvashem.org/righteous.html.

22. *Le Maitron* offers an alternative ending to Gaston's life: "It is more likely that he died of illness . . . or exhaustion at the Vercors hospital. Anyway, he was recognized 'dead for France' in a military capacity (AC 21 P 168952)." See https://maitron.fr/spip.php?article216151, notice VINCENT Gaston, Arthur [alias commandant Azur] par Frédéric Stévenot, version mise en ligne le 6 juin 2019, dernière modification le 4 mars 2022, accessed March 17, 2022.

23. Paldiel, *The Righteous among the Nations*, 230, summaries from Yad Vashem rescuer case file 6538, https://www.yadvashem.org/righteous.html. I am grateful to Franck Keller, who sent me his biographical article on Edmond Evrard via email: "Evrard Edmond" (Paris: SHPF et Ed de Paris 2020); he covers the same narrative in my text in greater detail.

24. Yad Vashem rescuer case file 6538.

25. Fred Coleman, *The Marcel Network: How One French Couple Saved 527 Children from the Holocaust* (Washington, DC: Potomac Books, 2013), 23, 25, 100, 175, 200.

26. Yad Vashem rescuer case file 6538.

27. Susan Zuccotti, *Père Marie-Benoît and Jewish Rescue: How a French Priest Together with Jewish Friends Saved Thousands during the Holocaust* (Bloomington: Indiana University Press, 2013), 76ff.; Patrick Cabanel, *De la paix aux résistances: les protestants en France 1930–1945* (Paris: Fayard Histoire, 2015), 303, 306.

28. Yad Vashem rescuer case file 6538.

29. J. H. Rushbrooke, ed., *Fifth Baptist World Congress: Berlin, August 4–10, 1934* (London: Baptist World Alliance, 1934), 236. The other delegate was Robert Farelly; see Thobois, *Henri Vincent*, 124–25. One documentary website, *Les Enfants & Amis Abadi*, claims that Evrard and his church in Nice welcomed German and Austrian Jewish children in 1930, a detail Keller repeats (https://www.lesenfantsetamisabadi.fr/fr/evrard1.htm).

30. The quote is from Trocmé's memoir, quoted in Christophe Chalamet, *Revivalism and Social Christianity: The Prophetic Faith of Henri Nick and André Trocmé* (Eugene, OR: Pickwick, 2013), 101.

31. Yad Vashem rescuer case file 6538. On Trocmé and Le Chambon-sur-Lignon, see Caroline Moorehead, *Village of Secrets: Defying the Nazis in Vichy France* (New York: Harper, 2014); and Richard P. Unsworth, *A Portrait of Pacifists: Le Chambon, the Holocaust and the Lives of André and Magda Trocmé* (Syracuse, NY: Syracuse University Press, 2012).

32. *Témoignage du Pasteur Edmond Evrard, recueilli par Monsieur Lazare Kelberine, rédacteur du centre de documentation sur la persécution nazie, le 28/03/1945* (Yad Vashem rescuer case file 6538), 3.

33. Yad Vashem rescuer case file 6538; see also Mordecai Paldiel, *Churches and the Holocaust: Unholy Teaching, Good Samaritans and Reconciliation* (Jersey City, NJ: KTAV, 2006), 123–24.

34. Walter O. Lewis, "News from Great Britain and Europe," *Watchman-Examiner*, April 23, 1942, 402. Keller states that Joe died on July 13, 1941.

35. *Témoignage du Pasteur Edmond Evrard*, Yad Vashem rescuer case file 6538; also quoted in Paldiel, *Churches and the Holocaust*, 124.

36. Correspondence from Louis Evrard to Mordecai Paldiel, March 22, 1995, in Yad Vashem rescuer case file 6538.

37. Anne Sebba, *Les Parisiennes: Resistance, Collaboration, and the Women of Paris under Nazi Occupation* (New York: St. Martin's Press, 2016), 63, 65–66.

38. Fath, *Les baptistes en France (1810–1950)*, 104; Jacques Poujol, *Protestants dans la France en guerre 1939–1945: Dictionnaire thématique et biographique* (Paris: Les Éditions de Paris, 2000), 205.

39. Madeleine Blocher-Saillens, *Témoin des années noires: Journal d'une femme pasteur—1938–1945*, ed. Jacques-E. Blocher (Paris: Les Editions de Paris, 1998). Relevant dated entries will be cited in the text.

40. Blocher-Saillens. Blocher-Saillens kept the article in her journal, and it is reproduced alongside the original handwritten journal page on p. 96.

41. Blocher-Saillens. Two months later Vincent informed her that Frankl was "on the run," and she sighed, "We live in terror" (April 9, 1944). At the end of August, a fire from a bomb blast destroyed part of the tabernacle (August 27, 1944; August 28, 1944).

42. "Report of Visit of Rev. C. H. Jenkins to France for the Baptist World Alliance," 7, Angus Library and Archive.

PART THREE

The Silence of German Baptists
Concerning Jews under Nazism

CHAPTER 7

German Baptists and the Arrival of Nazism

Welcoming Hitler and Baptists

No one who with open eyes experienced the revolution of 1933 and its subsequent development will ever forget the spiritual force with which Christians were carried away, Christians of all classes: Catholic bishops and Baptist preachers, Lutherans of all complexions . . . and especially those who were inclined to pietism.[1]—Professor Hermann Sasse, Erlangen University

Andrea Strübind describes Hitler's whirlwind takeover of the political, social, and economic aspects of German society as a veritable "upheaval" and states that German Christians viewed it as a "God-given turn of events." Even German Baptists were "carried along by a wave of enthusiasm for the incoming leadership," seeing the incoming Nazi regime "as the legitimate government, which according to Romans 13 was to be owed obedience."[2]

Observing the situation from across the Atlantic Ocean, the *Watchman-Examiner* requested prayers for German Baptists during this period of turmoil.[3] In July 1933 the newspaper lodged a protest against the ongoing anti-Semitic Nazi "brutality and terrorism . . . that so shocked civilized countries a few months ago,"[4] after Hitler seized control of the government. In contrast, Paul Schmidt, a key leader in the German Baptist Union throughout the Nazi period, and who himself had served in the Reichstag from 1930 to 1932 as a member of the Christian Social People's Service party (CSVD), supported the initial wave of National Socialist anti-Semitic legislation: "On the basis of our biblical knowledge, we have come to the insight that exceptional laws against Judaism are very possible for the State, yes, (and) may belong to its state obligations."[5]

The idea that the German Baptists might be useful to the new German government arose as the initial anti-Jewish actions provoked a widespread international negative response. German Baptists had relationships with their coreligionists across the globe and especially in Great Britain, France, and the United States. In the spirit of patriotism, the authorities encouraged German Baptists to counter the "atrocity" responses when dealing with their international partners[6]—a tactic that German Baptists used all the way up to the 1934 BWA World Congress.

J. H. Rushbrooke attended the German Baptist Union Annual Assembly in August 1933 and reported, "References to the political changes in Germany were inevitable, and it was evident from first to last that the overwhelming majority of German Baptists welcome the Nazi Government with the Chancellorship of Herr Hitler, chiefly on the ground that it has averted the peril of atheist-Communist domination."[7] Rushbrooke's impression was reinforced by German Baptist opinions subsequently expressed at the Berlin congress. German Baptist delegates explained that "the wholehearted support of Hitler by the Baptists and other Christian bodies was due to their faith in him as a bulwark against Communism and atheism."[8]

Another respected contemporary observer, Charles S. Macfarland, enjoyed great credibility in Great Britain and the United States, having served as the general secretary of the Federal Council of Churches of Christ in America. Following a fact-finding trip to Germany in the autumn of 1933, he published an influential book recording his impressions of the dynamics of the German religious scene in the first year of Nazi rule, including a personal interview with Hitler himself, which received attention in Baptist circles and journals.[9] *The New Church and the New Germany* surveyed the state of the Free Churches of Germany (including Baptists) in 1933. His Baptist contacts asserted that they were experiencing a measure of freedom in conducting their church activities—while also admitting that there were indeed Nazi Party members within the Baptist Union. They indicated that "Baptist officials reported that they had not been interfered with. Some of their own members who are National Socialists had proposed that fifty-one percent of the church officials should be members of the movement, but it had been given no serious consideration." Baptist leaders felt that the "chief danger" posed by the Nazis was that Baptists "would lose their youth to the Hitler Youth Movement."[10]

A German Baptist perspective was provided by Professor Julius Janssen, a faculty member of the Hamburg Baptist Seminary. He distanced Baptists from the challenges Roman Catholics and German Evangelicals faced: "The small German Freechurches [sic] are not involved in these difficulties." Baptists were most concerned about achieving legal and ecclesial recognition, without being coerced to merge with the State Church. He believed that "recognition of our Union by the state and church seems to be sure."[11]

In response to misgivings circulating among Baptists regarding attending the congress in Berlin, F. W. Simoleit, as chairman of the German Committee of Arrangements to the Berlin congress, sent a letter to the *Watchman-Examiner* in early March 1934. He sought to assuage any fears that Baptist delegates would be forced to "keep silence about their principles" and about "members of all races" being welcome in Germany. He was perplexed by the charge that it was not possible to quote from the Old Testament, writing, "We German Baptists still have the whole Bible, and use it all." Simoleit declared, "Our fellow-Baptists must come and see how things really are! They need not have the least fear about full freedom for the congress. If we had not been certain that our government would allow that, we should not have sent our invitation."[12]

The views of Baptist historical theologian Dr. Conrad Moehlman, who taught at Colgate-Rochester Theological Seminary, interested the publishers of the *American Hebrew*, since the Jewish paper hoped the BWA Congress represented an "opportunity for Christianity to make known its feelings in respect to the Nazi persecution of the Jews." Moehlman asserted that if Baptists did not seize this opportunity to criticize Nazism, for "such cowardice the Baptists would be despised in every country of the world." Would Baptists be "bold enough to call attention to Christianity's debt to Judaism and the shame of the ghetto, the inquisition and the pogrom? Will they dare affirm their faith in democracy, brotherhood and the Kingdom of God and their opposition to propaganda, race hatred and war in Berlin in 1934?" Baptists, he worried, might refrain from doing so out of concern for the stance's potential negative impact on their German Baptist hosts.[13]

Moehlman's fear that the BWA might lose its prophetic nerve out of concern for the welfare of the German Baptists was realistic. At the BWA administrative subcommittee meeting on April 30, 1934, in London, W. T. Whitley, T. G. Dunning, Grey Griffith, and George Truett joined Rushbrooke in considering a letter from R. A. Ashworth, recording secretary of the Board of Education of the Northern Baptist Convention. The letter contained a "suggestion as to the attendance of a leading Jewish rabbi to bring greetings to the Congress." Rushbrooke bluntly informed the subcommittee that he intended to respond to Ashworth's request in a negative fashion. He judged that having a rabbi share the plenary stage would be "inexpedient," and rationalized his rejection with a curious justification: "The Congress would undoubtedly express itself upon the racial question, and its action would be rather prejudiced than helped if Dr. Ashworth's proposal were endorsed."[14]

A Private Conversation on the "New Situation"

The BWA executive committee met in Berlin's Hotel Continental on August 2, 1934, just prior to the start of the Fifth World Congress. Many of that generation's Baptist luminaries were in attendance, including M. E. Aubrey, Gilbert Laws, J. A. Ohrn, George Truett, and Ruth Baresel, the daughter of Jewish-Baptist Julius Köbner and the author of his then recently published biography.[15]

Rushbrooke addressed a sensitive question that was on everyone's minds—how were German Baptists responding to the government's efforts to determine church policy and structure? His report cryptically indicated that the German Baptist leadership had acted "with a view to meeting the demands of the new situation in Germany."[16]

Since the BWA vice president and German Baptist leader F. W. Simoleit was temporarily absent, the conversation was adjourned. When the committee regathered, Simoleit spoke and there ensued a "long and frank conversation" about the issue. The minutes simply state that the committee "rejoiced to hear from Dr. Simoleit that in the present conditions of Germany German Baptists have not compromised on essential Baptist principles, but have steadfastly maintained as heretofore their witness to the spiritual freedom of the Church of Christ, and to the duty and privilege of the Church to serve all men of whatever race or nationality for whom Christ died."[17]

In essence, the committee's conversation focused on the same concerns raised by the German Evangelical Church's Barmen Declaration (May 29–31, 1934), composed in part by Karl Barth. Simoleit and Rushbrooke had corresponded about German Baptist strategy in facing the evolving religious situation. At the June 19, 1934, BWA administrative sub-committee meeting, the general secretary shared Simoleit's letter dated May 28, 1934, written one day before the start of the Barmen meeting.

Simoleit revealed that German Baptists and other Free Churches were working to "delay" negotiations to unify all Protestant churches into one administrative "Reichskirche." However, Simoleit expressed pessimism that German Baptists could retain their autonomy. He "feared that we shall be forced to action by the method of administrative demand which we dare not resist without risking *everything*."[18]

The Baptist leader's comments were revealing. As with the Barmen Declaration, the Free Churches reacted to the Nazi initiative primarily on an institutional level, perceiving it as a threat to their organizational independence and integrity, and not primarily as an expression of Nazi anti-Semitism. Neither the Barmen Declaration nor the German Baptist response focused on the plight of German Jews, but rather defended the right of the Christian church to control its internal affairs. For the global Baptist family, this oversight would be rectified during the forthcoming congress.

Extolling Hitler at the 1934 Congress

The BWA's Fifth World Congress in Berlin was a veritable vortex of diametrically opposed concerns. Baptists from the United States were worried about the independence of the conference and Nazi restrictions on speech and debate. Rushbrooke believed the congress was a symbol of Baptist unity that could transcend national boundaries and political divisions. Many Baptists viewed the congress as an opportunity for a truly courageous and prophetic witness against totalitarianism and racism. German Baptists saw the congress as a means of retaining their place of pride in the global Baptist movement while gaining favor with the German government and eventually securing legal recognition. The Nazis manipulated the event for their own reasons. The government "promoted and used" the congress "as a propaganda measure" against its international detractors. That the German Baptist Union's leadership acted with "readiness to conform to the conditions and demands of the state"[19] is generally accepted; what is debatable is whether their representation of the state was coerced or voluntary, excusable or indefensible.

At the center of the vortex was the issue of *racialism*. In the first half of the twentieth century, racialism as a field of inquiry focused on the similarities and differences between people of various so-called races as they related to one another. Racialism was a topic for discussion and thus was not necessarily a derogatory term. *Racism*, in contrast, was always a decidedly negative term, denoting the abuse and oppression of one race against another. Confusingly, the two terms sometimes were used interchangeably. The BWA investigated topics related to racialism and, based on those investigations, concluded that Nazi anti-Semitism was a grievous example of racism and thus should be opposed.

In Berlin several resolutions "hit at the heart of the Nazi ideology," and the congress "took a clear position against all forms of racial discrimination in the very capital of the country which had created a special jurisdiction for its Jewish citizens, in which these were defamed, deprived of their rights and persecuted." Paradoxically, "German Baptists felt themselves called to defend Nazi politics, but also supported the clear resolutions on all topics."[20]

Why did German Baptist delegates simultaneously welcome the Nazi revolution, including its anti-Semitism, and vote for the BWA resolutions on racialism and nationalism? Strübind is of the opinion that "German Baptists found themselves on the defensive, which was expressed in oaths of loyalty to the Nazi state."[21] In reality, German government officials, religious representatives, and even German Baptist leaders *seized the initiative* to promote a pro-Germany perspective. In the opening session, one German city official, "like many other speakers" during the congress, "spoke of the Fatherland with passion" and campaigned "for sympathetic understanding for the work done for the children of Germany, and the work of the Government for the relief of unemployment."[22] He did not mention that the government had been subjecting Jews to a series of oppressive economic and social sanctions. Reichsbishop Ludwig Müller, a "fanatical Nazi,"[23] greeted the Baptists and assured Baptist leaders that German Baptists would not be coerced into joining the proposed unified German Church.

On the first night of the congress (Saturday, August 4), Simoleit reframed the themes from his two invitation letters. It included universally accepted Baptist convictions, such as evangelism, the lordship of Jesus, and Baptist family unity, and juxtaposed them with subtle statements at odds with these convictions. He stated "even in quite recent times human error and evil raised barriers which threatened to hinder this Berlin Congress," and criticized unspecified others who manifested "the spirit that seeks to estrange and destroy the peoples, and from the lack of faith which everywhere sees spectres"—in other words, critics who had doubts about holding the congress in Nazi Germany. In a plenary hall draped with Nazi swastikas, Simoleit sought to circumscribe the boundaries of the congress, so that an event hosted by German Baptists would not offend their government's sensitivities. He declared that the congress would focus on "religious" discussions and not be "concerned with the political conditions in any land that is represented here."[24] Simoleit was protecting Germany, seeking to preemptively insulate the Nazi regime from prophetic critique.

Friedrich Rockschies and Paul Schmidt addressed the assembly during its opening plenary, but their text speeches were not included in the official congress book. However, the *Baptist Times* reported that Rushbrooke "graciously acknowledged the spirit of the welcomes, but without discourtesy he challenged a number of the speeches both on political and religious grounds." Rushbrooke hoped "the speakers would understand that, while acknowledging a true brotherhood, many in the audience would not be able to entirely agree with their sentiments."[25] In the second session, Rushbrooke declared that Baptists "hold no brief for any political party or for any national or economic programme." Furthermore, he made it clear that Baptists "limit our fellowship by no frontiers of race" and could not submit to "control by State or magistrate."[26]

An exchange took place between Rockschies and Rushbrooke during the seventh plenary session on Wednesday, August 8. The

Berlin pastor asserted that Baptists "have been National Socialists in the true sense for the past hundred years." Rushbrooke retorted: "If Pastor Rockschies' definition of National Socialism is correct then we are all Nazis. There are, however, elements in National Socialism, as we actually see it, which do not commend themselves to us." The general secretary did not hesitate to bring the plight of German Jews to the fore: "To stamp a race as inferior is no solution to the race problem."[27]

A most egregious example of German Baptist support for the Nazis was delivered during the ninth plenary session. Professor Carl Schneider, from the Baptist Seminary in Hamburg, presented a standard overview of the history of the German Baptist movement in honor of its centenary milestone and even acknowledged Julius Köbner as one of the three "Apostles of Experience" (although he did not mention Köbner's Jewish lineage). If Schneider had concluded here, his remarks would have been noncontroversial. However, he chose to add,

> The Centenary of the German Baptists synchronises with the re-birth of the German nation as a people. God the Lord has given us, in Adolf Hitler, a man who recognises the needs of the time and its perils, and who is directing and using the forces that make for health in order to subdue those that make for decay. As a force making for health, the German Baptist community has been recognised and used by the Third Empire and actively included in the process of renewal. Never before has our movement experienced so much in the way of public recognition and support as in the Third Empire, and to-day in Berlin. United by speech and blood with the German people and the homeland, in love for the Fatherland and in the consciousness of sharing the responsibility for its destiny, the German Baptist movement co-operates, on the basis of the Gospel, with all its power in the work of building up a self-reliant State, in which a physically and morally healthy generation can live free and confident, contented and self-disciplined.[28]

Schneider's remarks were confident, proud, and assertive, revealing that the seduction and submission of the German Baptist leadership, and indeed, the entire fellowship, was well established by the summer of 1934. German Baptists had embraced the dreams and aims of National Socialism with as much enthusiasm as other Germans. Schneider was enthusiastic about Nazi-Baptist cooperation and he believed that God had sent Hitler in a politically messianic way for Germany's sake. Months prior to the congress, Schneider boasted that at the centennial celebration of the First Baptist Church in Hamburg, representatives of the Nazi government were in attendance, including "Secretary of State Ahrens, and Senator von Allwörden." Both Georg Ahrens and Wilhelm von Allwörden were committed members of the National Socialist Party in the Hamburg region.[29] The professor proudly exclaimed, "All this is eloquent testimony of the public esteem which the German Baptists, once so despised, enjoy in Germany to-day."[30]

Paul Schmidt responded to the commission report on nationalism. In line with German Lutheran theology, Schmidt distinguished between "the realm of the Church . . . and the realm of the world State and its order." Although the Church "must stand against false nationalism, war, and social injustice, it must also respect the natural order and so there must be avoidance of direct political counsels." He echoed the racial focus of the Nazis in defining the church as "the fellowship of peoples to which by birth and race they belong." For Schmidt, the Nazi focus on race was not at odds with "healthy" manifestations of nationalism: "Facts of blood, speech, and mental outlook are a natural innate gift to a people, the basis of its self-consciousness and a guarantee of its continuance." He was not troubled by a nationalism that promoted "life-claims by methods of force, an instinctive faith in itself on the part of a people, [and] vigorous races overcoming weaker" ones.[31]

What might a sermon look like if it were influenced by the revolutionary Nazi spirit? Hamburg Seminary professor C. Neuschäfer's devotional, "Jesus Christ as Son of God," served as an eloquent example. The message was curiously devoid of any references to Jews, Judaism, or the Jewishness of Jesus. Neuschäfer presented a universalized, humanly generic Jesus of Nazareth who "2,000 years ago trod this earth . . . and spoke for all time and for all men." Although "born of the Virgin Mary," he is not called the Messiah of Israel, who defined his journey as a fulfillment of the predictions of the Hebrew prophets or who taught in light of the Old

Testament. Neuschäfer once mentioned God's "people, under the Old Covenant" but did not identify them as Jews.[32]

Simoleit spoke during the closing session of the congress on August 10. Outlining the three questions the congress raised for an "unchristian and indifferent world," and a like number of "brotherly pleas" to the global church, he declined to mention racism, especially as manifested by anti-Semitism. Simoleit and his German Baptist colleagues vigorously maintained that the congress had focused on spiritual and not political issues. And yet he felt it necessary (perhaps out of politeness) to express "hearty thanks" to "the official circles of the Reich, of the Church, and especially of the City of Berlin."[33]

A Church Struggling to Remain Free

Between 1935 and 1938, the German Baptist Union struggled to maintain its "free church" identity. Once it permitted itself to become ensnared in the Nazis' political and cultural orbit in 1933–34, it could discover no satisfactory escape from the totalitarian trap. The Führer Principle fight caused division within the fellowship and was eventually rejected. German Baptists did not wish to emulate the State Church in adopting a Nazi influenced leadership structure, but over time, the course of the Union nevertheless was dominated by a few powerful leaders who were unwilling to oppose the Nazis' political agenda.

Nazism also impacted how German Baptists related to their Jewish neighbors. The loosening of ties with the Jewish community was due to "fear of conflict with the Gestapo" and manifestations of anti-Semitism that were already embedded within the German Baptist family.[34] In August 1935 Simoleit released a confidential message to the clergy of the German Baptist Union, warning against "accepting members of forbidden communities"[35]—a not-so-veiled reference to non-Aryans or Jews. Andrea Strübind summarizes the German Baptist relationship with their Jewish neighbors during the prewar period:

> One can only speak about a discussion in the Baptist churches about the Jewish question during the first phase of the Nazi dictatorship, as publications from 1933 show. In the face of

state persecution of the Jewish population, Baptists behaved passively throughout. Given the small number of Jewish members in Baptist churches, Baptists dispensed with a general ruling. The so-called "non-Aryan Laws" were not put into practice in the churches, thus Jewish members were not removed from membership and . . . they were admitted into membership of the church. Nevertheless, Jewish members had to endure a certain amount of discrimination in the churches. Assistance from a few individuals contrasted with the isolationist policy which the majority of church members pursued.[36]

The German Baptist Union celebrated Hitler's birthday through its denominational magazine, which also supported Hitler's economic policies that included oppressive measures against Jews. It reported that on August 31, 1936, "the chairman of the Federation of Baptists' Annual Conference had expressed thanks to the Führer particularly for the protection he had brought from the destructive forces of Bolshevism" as well as for "the magnanimous support" German Baptist ministries "had received in bringing health to the soul of our people."[37]

Supporting Nazi policies while remaining silent about anti-Semitism had two effects. First, it effectively denied the free-church heritage upon which European Baptists had stood for a century. In the fall of 1937, Jacob Köbberling, a German Baptist from East Prussia, expressed his dissatisfaction with how Paul Schmidt had represented German Baptists at the Oxford Conference (see Chapter 8), and asserted something truly astounding: "This is a church in bondage, an unfree church, even if it proudly calls itself a 'Free Church.'"[38] Schmidt disagreed, boasting that the German Baptist support for the Hitler regime had produced "positive effects over and over again for ourselves and our ministry."[39]

Second, Baptist allegiance to the German governmental authorities virtually guaranteed that they would not, and indeed could not, protest the treatment of Jews under German control. The Nazis would have denied freedom to Baptists if they had acted in a prophetic way. More insidiously, the passive bystander behavior of the German Baptist Union and its leadership infected the very soul of the movement, making it callous or indifferent to the plight of persecuted Jews. Throughout the first six years of the Hitler regime,

German Baptists embraced a "desolidarisation[40] of Jewish citizens (out of fear for their own existence)."[41] This in turn, led to the morally indefensible response of the German Baptist Union to Kristallnacht—they sought to profit from Jewish persecution and loss:

> Looking back, it is particularly shameful that on the night of the Reich's pogrom in November 1938 the German Union looked into the possibility of buying up synagogues cheaply. After the pogrom the Union was advised against buying synagogues because former Jewish prayer houses, which had been bought up by the Baptists, had already been demolished and burnt down. Attempts were made to reduce the material losses for the Baptist churches by suing for repayment of the purchase price![42]

Fleischer notes that German Baptist "official statements on the November pogrom are completely missing," but rare individual narratives do exist.[43] In English, Reinhold Kerstan recounted his experience of Kristallnacht as a seven-year-old. In Berlin he observed a synagogue on fire and read slogans like "We don't buy from Jewish rats" and "Jews out." His father, a Baptist pastor, expressed his opposition to such anti-Semitism by reminding his son that both the apostles and Jesus were Jewish.[44]

It was just a small step from the passivity of indifference to the amorality of greed that seeks advantage from another's suffering. But once such an ethical slide gains momentum, gravity can precipitate further moral descent. Following Kristallnacht, the German Baptist Union remained steadfastly silent, abandoning the Jewish people to the horrors of the coming Holocaust. As Strübind states, "The last phase of the persecution of the Jews was clothed in silence by the Baptists."[45] That silence, as we shall see in Chapter 10, was facilitated by an intentional de-coupling of German Baptists from their historical Jewish heritage and influence, which had been gifted to them through the apostolic ministry of Julius Köbner.

Judenchristen Baptists

In Hitler's Germany, several categories of Jews were created to support legal discrimination and persecution. Jewish identity had both racial-genetic and religious components. Jews with four Jewish

grandparents were considered fully Jewish and faced systemic oppression throughout the Nazi era. Jews with two Jewish grandparents were derisively labeled as *Mischlinge* in the first degree. People
with one Jewish grandparent were *Mischlinge* in the second degree.
Mischlinge had one parent who was Jewish and one who was Gentile. A *Mischling* who practiced Judaism was considered to be *Gel-
tungsjude* and treated as full Jews. In general, *Mischlinge* were less
likely than full Jews to be sent to concentration camps and killed,
and many survived the war.[46]

A small minority of Jews, who had personally embraced Christian faith and joined churches, often found themselves at odds
with the authorities. Judenchristen Baptists, like all other Jews, felt
threatened by the oppressive measures taken against Jews in Germany and Nazi-occupied countries. On May 11, 1939, Hamburg
pastor Hans Fehr wrote a plaintive letter to Rushbrooke on behalf
of some Judenchristen. Six months after Kristallnacht, these believers knew they were facing a dangerous predicament:

> I am repeatedly used by Judenchristen as a pastor. In general,
> it can be said that those who have a different view of things
> through Christ fully understand the measures taken by our
> Reich against the Jews. Now they are in a special situation, on
> the one hand I only deal with poor Judenchristen, on the other
> hand, and that weighs more heavily, they are shown contempt
> by their fellow race who refuses to help them. It has been sug-
> gested to me to ask you, who has a large heart, whether you
> know an organization that could take care of the Judenchristen.
> I would be very grateful for a friendly answer.[47]

Fehr had no confidence that his German Baptist denomination
would be willing to protect Baptist-affiliated Jewish Christians, and
so he looked to the BWA for assistance. The Judenchristen also
faced a similar lack of support from their fellow Jews and the Jewish relief organizations outside Germany, who no longer accepted
them as authentically within the Jewish community.[48]

Some German Baptists "conformed to the official state policy regarding Jews" and some acted in an "overtly anti-Semitic"
manner. Other individuals "offered clandestine resistance." Some
Jewish Baptists were "forced out of the churches and left to face

persecution from the state." In general, "a lack of solidarity and sympathetic help existed side by side,"[49] but by no means was assistance to Baptist-affiliated Judenchristen (or to Jews outside the fellowship) widespread or common.

Fleischer has identified forty-four German Baptist Jews, accompanied by brief biographies. Seven lost their lives at the hands of the Nazis, and "by the summer of 1941 there were practically no Baptists of Jewish descent left in Baptist churches" in Germany. A few accounts of individual Baptist Jews being helped by German Baptists have been preserved; for example, Lucie Seiffert hid Frieda Schmal in her Berlin apartment from 1942 to 1945. However, Fleischer acknowledges that such "courageous actions did not have their origin in the Baptist leadership nor in individual churches, but were done discretely by ordinary church members."[50]

Arnold Köster's Courageous Pastoral Ministry

An impressive Baptist protest against Nazism and its anti-Semitic agenda on a local church level took place in Vienna, Austria, where Arnold Köster served as pastor beginning in 1929. Köster remains "the only known German pastor from the Free Church congregations who continuously criticized the Nazi regime."[51] Following Hitler's ascension to power, Köster engaged in a debate with German Baptist leaders, who "laughed" at his rejection of Nazism as "antichristian thinking." He remembered, "I was sitting together with leading members of the German Baptist Union at a decisive moment in 1933. They thoroughly grilled me for several hours; 'What is your argument with National Socialism? Why don't you keep your mouth shut? After all, you endanger the whole Baptist movement.'"[52] He remained steadfast in his political opposition throughout the Nazi period.[53]

How did Köster relate to and serve Baptist Judenchristen and other Jews following the Anschluss of March 1938? Gottfried Rabenau states, "When the persecution of Jews began, many Jews sought pastoral advice and strengthening of their faith" from Köster. He was able to baptize approximately fifty of them, "despite difficulties from the Gestapo."[54] Köster's colleague, Rupert Ostermann, praised Köster's prophetic preaching from both "the

Old and New Testaments" and recalled that "numerous members of the persecuted people of Israel found refuge and a home"[55] in Köster's church.

Following Kristallnacht, a woman who was married to a Jewish husband was so concerned for the future welfare of their thirteen-year-old daughter that she was willing to send her to England to live in the home of a Baptist minister. Köster asked Rushbrooke to provide a reference for the family who was willing to accept the girl, to provide peace of mind to her parents.[56] Further accounts of Köster's helpfulness have been supplied by witnesses from Vienna.[57]

Köster's preaching clearly indicated that he rejected Nazi philosophy and its racism. Based on Köster's sermons, Franz Graf-Stuhlhofer lists eleven reasons why Köster should be seen as a philo-Semite. He appreciated and preached often from the Old Testament; appropriated a Hebrew mode of thinking, especially from the prophetic perspective; worshipped Jesus while affirming Jesus' Jewish background; respected Paul; believed in the Jewish covenant and Israel's place in salvation history beside the Church; proclaimed that Jesus was the one means of salvation for both Jew and Gentile; asserted that racism could not be part of church life; and interpreted the sufferings of the Jewish people from an eschatological perspective in which there would be a bright future for the Jewish people.[58]

NOTES

1. Quoted in Stewart W. Herman, *The Rebirth of the German Church* (New York: Harper and Brothers, 1946), 50–51.

2. Andrea Strübind, "German Baptists and National Socialism," *Journal of European Baptist Studies* 8, no. 3 (May 2008): 9.

3. "Men and Things," *Watchman-Examiner*, July 13, 1933, 666.

4. "Sympathy for German Jews," *Watchman-Examiner*, July 20, 1933, 697.

5. The original German quote is from *Der Hilfsbote* 7 (1933): 157, cited in Andrea Strübind, "'Wir Christen unter Zuschauern': Die deutschen Baptisten und die Judenverfolgung in der Zeit der NS-Diktatur," in *Freikirchen und Juden im "Dritten Reich,"* ed. Daniel Heinz (Göttingen: V & R Unipress, 2011), 159. A slightly different translation is found in Roland Fleischer, "The German Baptists and Their Conduct towards Jews and Jewish Christians, Especially during the Third Reich," in John H. Y. Briggs and Paul S. Fiddes, eds., *People of God: Baptists and Jews over Four Centuries* (Oxford: Center for Baptist Studies in Oxford Publications, 2019), 197.

6. Johannes Hartlapp, "Evangeliumsverkündigung um jeden Preis—deutsche Freikirchen in der Zeit des Nationalsozialismus," *Kirchliche Zeitgeschichte* 30, no. 1 (2017): 85.

7. "The German Baptist Meetings," *Baptist Times*, September 7, 1933, 598.

8. Open Forum Letters, "Germany and Liberty," *Baptist Times*, January 4, 1940, 4.

9. See "An Interview with Hitler," *Missions*, January 1934, 21; "A Book of Great Interest," *Watchman-Examiner*, January 25, 1934, 81.

10. Charles S. Macfarland, *The New Church and the New Germany* (New York: Macmillan, 1934), 57–59.

11. Julius Janssen, "German Christianity and Baptists," *Watchman-Examiner*, January 18, 1934, 59.

12. "A Letter from Germany," *Watchman-Examiner*, April 12, 1934, 395. A second invitation was published in "A Word of Welcome from German Baptists," *Watchman-Examiner*, June 14, 1934, 677.

13. "Christian Resentment against Hitlerism Grows in This Country as Nazis Assault Jesus," *American Hebrew*, February 16, 1934, 276. Moehlman's original statements were from the *Christian Century*.

14. *Baptist World Alliance: Minutes of Administrative Sub-Committee Meeting on Monday, 30th April, 1934, at the Offices of the Alliance, London* (London: Baptist World Alliance, 1934), item 5a, Berlin Congress Programme, 2.

15. Ruth Köbner Baresel, *Julius Köbner: Sein Leben* (Kassel, Germany: J. G. Oncken Nachfolger, 1930).

16. *Baptist World Alliance: Minutes of Meeting of Executive Committee, Held at Berlin, Germany on Thursday, August 2nd, 1934* (London: Baptist World Alliance, 1934), item 14, German Baptists as Free Churchmen, 5.

17. *Baptist World Alliance, Minutes of Meeting of Executive Committee*, item 23, German Baptists as Free Churchmen, 7.

18. *Baptist World Alliance: Minutes of Administrative Sub-Committee Meeting on Tuesday, 19th June, 1934, at the Offices of the Alliance, London* (London: Baptist World Alliance, 1934), item 5, Germany, Relations of the Reichskirche and Free Churches, 2.

19. Andrea Strübind, "German Baptists and National Socialism," 12.

20. Strübind, 12–13. For example, the *Detroit Jewish Chronicle* (August 17, 1934, 1) reported that German Baptist pastor Heinrich Fiehler (misidentified as Ernst Siedler), parent of the Nazi-affiliated mayor of Munich, declared that although "all races are equal before the face of God," he believed that "when a race is destructive by nature, then a government is forced to do to it what the race wanted to do to the nation as a whole." This assertion, in German, is also quoted in Strübind, *Die unfreie Freikirche: Der Bund der Baptistengemeinden im "Dritten Reich,"* (Berlin: Neukirchener, 1991), 166.

21. Strübind, 12.

22. "Baptists in Berlin," *Baptist Times*, August 9, 1934, 563. See also C. T. Le Quesne, "The Significance of the Berlin Congress," *Fraternal* 17 (January 1935): 4–5; Bernard Green, *European Baptists and the Third Reich* (Didcot, UK: Baptist Historical Society, 2008), 46–50.

23. K. W. Clements, "A Question of Freedom? British Baptists and the German Church Struggle," in *Baptists in the Twentieth Century: Papers Presented at a Summer School July 1982*, ed. K. W. Clements (London: Baptist Historical Society, 1983), 96.

24. F. W. Simoleit, "Address of Greeting," in *Fifth Baptist World Congress: Berlin, August 4–10, 1934*, ed. J. H. Rushbrooke (London: Baptist World Alliance, 1934), 198–99.

25. "Baptists in Berlin," *Baptist Times*, August 9, 1934, 563.

26. "Baptists in Berlin," 564.

27. "Baptists Attack Anti-Semitism," *Yorkshire Post*, August 9, 1934, 5; "Anti-Semitism Condemned" sub-section in "Nazi Bishop as Church Dictator," *Belfast News-Letter*, August 9, 1934, 11.

28. Carl Schneider, "The Centenary of the German Baptists," in *Fifth Baptist World Congress*, ed. Rushbrooke, 191–93.

29. "Georg Ahrens (Politician)," Wiki, last updated November 26, 2020, https://second.wiki/wiki/georg_ahrens_politiker.

30. Schneider, "Centenary of the German Baptists," 193.

31. Paul Schmidt, "Address," in *Fifth Baptist World Congress*, ed. Rushbrooke, 63–65.

32. C. Neuschäfer, "Jesus Christ as Son of God," in *Fifth Baptist World Congress*, ed. Rushbrooke, 78–83.

33. F. W. Simoleit, "The Congress Message to World and Church," in *Fifth Baptist World Congress*, ed. Rushbrooke, 213–15.

34. Sandra Zimmerman, *Zwischen Selbsterhaltung und Anpassung: Die Haltung der Baptisten und Brüdergemeinden im Nationalsozialismus* (Germany: Brüderbewegung, 2004), 47–50.

35. Veit Claesberg, *Der pastorale Leiter als Prophet: Der Baptistenpastor Arnold Köster (1896–1960) im Widerstand gegen den Nationalsozialismus* (Elstal, Germany: Oncken-Archiv, 2018), 69.

36. Strübind, "German Baptists and National Socialism," 14–15.

37. Nicholas M. Railton, "German Free Churches and the Nazi Regime," *Journal of Ecclesiastical History* 49, no. 1 (January 1998): 125.

38. Railton, 126. The original quote, in German, can be found in a collection of Köbberling's writings edited by Roland Fleischer, *Der Streit über den Weg der Baptisten im Nationalsozialismus* (Elstal, Germany: Onchin-Archiv Elstal, 2014), 34.

39. Railton, "German Free Churches and the Nazi Regime," 129.

40. "Desolidarisation" is best understood in English as disassociation or disconnection from something or someone; a more direct translation is the French *désolidarisation*.

41. Strübind, *Die unfreie Freikirche: Der Bund der Baptistengemeinden im "Dritten Reich,"* 263; see also Roland B. Fleischer, "'Das verachtete Volk der Juden': Baptisten, die Pogromnacht 1938 und das Verhältnis zum Judentum," in *Freikirchen-forschung* 17 (2008): 202. An example of such "desolidarisation" was the changing of Deacon- ness House ministry names that had Jewish or Old Testament roots (Strübind, 268 and n. 69).

42. Strübind, "German Baptists and National Socialism," 15. At least one example was in East Prussia; see Zimmerman, *Zwischen Selbsterhaltung und Anpassung,* 8. See also Fleischer, "'Das verachtete Volk der Juden,'" 210–13.

43. Fleischer, "'Das verachtete Volk der Juden,'" 196, 206–9.

44. Reinhold Kerstan, *Blood and Honor* (Elgin, IL: Cook, 1983), 34–35; also cited in Roland B. Fleischer, "'Das verachtete Volk der Juden,'" 206–7.

45. Strübind, "German Baptists and National Socialism," 15.

46. James F. Tent, *In the Shadow of the Holocaust: Nazi Persecution of Jewish-Christian Germans* (Lawrence: University of Kansas Press, 2003), ix–x, 1–4, 16, 21. Tent does not investigate the Judenchristen who consciously chose to believe in Jesus.

47. Correspondence, Hans Fehr to J. H. Rushbrooke, May 11, 1939, Angus Library and Archive. Trans. from German.

48. See Tent, *In the Shadow of the Holocaust,* 15.

49. Roland Fleischer, "The German Baptists and Their Conduct towards Jews and Jewish Christians, especially during the Third Reich," in *People of God: Baptists and Jews over Four Centuries,* ed. John H. Y. Briggs and Paul S. Fiddes, 218–19.

50. Fleischer, 222–23. See also Roland Fleischer, "Judenchristliche Mitglieder in Baptistengemeinden in Dritten Reich," in *Wie alle andern Auch: Baptistengemeinden im Dritten Reich im Spiegel ihrer Festschriften,* ed. Hans-Joachim Leisten (Hamburg: VDL Verlag, 2010), 159–83.

51. Claesberg, *Der pastorale Leiter als Prophet,* 17.

52. Quoted in Paul Spanring, *Dietrich Bonhoeffer and Arnold Köster: Two Distinct Voices in the Midst of Germany's Third Reich Turmoil* (Eugene, OR: Pickwick, 2013), 36.

53. See Franz Graf-Stuhlhofer, Öffentliche *Kritik am Nationalsozialismus im Grossdeutschen Reich: Leben und Weltanschauung des Wiener Baptistenpastors Arnold Köster (1896–1960)* (Neukirchen-Vluyn, Germany: Neukirchener, 2001).

54. Quoted in Claesberg, *Der pastorale Leiter als Prophet,* 116.

55. Claesberg, 129.

56. Correspondence Arnold Köster to J. H. Rushbrooke, March 2, 1939, Angus Library and Archive, Regent's Park College, Oxford, England.

57. See Spanring, *Dietrich Bonhoeffer and Arnold Köster,* 246–47.

58. See Graf-Stuhlhofer, Öffentliche *Kritik am Nationalsozialismus im Grossdeutschen Reich,* 229–39.

CHAPTER 8

Hitlerism's Emissaries

Church and State

Hans Luther served as the German government's ambassador to the United States following the Nazi Party's coming to power in 1933. In July 1934 Rufus W. Weaver, pastor of First Baptist Church of Washington, DC, secured from him a warm letter of invitation for the 1934 BWA Congress.[1] By 1937, however, his term of service was coming to a dismal end. Luther's mission to promote positive relations with the United States was sabotaged by the Nazis' "violent anti-Semitism" as well as its policies regarding economic trade and debt. By May Luther was replaced, and he returned to the homeland.[2]

Prior to Luther's departure, a luncheon was arranged in his honor, during which Southern Baptist denominational leader Archibald C. Cree was invited to speak. Addressing the question of "Are the Baptists in Germany being persecuted?" Cree echoed the position of German Baptist leadership, who argued that Baptists were not in the same boat as Lutherans since Baptists refused tax dollars to compensate clergy.[3] To be fair, Rushbrooke had expressed this same criticism of State churches, but Cree apparently ignored the German Baptist cooperation with the government and its persecution of Jews.

When the members of the BWA's executive committee met in London on June 19, 1937, the German Baptist Union's position on the Confessing Church could not be ignored. Considering it "unwise to attempt to deal with matters concerning which it is not specifically informed," the committee passed a general resolution "reaffirming the historic position of Baptists as to Church and State and as to freedom of religious belief and practice."[4] The resolution quoted in full the 1934 Congress Resolution on Church and State,[5] and added that the global Baptist family was "resolutely opposed to religious repression of every kind, whether directed against Baptists or others, and it expresses the unwavering sympathy of all our people for the victims of persecution or repression, whether belonging to our own or any other communion."[6]

In expressing sympathy for "victims of persecution or repression," the executive committee implicitly critiqued German Baptist passivity regarding the struggles of both the Confessing Church and the Jewish population of Germany. But if they imagined that this gentle diplomatic expression of concern would influence the German Baptist leadership, they were sadly mistaken—as Paul Schmidt's participation in the 1937 Oxford Conference would demonstrate.

Paul Schmidt and the Oxford Conference

The Oxford Conference on Church, Community, and State took place July 12–26, 1937. Its aim was to articulate an inclusive Christian perspective on the church's relationship to society (the intended meaning of "Community").[7] Many denominations were represented, with two notable exceptions: the Roman Catholic Church was absent, while the German Evangelical Church (including the Confessing movement) was prohibited from sending representatives. Baptists were well represented, with a dozen leaders from North America, three from Great Britain, and individuals from China and New Zealand.[8]

Oxford's most controversial delegates were two leaders of the Protestant Free Churches of Germany—Methodist bishop Otto Melle and German Baptist Paul Schmidt. They traveled to Oxford "with the complete agreement of the Reich Ministry for the Churches."[9] Aubrey spoke for others in the international Baptist camp when he admitted being "embarrassed" that the "so-called Free Churches of Germany could have representatives in Oxford, one Methodist and one Baptist, while the Evangelical Churches of Germany had refused to send their representatives because of the refusal of the German Government to allow the German Confessional Church, which is fighting for freedom, to come over." Aubrey charged that "the German Government may use their presence there, as it did our Baptist World Congress in Berlin, for propaganda purposes—to demonstrate that religious freedom is not denied! That will deceive nobody."[10]

The conference overwhelmingly approved sending a sympathetic letter of support to Germany's Evangelical churches,[11] with the only "dissenting voices" being the "German delegates who were actually present." Northern Baptist Austen de Blois quoted Melle, who claimed that "the Federation of Free Churches of Germany are grateful for the full liberty to proclaim the Gospel of Jesus." The Free Churches interpreted "the National rule of the German people as a deed of divine providence." God had sent Hitler to Germany "to rescue a nation . . . from the abyss of despair, and to give this nation a new faith in its mission and in its future." Melle dismissed the Oxford letter, arguing, "it will not render a mediating ministry, but will rather tend to deepen existing tensions."[12]

Aubrey was mortified by Schmidt's refusal to sign on to the letter, saying, "It might be thought that a statement so Christian and so carefully worded would have been acclaimed by all real Christians." He also was horrified that both German representatives were unwilling to express "condemnation of the treatment of the Jews, who include many Jewish Christians." He was not alone in his reaction: "Feeling, I found, was running high and especially among Baptist members of the Conference."[13] Oxford's Baptist delegates feared that German Baptists had abandoned their professed neutral political stance, surrendered to Hitler, and were tacitly supporting the oppression of the Jewish people:

> The German Free Churches have now, through their representatives, chosen to praise Hitler and pay some sort of tribute to him. They can scarcely any longer be regarded as non-political. . . . They, on their part, must realise that their fellow believers in Britain and America cannot stand by them, for we have our tradition of protest against every form of tyranny. We raised our voices for the emancipation of the Roman Catholics and of the Jews . . . [while] some of our own faith in Germany have no words of condemnation of the Hitler régime.[14]

Schmidt served on the Church and Community committee, a significant platform from which to advocate for the legitimacy of social orders based on the German understanding of *Volk* (see

Chapter 10). The committee report considered the relationship between the church and the National Community—Volk—and conceded that "the primary call on the loyalty and service, both of the
church and the individual Christian believer, will be, as a rule, the
community in which God has set him. Every church should regard
itself as a church for the whole people."[15]

However, there was a caveat: "It does not mean that it subor-
dinates itself to the national life." In fact, contra Nazi philosophy,
when "the love of one's own people leads to the suppression of
other nationalities or national minorities" or tries to "give the nation divine status," the social order is in a state of sin! Such a dis-
torted social system must be "utterly repudiated and irreconcilably
opposed by the Christian conscience in the name of God and for the
sake of the nation it is called to serve." Similarly, the church must
reject all forms of racism, including "racial pride, racial hatreds and
persecutions and in the exploitation of other races."[16]

The report concluded with a list of practical suggestions for im-
plementing this perspective. It called for the church to demonstrate
a "more passionate and costly concern for the outcast, the under-
privileged, the persecuted and the despised in the community and
beyond the community." Regarding the specific plight of German
Jews, the report continued: "The recrudescence of pitiless cruelty,
hatreds and race discriminations (including anti-Semitism) in the
modern world is one of the major signs of its social disintegration.
To these must be brought not the weak rebuke of words but the
powerful rebuke of deeds."[17]

Schmidt and Melle must have been crushed by these words,
which constituted a clear repudiation of their churches' position. It
also could have caused them trouble upon their return home. Could
this be why the explicit reference to "anti-Semitism" was missing
from the German translation of the report, as was soon discovered?
Committee chair Walter Moberly unconvincingly "assured all present, however, that it was purely an inadvertence, an unintentional
oversight by the translator."[18]

International Youth Exchanges

British youth ministry leader T. G. Dunning was undeterred by what
had transpired at the Oxford Conference. He brushed aside concerns raised that the Second Young Baptist International Congress

scheduled for August 1937 would be tainted by German youth participating "under the instructions from Hitler." He retorted, "That may be doubted, but, if they are so instructed, let them come. We will hear what they have to say, and all, having first sought the guidance of the Spirit, will surely come to a closer unity of heart and mind, already so splendidly achieved at Oxford."[19] Among the 1,500 participants, 120 young people from Germany traveled to Zurich for the conference.[20]

The youth considered a diverse array of subjects, including social responsibility and Baptist persecution in Romania, but the published record does not indicate that Jewish oppression was addressed. Nationalism and the duties of a Christian citizen were a focus of several of the speakers, including Dunning, who acknowledged, "There is a place for a true nationalism. But it was not the will of God that one national character should obliterate all others and reduce them to its own likeness."[21] American W. H. Jernagin urged his listeners to "clean up the world mess of ignorance, race prejudice, family instability, economic injustice" and to be a "living example of what we mean by world brotherhood."[22] Hans Rockel, secretary of the Young People's Department of the German Baptist Union, steered clear of directly addressing the challenge of Nazism.

An English pastor, W. Taylor Bowie, spoke on "Christian Individualism and the Modern State." Since the New Testament affirmed both individualism and community, Taylor applied "the two complementary truths" to contemporary politics. Democracy was based on individualism, while totalitarianism favored community. There were dangers to both approaches. Democracy could foster unrestrained and irresponsible individualism, while the "danger of the Totalitarian State is that it achieves the values of community at the expense of personality."[23]

The Second Young Baptist International Congress was considered to be a huge success, and it was hoped that it would be a springboard for international correspondence and exchange trips.[24] In April 1938 W. D. Kassul visited Plymouth's Hope Baptist Church, where he brought greetings from Paul Schmidt and the "71,000 Baptists in Germany," and declared, "We feel that our great nations belong together, and in order to tie the bond of friendship closer I have come over here to tell you that we love the English people, especially those of the same faith." He even referred to the "blood relationship between England and Germany."[25]

Kassul defended the Baptists' relationship with the Nazi government, saying, "We have full liberty to preach the pure Gospel, not only from the pulpit, but in the streets and villages. . . . The Government gives us full permission to go to into the open and preach the Gospel and if there should be any trouble, as soon as approach is made the difficulty is soon obviated." The newspaper article of the event did not note if Kassul mentioned restrictions on Baptist youth work or the German Baptist stance on Jewish persecution, but it did quote him as stating, "We have nothing to do with politics, and the people rejoice in their faith."[26]

In actuality, German Baptists could only have facilitated such exchanges if they were viewed as useful by the government. In a letter dated October 1, 1938, to Rushbrooke, Kassul expressed hope "for the knitting of a closer friendship between the English and Germans." He was pleased that "30 English friends" came to Königsfeld in the summer of 1938, and he had accepted an invitation from English leaders (including Dunning) "to bring a group of young German Baptists to England" in July 1939.[27]

Hans Luckey—"Why Should We Be Silent?"

Dr. Hans Luckey (1900–1976) was a leading German Baptist voice in the twentieth century. A professor (and later rector) at the Baptist Seminary in Hamburg, Luckey mentored a generation of German Baptist clergy who served churches while Hitler reigned. He defended Schmidt's performance at Oxford in the German paper *Der Hifsbote*, writing, "National Socialism has kindly let us do as we like because we stay away from politics."[28] He also played a central role in formulating the revised 1944 Confession of Faith (see Chapter 10). Luckey served as BWA vice president from 1939 through 1946, and he had responsibilities in the 1934 and 1939 World Congresses. Following the war, Luckey was permitted to remain in European Baptist leadership and even rose to the position of president of the European Baptist Federation.[29]

Luckey's willingness to defend the German Baptist position under Nazism put him at odds with the *Baptist Times* and its editor, J. C. Carlile. Arthur Porritt, columnist for the *Baptist Times*, regularly covered the plight of persecuted Jews under Nazi oppression. In January 1938 he focused on Romania, where "unfortunate Jews are to be cleared out of their jobs in industrial, journalistic and professional life. They are, in fact, being given notice to quit the country."[30] In a letter dated May 16, 1938, Luckey expressed his outrage to Carlile over the "false" accusations against Germany that Porritt allegedly made in recent columns. The criticisms are too numerous to detail, but one stands out. Luckey criticized Porritt for his sympathy toward the Jewish people: "Or should we remember how Herr Porritt mourns the poor Jews who are rejected/eliminated by outraged peoples, but how he does not know or want to know about the terrible misery that Jewry has brought upon our plundered people?"[31] The charge that the Jewish people in Germany and Europe had plundered non-Jews ("Volk") is astonishing, for it served as a standard trope of Nazi propaganda and justification for Hitler's anti-Semitism. Nor was it merely a momentary outburst of irrational emotion; six years earlier, in 1932, he negatively portrayed Jews as "hungry for gold."[32] Luckey's charge was an outright and clear expression of anti-Semitism.

Luckey also debated Porritt's columns with Rushbrooke, whom he knew to be a sympathetic conversation partner. Rushbrooke sought to maintain bridges with his friend while standing firm on Baptist principles that were at odds with German political trends. In a letter responding to prior correspondence, the general secretary reminded Luckey that he had "always recognized the significance" of German Baptists and their role in European Baptist life, but that he felt "sorrow" over "racial separations among Baptists." By this Rushbrooke meant German versus English separation, but he also issued a warning: "The over-valuing of race or nation (which of course have values) easily leads to the denial of the New Testament idea that we are one in Christ." He repeated in German a sentence from Luckey's communication[33] and wondered whether he fully understood its true meaning for Luckey; in English Luckey asserted, "It is not nationalism in an exclusive tendency, but respect for the ethnic realities with fraternal understanding and alliance, that is my line." Rushbrooke wondered if Luckey was "getting rather deeply entangled in worldly politics," and he hoped Luckey would write about, in future pages of the German Baptist preacher's journal, *Hilfsbote*, "the conception of the Kingdom of God as something transcending nationalism and racialism."[34]

On May 11, 1938, the BWA's executive committee considered Luckey's charge that "some of our brethren in Germany have been troubled by some articles and expressions in Baptist newspapers of other lands." In a follow-up letter, Rushbrooke reiterated the "strong fraternal affection" of Baptists for "their German brethren," but that "independence of expression" was a Baptist norm that deserved respect. He stated that "differences of judgment on matters that are not vital issues affecting our common faith" should not be a cause for alienation and closed with the hope that German Baptists would not boycott the 1939 World Congress, where they would "enjoy full liberty to express themselves."[35]

Luckey was not satisfied. In a letter composed on June 15, 1938, he continued to criticize Porritt for his critical pieces on Hitler's policies and actions and concluded with a rhetorical reply, "Why should we be silent when our people ('Volk') and our Führer are reviled?"[36]

Luckey's Defiant Defense of the German Perspective

Luckey did not remain silent. Perhaps to mollify the German Baptist leader, in August 1938 the *Baptist Times* published an article by Luckey that painted the relationship between German Baptists and the Nazi government in a positive light, while ignoring the hardships the same government had consistently and progressively imposed upon Jews. Luckey claimed that Hitler's crackdown on political debate represented a "desire for community and the sense of subordination to the common weal" which among Germans was "felt to be natural." The political revolution was fostering discussions that were leading to greater closeness and even the growth of the Union of Free Churches. For Baptists, Hitlerism was a veritable blessing:

> We add that there are not only no difficulties made by the State but that we have even had every opportunity to experience the helping hand of the Ecclesiastical Ministry and the Ministry of the Interior. We have been greatly supported also in another manner. While all corporations not of a public character are liable in principle to a new tax, we have been exempted from this burden: this means a saving of many thousands of marks for us. Thus we have not the slightest reason whatever to complain about a limitation of our evangelistic work. We can freely

preach the Gospel of Christ as the Saviour of all human beings
and all races and both sexes.[37]

Luckey proudly announced that German Baptists had also made
"good progress" in international mission, having launched a "new
branch of the Union's work . . . in Austria."[38] He omitted the fact
that this mission field became available because of the Anschluss—
the forcible annexation of Austria by the Nazis in March 1938,
which was devastating for that country's Jewish population.

Within a month of the invasion, Luckey was in communication
with Arnold Köster in Vienna. Köster had written to Luckey for
advice regarding how to encourage other Austrian Baptist pastors
to embrace creative forms of mission. Luckey thought it might be
possible to plant a deaconess house and clinic in Vienna, although
start-up funds would be hard to come by. He encouraged Köster to
investigate property options, callously noting that "experience has
shown that Jewish emigration releases all kinds of cheaper real es-
tate."[39] Luckey was more than willing to have German Baptist mission work benefit from Jewish dislocation, suffering, and calamity.

Carlile countered Luckey's published claims with an unprecedented rebuttal. Arguing that "the right to liberty" has its "foundation in the conception of the value of human personality," his
editorial declared, "Baptists throughout their history have been
characterised by their insistence upon freedom for the soul." It
was "incomprehensible that any Christian leaders should defend
Governments which are engaged in destroying the freedom of the
individual." Carlile also attacked Luckey for ignoring the plight of
German Jews: "The Baptist professor cannot dispute the horrible
facts concerning the persecution of God's ancient people. The Jews
have suffered and are still suffering which has been reduced to an
art of torture."[40]

Luckey defended himself in the September 1 issue. Ignoring Carlile's points, he applauded the Nazi Party's embrace of "positive
Christianity," and described Hitler as "a religious romantic who
looks too far to be an atheist." He claimed that the Baptist movement had prospered under Nazism: "Before 1933 we were not able
to proclaim the Gospel so well as we can now." Luckey defended the German government's actions to transform social norms:
"The street battles, the moral purification of the community, the

destruction of noxious literature, social peace, the increase of mat-
rimonial morality—all these things give greater possibilities for the
proclamation of the Gospel than ever before." He criticized state
church leaders who opposed the Nazis, saying their "empty places
of worship mock at Bishops who talk politics."[41] In a striking second rebuttal, Carlile decisively rejected Luckey's arguments, declaring that nothing Luckey praised regarding Nazism could serve as "a
justification of the horrors of the treatment of the Jews."[42]

In his August article, Luckey conceded that Sunday school
youth ministry was "in an unfortunate position . . . for the State
takes much of their time."[43] In the follow-up article, Luckey reasserted the "fact" that the German government had preserved Sunday for "the exercise of religious duties by youth." He then made
a startling admission: "I can add as a father that my three sons,
who go to Sunday School and at the same time are members of the
Hitler Youth Movement, have not been hindered so far and have
never been persecuted for their faith's sake. And my experience is
not the exception."[44] It is profoundly disturbing that Luckey and
other German Baptists so unashamedly accepted their children's
participation in a Nazi-controlled organization dedicated to inculcating anti-Semitism[45] and did not see it as a corrupting influence
on the spirituality of the church's youth. One might argue that these
parents had no choice in letting their children become part of the
movement, but that was not Luckey's point; addressing an English
Baptist audience, Luckey justified German Baptist accommodation
to the Nazi reordering of society (which had no place for Jews) and
church life, in line with the positions taken by Schmidt and Kassul.

Inviting a Rabbi to the Atlanta Congress

In the year leading up to the BWA's Sixth World Congress in Atlanta, Georgia, Rushbrooke and the organizers of the conclave had
to deal with two thorny issues that threatened to undermine the
witness and success of the event. The segregation of black Americans could not be ignored, especially after passing the racialism
resolution during the prior congress. To address the racist culture
of the American South, National Baptist leaders worked alongside
their Southern and Northern Baptist white colleagues, ensuring that
the Atlanta congress would be fully integrated and feature several

African American speakers, musicians, and choirs. The other racially based challenge to the congress concerned German Baptist sensitivity toward an invitation to a Jewish rabbi to bring greetings during the opening night's plenary session.

German Baptist opposition to this invitation was a manifestation of a larger issue—the souring relationship between the United States and Germany. Rushbrooke continued seeking ways to keep the German Baptists invested in the 1939 Atlanta World Congress. On December 8, 1938, Luckey penned a reply to the BWA general secretary, supporting the idea of bringing historians together. However, he warned that the current relationship between the host country and Germany could preclude German Baptist attendance: "The question of whether we can appear as a German delegation in Atlanta depends largely on the political situation. At the moment there is a rather cloudy sky between America and Germany." He offered to compose an article about the significance of American Baptist support for "the German work in preparation for the Congress."[46]

Rushbrooke denied that there was "any political risk involved" in German Baptist attendance. Luckey believed the Friday morning session, focused on international issues and political ideologies, contained a slate of speakers unbalanced toward the democratic perspective. To make peace, Rushbrooke accepted his suggestion that Paul Schmidt be invited to speak.[47]

Perhaps emboldened by Rushbrooke's conciliatory response, Luckey went on the attack. He asserted that international Baptist criticisms of Hitler and the German Nazi regime were unacceptable and causing difficulties for the German Baptists. The Nazis were *monitoring* German Baptist relationships: "The fact that Atlanta poses a risk for us in many ways is hardly a new message for you. Our relations with international alliances are of course closely monitored, especially when leading Baptists in England and America are part of the anti-fascist front." Luckey was exasperated by one glaring example of this "anti-fascist" agenda—"How far this is the case can be seen from the fact that a Rabbi David Marx has been included as a most welcome personality bringing greetings at the Congress."[48]

Luckey could not accept such a scenario; the imagined negative reaction from the Nazi authorities no doubt made him shudder.

How could German Baptists, traveling to Atlanta by permission of their Nazi government, be part of a crowd receiving and applauding a Jewish rabbi? Luckey appealed to Rushbrooke to help "bridge all political and ideological differences" among Baptists so that the Germans could attend the congress. German Baptists were not among the "politicizing pious," but he warned that if the British and Americans continued to attack fascism, they were prepared to "emphasize our beliefs—as Oxford has shown," and that their critique of democratic countries would be "quite harsh."[49]

The rest of Luckey's letter demonstrated the threat. Rushbrooke would have none of it. He immediately fired back:

> Let me say in regard to Rabbi Marx that it has for many years been the custom in America, when a religious gathering is held in any city, for a welcome to be expressed by leading citizens. Rabbi Marx has lived in Atlanta for many years, and has the respect of the whole city. We should be acting altogether unworthily if we had refused the local request that he should give one of the short speeches of welcome on behalf of the general community.[50]

Rushbrooke's tactic of describing Marx as a civic representative of the whole community of Atlanta, and not as a religious representative of the city's Jewish community, could hardly satisfy someone as sophisticated as Luckey. In fact, it could be criticized as a less than forthright response. Although Marx did offer a "hearty welcome to our Baptist brethren from many climes and many nations,"[51] he also "spoke out of a full heart, since these last years have been crowded with new sorrows and suffering for his oft-afflicted people. Gratefully he paid tribute to the stand which Baptists have always taken for religious liberty."[52] The Jewish rabbi praised Baptists for their stance on separation of church and state, an important issue for American Jews, and called for a rejection of racism based on the theological and biblical tradition that Jews and Baptists held in common:

> The foundations of civilization are bedded in the intangible, spiritual qualities of man. It is of supreme value that religion transcend national and racial boundaries and in its universal

character strive for the full brotherhood of man. The contributions made by the Baptists to the rights of the individual to freedom of worship have become the possession of myriads of men outside the Baptist affiliation.[53]

Conscience and Racialism

Rabbi David Marx addressed the Sixth Baptist World Congress on the evening of Saturday, July 22, 1939.[54] During his welcome, in addition to what was previously discussed, he declared that "God does not give to man power over the conscience of man."[55] In a single sentence, the rabbi identified with core Baptist convictions, prophetically opposed totalitarian ideology, and challenged his Baptist friends to consider how to live up to their ideals in a world gone awry.

Outgoing BWA president George W. Truett preached the next morning, at the third plenary session. He, too, was concerned with how the global Baptist family would respond to the challenges facing them: "You have come together in one of the most ominous and epochal hours in the life of the world." Truett specifically cited racial prejudice as a threat to a Christian sensibility of how the world should be: "The astounding fact of ghastly persecutions, both racial and religious, continues to challenge the whole world with horror, and to make a blot that is an unspeakable disgrace to civilization." Speaking about nine months after Kristallnacht, Truett surely had the ongoing Nazi persecution of the Jewish people in mind. Extending the Baptist conviction of freedom of conscience to all people and citing Catholics and Jews as examples, Truett called for a devotion to radical liberty and not mere tolerance.[56]

Norwegian leader Arnold T. Ohrn connected the spiritual awakening of the individual disciple of Jesus to the "great human problems of the hour." He cited racialism as an example: "The Christian protest against racialism or against any form of tyranny rests on the Christian valuation of man. This grows out of the Christian idea of God, and this again rests upon the revelation given in Christ, which revelation reaches its peak and receives its guarantee in Christ's death for all men without regard to race or class or grade of culture."[57]

Speaking from an African American perspective, Virginia Union University professor Gordon B. Hancock focused on "color-consciousness," which was synonymous with racial prejudice. The desire to promote "race integrity" (for example, as practiced by the Nazis in pursuit of the purity of the Aryan race) constituted "one of the mightiest moral challenges of modern times," as illustrated by the Italian takeover of Ethiopia and the German dismemberment of Czechoslovakia. It was his considered judgment that "what is transpiring here and there throughout the world in the name of racialism . . . must be Christianized or destroyed."[58]

For Hancock, contemporary ideologies of "bigoted racialism" threatened to destroy Christianity, and "unless the Church will accept the challenge that racialism has thrust in its pathway through the Twentieth Century world, it too must decline and die. Already in Communism and Nazism the axe is lying at the root of the tree." Accordingly, the gauntlet has been laid down: "For the Church of today it is either the Barabbas of racialism or the Jesus of fraternalism. The Church must make its choice."[59]

Throughout the congress, Baptist young people were encouraged to fight prejudice. In the "Young People's Demonstration," everyone rose "in support of a message of sympathy for the Romanians, and especially the Christian Jews."[60] During the Young People's business meeting, T. G. Dunning praised the international links that had been promoted by BWA youth events and claimed that such friendships could even save Jewish lives. For example, a "non-Aryan family" was able to resettle in South America due to the generosity of a Baptist youth group. Dunning shared another case—of a Baptist Jew:

> Thus, when the Jewish pogroms started, many a noble Baptist Jew found himself in a painful situation. One man whose time for the concentration camp was drawing near, secured a permit to enter Belgium. He had, however, been deprived of all his possessions and could not pay his fare. But he was known to the young Baptists of another land, who, on hearing of his peril, wired £10 to him, and ultimately brought him to their own land and provided employment and a good home for him.[61]

Racialism could not be avoided during the congress. The Baptist core conviction of freedom of conscience collided with Nazi racist ideology. It could even induce youth to sacrificially reach out to persecuted Baptist Jews. Racialism could furthermore expose a growing rift in the very fabric of Baptist fellowship and unity, as evidenced by a riveting debate between an English Baptist leader and his German Baptist colleague.

The Great Debate

The six German Baptist leaders who participated in the 1939 World Congress came well prepared to represent their homeland and defend the Baptist Union's position under Nazi rule.

Three hundred attendees heard presentations by William Kuhn and Friedrich Rockschies at a German-language sectional meeting on Wednesday, July 26, 1939. Hans Luckey attended, while Paul Schmidt served as moderator. Rockschies declared, "We are convinced that the German Fuehrer has full confidence in the Baptists and their loyalty to the present government. With God Almighty still in control of human affairs, and with Adolf Hitler, who has led the German people out of a desperate situation into unity and strength, our fate is in good hands."[62] Luckey offered a glowing assessment of Baptist life under Nazism: "German Baptists are experiencing a happy time. Evangelism is growing at a tremendous pace and congregations are constantly increasing. It is our great desire that peace be kept in the world, both for you and ourselves."[63]

Schmidt denied a charge that "the German government is trying to eliminate the doctrine that Christ was a Jew," claiming that it didn't care about "the elimination of the Jewish element in the Bible. While there are people in Germany, and other parts of the world who would not be willing to believe that Jesus was a Jew, we, as Baptists, do not consider these people to be a real danger to the Christian faith, and their number is constantly decreasing."[64]

At the English-language sectional meeting, Gilbert Laws declared that freedom of conscience and totalitarianism could not coexist. Laws raised doubts about the legitimacy of German Baptist conduct and practice under Nazism: "A totalitarian state, with its tremendous claims on all its subjects, cannot endure a church which is not an expression of its will. A truncated, reduced, emasculated

Gospel is all that can be tolerated. . . . It must speak only as permitted, or be silent, or suffer the consequences." The German Baptist Union could not claim faithfulness to Christ while submitting to the Nazi constrictions on its activities, supporting Nazi positions in conferences, and remaining silent about the Nazi persecution of the Jews. Laws specifically addressed this last point:

> Moreover, this permitted and tolerated church must be limited by race-barriers. It must be closed against the very people (the Jews) through whom the Gospel first came to us, and of whom, according to the flesh, Christ Himself came. A doctrine of racial pride and racial hatred entirely forbidden by the Gospel is imposed on the minister of Christ. Any refusal to tune the pulpit to these unchristian notes of pagan conceit and race-hatred can bring condign punishment upon the preacher bold enough to make such refusal.[65]

Perhaps the most dramatic stage debate in BWAs history took place at the thirteenth session on the morning of July 28, 1939. M. E. Aubrey, a consistent opponent of totalitarianism, and Paul Schmidt, representing the German Baptist Union, took turns discussing the relationship between the church and political systems.

Aubrey declared that the totalitarianism regimes of "Germany, Russia and Italy" posed "as great a challenge" to the church "as any it has faced since the fall of the Roman Empire." He insisted that "the first loyalty of every Christian is neither to class, nor sect, nor state, nor race, but to Almighty God who has revealed His nature and His will in Jesus Christ our Lord." Totalitarianism destroyed freedom of conscience, while democracy was in accord with Baptist core convictions concerning freedom of the human soul and "the dignity of human personality." Thus, "Tyranny and evangelical Christianity cannot exist together. Dictators know it." Aubrey reminded the congress that the successes of totalitarianism, lauded by German Baptists, "cannot last," for "no good can come in the end of pride, cruelty and hate."[66]

Schmidt rued the fact that congress delegates exhibited "a conspicuous lack of understanding . . . for the real situation in our native land," and criticized Baptist leaders who sided with the Confessional Church instead of the German Baptist Union. He complained that German Baptists "might well have given an account of actual conditions in Germany, but no one at this Congress has thus far asked us to do so."[67]

The German Baptist asserted that the church may thrive under any political system, and "Baptist ideals" were not "necessarily identical with any political ideology." It was not the responsibility of the church to "meddle in the affairs" of empires. He claimed that throughout history, the church sought to "share in and help to fulfill the destiny of their own people within that people"—implying that German Baptists should indeed work within the German political reality: "Thus Baptist Churches will participate in the life of their nation, no matter whether this life is determined by liberal or collectivist tendencies, and declare and bear the gospel." German Baptists bore no responsibility to challenge or oppose the Nazi political regime but to find ways to work within it. He concluded, "The Churches of Baptists in Germany assume this attitude, and they stand forth in missionary power and are entering through open doors. This is the God-given attitude which God would have His church take in the world."[68]

During their debate, neither leader mentioned the persecution of Europe's Jewish population, but it is not difficult to extrapolate their stances from their presentations. No doubt, many at the congress did so. For Aubrey, Jews deserved freedom and dignity, and their persecution and loss of civil rights under Hitler's totalitarianism was an evil to be opposed vigorously. Solidarity with oppressed minorities, like the Jewish people, was within the church's prophetic witness and required by Baptist core convictions. For Schmidt, it was not the responsibility of the German church to actively oppose Hitler's political agenda, even if it was anti-Semitic. The church bore no direct responsibility to protect Jews, who had been defined as outside the German people.

In a fine example of British understatement, the *Baptist Times* reported that the exchange between Aubrey and Schmidt "produced some mild excitement."[69] In fact, the interpreter, Dr. William A. Mueller, felt it necessary to go outside his official role and share (in German) his own opinions. Contra Aubrey, he did not believe that Christianity was inseparably tied to democracy, even though it "was the best form of government." Rushbrooke himself intervened and "appealed to the delegates not to fight over political questions." He sought to clarify Aubrey's position and affirmed that "there are certain definite human values implied in the New Testament and that the finest opportunity for bringing these values into being is afforded by democratic forms of government."[70]

Closing Arguments

In the official report of the 1939 Baptist World Congress, Rushbrooke, as its editor, inserted an address by Mueller immediately following the presentations made by Aubrey and Schmidt "because of its direct bearing in the differing points of view in the two addresses immediately preceding."[71] As a German-born Baptist who came to the United States in 1923 and was naturalized in 1929,[72] Mueller exemplified the close ties between German- and English-speaking Baptists, and so was the perfect choice to address the perspectives of the two adversaries. Rushbrooke needed a symbolic peacemaker, and Mueller's life was an illustration of Baptist transnational unity.

Mueller shared his reflections in his speech "Baptist Emphasis East and West of the Atlantic" at a sectional meeting of German-speaking delegates. He insisted that Baptists on both sides of the ocean shared "a common faith in Jesus Christ's Lordship and absolute sovereignty."[73]

Turning to the German Baptist situation, Mueller then launched a sensitively crafted critique. Contrasting what he experienced when he was younger to recent visits, including during the 1934 congress, he observed, "A complacent bourgeois mentality seems to be gripping increasing numbers of your people, Again, German Baptists seem to withdraw more than in the post-war era into their own shell." In the past, German Baptists "wrestled long and deeply with the conflicting philosophies then claiming the soul of your people," but under the Nazi regime, "today it seems to us on this side of the Atlantic that the Baptists of Germany are too easily adapting themselves to the prevailing spirit."[74]

The "prevailing spirit" of National Socialism had silenced German Baptists regarding Nazi oppression of Jews: "Thus far, we have not heard of a clear word from our Baptist brethren in Germany concerning the racial problem that is a burning issue in your land as well as in ours." He accused Baptist leaders of duplicity and deception in maintaining that their movement experienced no interference: "Is it not a fact that again and again even your work has been interfered with by the authorities?" Rejecting German Baptist unwillingness to face the issues raised by Nazism, Mueller asked, "Are the Baptists of Germany forgetful of the fact that to a real disciple of Jesus Christ any political, economic, educational or scientific issue is at every moment a deeply Christian issue to be met in obedience of faith (Col. 3:17)?" Quoting John Clifford, one of the founding leaders of the BWA, Mueller reaffirmed that Baptists should be "an insuppressible race of protestors."[75]

C. Oscar Johnson, pastor of the Third Baptist Church of St. Louis, preached the Coronation Address at the closing plenary session. Johnson specifically addressed "our German friends who are here" and shared an illustration about a hotel message sign he saw on a Hamburg bus, which said, "*Wir haben ein lift.*" He learned it meant simply that the hotel had an elevator on its premises. Johnson, a consummate preacher, declared that "the lifting power of the Son of God" was a recurring theme of a panoply of great Protestant leaders, including Martin Niemöller—"lifted from a submarine to a concentration camp." His German Baptist listeners must have winced when Johnson confessed, "I would rather have been lifted to that height and be privileged to live in a concentration camp with the presence of Christ in my heart than to be the dictator of both Germany and Italy, aye, of the world. . . . He has lifted a race, He has lifted a nation, He has lifted the world closer to the heart of God."[76]

The *Baptist Times* published a more caustic reaction to the German Baptist witness at the World Congress. Columnist Basil Mathews quoted an editorial from the *Minister*, a Baptist periodical from Chicago, which charged that German Baptists "took every opportunity to defend Adolf Hitler," and then asked, "Is the so-called freedom of Baptists in Germany to-day due to the fact that German Baptists take the 'easy' road and play Hitler's game?" The editorial then posed a follow-up question: "If German Baptists were to stand on their own feet and denounce an international brigand like Hitler, denounce racial prejudice, and show their horror at the suffering and destruction of minority groups, what would Hitler do? Would Baptists then be free in Germany?" Citing Nazi persecution against Jews in conquered Czechoslovakia, the editorial asked, "Do

German Baptists condone this sort of thing? Is this why German Baptists are 'free'?"[77]

NOTES

1. "An Invitation from the German Ambassador," *Watchman-Examiner*, July 19, 1934, 810.

2. C. Edmund Clingan, *The Lives of Hans Luther, 1879–1962: German Chancellor, Reichsbank President, and Hitler's Ambassador* (New York: Lexington, 2010), 120.

3. "Men and Things," *Watchman-Examiner*, June 17, 1937, 707.

4. Minutes of Executive Committee Held at the Offices of the Alliance, London, on Tuesday, June 29th, 1937 (London: Baptist World Alliance, 1937), 8.

5. *BWA World Congress Resolution 1934.8 Church and State*, in J. H. Rushbrooke, ed., *Fifth Baptist World Congress: Berlin, August 4–10, 1934* (London: Baptist World Alliance, 1934), 18.

6. *BWA Executive Committee Resolution 1937.3 Church and State and Religious Freedom*, Minutes of Executive Committee Held at the Offices of the Alliance, London, on Tuesday, June 29th, 1937, 10.

7. J. H. Oldham, *The Oxford Conference (Official Report)* (Chicago: Willett, Clark, 1937), i–xiii.

8. Oldham, 2–3; 277–82; and R. Birch Hoyle, "Oecumenical Conference at Oxford," *Baptist Times*, July 29, 1937, 573.

9. Quoted in Nicholas M. Railton, "German Free Churches and the Nazi Regime," *Journal of Ecclesiastical History* 19, no. 1 (January 1998): 120.

10. M. E. Aubrey, "The Religious Situation in Germany," *Baptist Times*, July 22, 1937, 551.

11. Oldham, *Oxford Conference*, 259–60.

12. Austen De Blois, "Ecumenical Fellowship: The World Conference at Oxford," *Watchman-Examiner*, September 23, 1937, 1060–61; Arthur Porritt, "German Free Churches and Hitler," *Baptist Times*, July 29, 1937, 571; and Railton, "German Free Churches and the Nazi Regime," 121.

13. M. E. Aubrey, "Oxford and Germany," *Baptist Times*, July 29, 1937, 567.

14. Aubrey, 567.

15. Oldham, *Oxford Conference*, 59.

16. Oldham, 59–60.

17. Oldham, 62.

18. William B. Lipphard, "The Christian Church in the Modern World," *Missions*, October 1937, 463.

19. T. G. Dunning, "Baptists and Germany," *Baptist Times*, August 26, 1937, 632.

20. Baptist World Alliance Youth Committee, *Christ Our Life: A Permanent and Illustrated Record of Addresses Given and Resolutions Passed at the Second Young Baptist International Congress, Zurich, 1937* (London: Baptist World Alliance, 1937), xvi.

21. Baptist World Alliance Youth Committee, 6.

22. Baptist World Alliance Youth Committee, 9.

23. Baptist World Alliance Youth Committee, 52–53.

24. Baptist World Alliance Youth Committee, 91–92.

25. "71,000 Germans Send Greetings LOVE FOR ENGLISH Plymouth Visit by Berlin Pastor," *Western Morning News and Daily Gazette* (Devon, England), April 25, 1938, 5.

26. "71,000 Germans Send Greetings," 5.

27. W. D. Kassel to J. H. Rushbrooke, October 1, 1938, Angus Library and Archive, Regent's Park College, Oxford, England.

28. Quoted in Railton, "German Free Churches and the Nazi Regime," 126.

29. Günter Balders, ed. *Ein Herr, ein Glaube, eine Taufe: 150 Jahre Baptistengemeinden in Deutschland, 1834–1984 Festschrift* (Wuppertal und Kassel, Germany: Oncken, 1985), 351–52.

30. Arthur Porritt, "The Unfortunate Jews," *Baptist Times*, January 6, 1938, 7.

31. Hans Luckey to J. C. Carlile, May 16, 1938, Elstal Seminary Archive Collection, Berlin, Germany, translation mine.

32. Herbert Gezork and Hans Luckey, "Unsere Stellung zu Rasse und But," in *Unsere Jüngerschaft und Unser Zeugendienst im Blick auf die Gottlosenbewegung* (Kassel, Germany: Oncken, 1932), quoted in Roland Fleischer, "The German Baptists and Their Conduct towards Jews and Jewish Christians, Especially during the Third Reich," in *Peoples of God: Baptists and Jews over Four Centuries*, ed. John H. Y. Briggs and Paul S. Fiddes, 201.

33. "Nicht Nationalismus in exklusiver Tendenz, sondern Achtung der völkischen Gegeben-heiten bei brüderlicher Verständigung und Allianz, das ist meine Linie."

34. J. H. Rushbrooke to Hans Luckey, March 29, 1938, Elstal Seminary Archive Collection. The conversation continued in an exchange of letters in April; see J. H. Rushbrooke to Hans Luckey, April 11, 1938. See also Lee B. Spitzer, "The British Baptist Union and Nazi Persecution of the Jews, 1933–38," in *Peoples of God: Baptists and Jews over Four Centuries*, ed. Briggs and Fiddes, 183–85.

35. J. H. Rushbrooke to Hans Luckey, May 20, 1938, Elstal Seminary Archive Collection.

36. Hans Luckey to J. H. Rushbrooke, June 15, 1938, Elstal Seminary Archive Collection, translation mine. The original German sentence is "Warum sollten wir schweigen, wo man unser Volk and unsere Führer schmäht."

37. Hans Luckey, "German Baptists and Religious Freedom: Baptist Work in the Third Reich," *Baptist Times*, August 11, 1938, 625.

38. Luckey, "German Baptists and Religious Freedom," 625.

39. Arnold Köster to Hans Luckey, April 7, 1938; and Hans Luckey to Arnold Köster, April 30, 1938, Elstal Library Archive, Berlin, Germany, translation mine.

40. Editorial, *Baptist Times*, August 11, 1938, 625.

41. Hans Luckey, "Freedom of Religion in Germany," *Baptist Times*, September 1, 1938, 673. It was also published in the *Canadian Baptist*, September 4, 1938, 4–5.

42. Rebuttal, *Baptist Times*, September 1, 1938, 673.

43. Luckey, "German Baptists and Religious Freedom," 625.

44. Luckey, "Freedom of Religion in Germany," 673.

45. See Nico Voigtländer and Hans-Joachim Voth, "Nazi Indoctrination and Anti-Semitic Beliefs in Germany," *Proceedings of the National Academy of Sciences*, June 2015, 7931–36.

46. Hans Luckey to J. H. Rushbrooke, December 8, 1938, Angus Library and Archive.

47. J. H. Rushbrooke to Hans Luckey, December 23, 1938, Angus Library and Archive.

48. Hans Luckey to J. H. Rushbrooke, December 28, 1938, Angus Library and Archive.

49. Hans Luckey to J. H. Rushbrooke, December 28, 1938, Angus Library and Archive.

50. J. H. Rushbrooke to Hans Luckey, January 3, 1939, Angus Library and Archive.

51. Rabbi David Marx, "To the Baptist World Alliance," *Atlanta Constitution*, July 23, 1939, 10B.

52. Ernest A. Payne, *Baptists Speak to the World: A Description and Interpretation of the Sixth Baptist World Congress, Atlanta, 1939* (London: Carey, 1939), 44.

53. "Pastors from Atlanta Churches of All Denominations Express Sincere Interest and Welcome to Baptists," *Atlanta Constitution*, July 23, 1939, 10B.

54. J. H. Rushbrooke, ed., *Sixth Baptist World Congress Atlanta, GA USA July 22–28, 1939* (Atlanta: Baptist World Alliance, 1939), 3.

55. Rushbrooke, 294.

56. Rushbrooke, 23–36.

57. Rushbrooke, 51.

58. Rushbrooke, 269–70.

59. Rushbrooke, 270–71.

60. Rushbrooke, 16.

61. Rushbrooke, 241.

62. "Baptists' Status in Reich Described," *Atlanta Constitution*, July 27, 1939, 11. *Watchman-Examiner* published a slightly different quote, substituting "faith" for "fate"; see "More Gleanings from the Atlanta Congress," *Watchman-Examiner*, August 17, 1939, 922–23.

63. "Baptists' Status in Reich Described," 11.

64. "Baptists' Status in Reich Described," 11.

65. Rushbrooke, *Sixth Baptist World Congress Atlanta*, 191.

66. M. E. Aubrey, "Christianity and the Totalitarian State," in *Sixth Baptist World Congress Atlanta*, ed. Rushbrooke, 198–202.

67. Paul Schmidt, "Liberalism, Collectivism and the Baptists," in *Sixth Baptist World Congress Atlanta*, ed. Rushbrooke, 203–6.

68. Schmidt, 203–6.

69. "Mr. Aubrey Challenged," *Baptist Times*, August 10, 1939, 621.

70. "Baptist World Alliance," *Watchman-Examiner*, August 10, 1939, 915.

71. Rushbrooke, *Sixth Baptist World Congress Atlanta*, 207.

72. "Students Met Are 'Enjoyable' Says Mueller," *Richmond Collegian*, February 10, 1950, 3; William Mueller's Deposition of Witness for Alfred Cierpke's Naturalization,

September 12, 1945, Ancestry.com; https://www.ancestry.com/imageviewer/collections/2505/images/40339_1821100522_0978-00045.

73. William A. Mueller, "Baptist Emphasis East and West of the Atlantic," in *Sixth Baptist World Congress Atlanta*, ed. Rushbrooke, 207–9.

74. Mueller, 207–9.

75. Mueller, 207–9.

76. C. Oscar Johnson, "The Uplifting Christ," in *Sixth Baptist World Congress Atlanta*, ed. Rushbrooke, 288–89.

77. Basil Mathews, "How American Baptists Look at Britain," *Baptist Times*, October 10, 1939, 762.

CHAPTER 9

The Journeys of
Two German Baptist
Exiles

Dunning's Veiled Reference

In November 1942 T. G. Dunning anticipated resuming BWA-related youth ministry when the war was over. In the meantime, he was eager to share that not all of Europe's Baptist youth ministry leaders were trapped in Hitler's grasp—some had escaped to America: "They are not lost to the Continent but will be able to acquaint our American brethren with the life and work of the Continental Baptists."[1] Two of these leaders were German Baptists: Herbert Gezork and Alfred Cierpke. The former became a prominent leader within Northern Baptist circles, while the latter found a spiritual home among the Southern Baptists.

Herbert Gezork (1900–1984) received his ministerial training from the Baptist Seminary in Hamburg and served as a pastor at the First Baptist Church in Berlin. He earned his doctorate from Southern Baptist Theological Seminary in the United States in 1930 and returned to Germany to assume leadership of the German Baptist Youth ministry until it was closed by the Nazi authorities. Fleeing in 1936 to the United States, Gezork reinvented himself as an academic, securing positions at Furman University, Wellesley College, and Andover Newton Theological Seminary, where he ultimately served as president from 1950 to 1965.[2]

Although the two men shared much in common, Alfred Cierpke's spiritual journey (1901–74) differed significantly from that of Gezork. Cierpke also attended the Hamburg Baptist Seminary and received his doctorate from an American school, Eastern Baptist Theological Seminary. Following his Eastern education and a stint as pastor of the Erie Street Baptist Church in Cleveland, Ohio, in 1940 (also known as Second Baptist Church), Cierpke spent the rest of his vocational life in Southern Baptist circles. He was a professor at Tennessee Temple College in Chattanooga (1947–48) and then dean at Temple Baptist Theological Seminary (1948–61).[3]

Herbert Gezork: Youth Ministry Leader, Exile, and Seminary President

GERMAN BAPTIST YOUTH MINISTRY AND THE RISING HOPE

The English Baptist's Young People's Department welcomed a delegation of some two dozen German Baptist young adults in July 1932. They visited Baptist churches in several towns, including Oxford, Birmingham, Cardiff, and Bristol. Rev. Dr. Herbert Gezork, secretary of the German Young People's Baptist Movement, thanked the Mill Street Baptist Church in Bedford for the welcoming attitude of British Baptists, while one of the female members shared about youth ministry in her homeland.[4] In Coventry the hope was expressed that a follow-up tour of English Baptist youth might visit Germany the next year.[5] In Bath Gezork expressed satisfaction that the aim of the visit—to promote bonds of friendship and solidarity between German and English Baptist youth—had been actualized: "Though we belonged to different nations and to different churches, we were all one in Jesus Christ."[6]

Youth exchanges served to create "mutual understanding and appreciation upon which alone firm and lasting peace can be built."[7] T. G. Dunning, chairman of the BWA's youth committee, was in Germany's Black Forest while the German youth toured England, cofacilitating a youth conversation with the German Baptist Dr. Herbert Patrick, European secretary of the World Alliance for International Friendship through the Churches. Among the topics covered were "the future of Hitlerism."[8]

Hitlerism became a present reality for German Baptists in January 1933. In an article originally written for the *Baptist Leader*, an English Baptist youth ministry journal, Gezork analyzed how Baptist young people were responding to Hitler and the Nazi message.

He acknowledged Hitler's charismatic personality and outlined the pillars of Nazi ideology—nationalistic pride, opposition to Communism, Jew hatred, and the eradication of Jewish elements in Christian religious life, including the Old Testament. Gezork stated that Hitler aimed to "break the power" of Jewish financiers and diminish their political influence. Gezork described the future leader's race-based anti-Semitism:

> The Jews, Hitler says, are strangers. Their concepts of morality are significantly different from those of the German people. They screw up the breed through mixed marriages with Germans. They are the bearers of a fateful world politics and the propagandists of Marxism. Because of their extraordinary ability to trade, they have managed to attain a position of undue influence on the economic and political life of the German people, a position they have not used for the benefit of the community. That is why Hitler longs, that in the Germany of the future, the Jews will not be given full civil rights, but that they will be treated as strangers.[9]

Gezork revealed that German youth (young adults) were attracted to Hitler's nationalistic message, as well as its opposition to Marxism. He estimated that "about 35 percent of German Baptist youth voted for the Hitler party," and that perhaps "5 percent" were "affiliated members." However, Gezork maintained that most Baptist young adults opposed Nazi militarism and the party's "racial glorification and racial hatred." He hoped that "in a conflict between their religious beliefs and the demands of their political party, most German Baptist youth, who have now rallied under Hitler's banner, will remain faithful to their faith in Jesus Christ."[10]

Rushbrooke attended the German Baptist Union Annual Assembly in August 1933. He reported that Gezork "spoke wisely and strongly on loyalty to Christ," and was "the rising hope of young German Baptists."[11] Gezork was also the "rising hope" of the German Baptist Union. He was added to the BWA's Commission on Racialism in 1932, in anticipation of the congress originally being held in 1933.[12] Gezork also served on the German Congress Committee, which organized the logistics and hospitality arrangements for the gathering.[13] On Sunday afternoon, August 5, the second day of the 1934 congress, Gezork led the United Young People's worship service.[14] He interpreted presentations and attended Hindenburg's funeral alongside the Northern Baptist W. B. Lipphard, "as guests of the German government."[15] In the congress's official report, his photograph appears alongside Rockschies' headshot.[16]

Prior to the congress, Gezork was called upon to represent the host denomination as it sought to encourage global Baptist attendance in Berlin. In a two-page article for *Missions*, Gezork presented the standard historical narrative of the German Baptist movement. Oncken, of course, received attention as the movement's pioneer, but Julius Köbner's Jewish background was also acknowledged: "The former was by birth a Jew. He was led to Christ by Oncken's preaching in Hamburg and very soon became one of Oncken's most zealous co-laborers. In him German Baptists had their poet and hymn writer. Scarcely a Sunday passes in which German Baptists do not sing at least one of Koebner's [sic] glorious hymns."[17]

Gezork also toed the party line when he rejoiced that "in the new Germany under the leadership of Chancellor Adolf Hitler," German Baptists "have up until the present had full freedom to preach the gospel." He asserted that adult evangelism was possible, unhindered by atheist attacks, since the Nazis "dissolved their bands."[18]

However, the youth leader also had to admit, without any public protest, that his own work had been shut down by the Nazis: "In the young people's work, as a result of political changes which have taken place in Germany during the past year, our National Young People's Union has been dissolved."[19] This had taken place in February 1934.[20] The Nazi leadership grasped the strategic value of organizing Nazi-controlled youth organizations (the Hitler Youth) which first competed with, and fairly rapidly replaced, other youth organizations, such as the youth ministries of the churches. As James F. Tent observed, "Given their success in creating the Hitler Youth as their organization of choice, the Nazis took a dim view of any competing group."[21]

"That's How I Saw the World"

With denominational youth ministry prohibited, the "rising hope" of the Baptist Union found it increasingly difficult to serve God under Nazi rule. In early 1936 Gezork corresponded with his mentor and spiritual advisor, Hans Luckey. A Baptist church was consider-ing calling Gezork as its next pastor, but ultimately he declined the invitation, to Luckey's dismay.[22]

On May 26, 1936, Gezork shared with Luckey that a planned trip to the Balkans had been canceled due to "foreign exchange difficulties." He also confessed that he felt a sense of "great restless-ness," and joked, "Have you heard that my book should be put on the 'Harmful Literature' list? Because of the comments about the Zionist settlements in Palestine. Ha Ha!!"[23]

Gezork was referring to his observations of kibbutz life dur-ing an around-the-world excursion he enjoyed between 1928 and 1930, which he published in 1933 under the title of *So sah ich die Welt* (That's How I Saw the World). His adventure began in New York City, and its Lower East Side revealed the city's "great melting pot of many races and peoples."[24] After traversing the American continent, Gezork toured Japan, China, India, and Egypt before finally arriving in Jerusalem—one of his "heart's longest dreams." Observing Jews praying at the Temple Mount, he began to appreci-ate the Zionist dream: "The strangest Jewish types from all over the world can be found here: Galician, Spanish, African, Mesopo-tamian Jews, men in long, greasy caftans, with reddish curls over their ears, here they are, the scattered people of Israel, from the ends of the earth they came to cry over the lost glory of their holy city, their temple."[25]

Gezork experienced the vigorous energy of Zionism in northern Israel while visiting "a Zionist settlement." He was impressed by the gracious hospitality of a young female resident of the kibbutz: "She came from Austria and moved to Palestine with her husband a few years ago. They joined this colony and now they, both academ-ics, are working side by side with the other, very simple Jews from Galicia and Lithuania. Their shared love for their fathers' old coun-try, which is to become their new home, binds them all together." Watching kindergarteners absorbing their lessons, the female Zion-ist remarked "with a smile that they will soon be out of the worst, that the first great difficulties have finally been overcome, that the earth is willing and gives them what they need." Gezork could not hide his astonishment: "Her beautiful, dark eyes shine with a firm belief in the future."[26]

In his diary, Gezork unreservedly praised Zionism, "which aims to give the Jewish people in Palestine a national and cultural home again." He praised the Jews' "heroic . . . struggle for their old homeland," as well as "the strength of their passionate love" and their "tenacious persistence" to create a new future "under the blazing Palestinian sun." Gezork had nothing but admiration for this "scattered, hated, unhappy people" as they sought to "finally return from their long exile and find their home in the land of their fathers."[27]

Gezork's admiration of the Jewish people he met on his global quest and positive portrayal of Zionism earned him the disdain and reproach of the Nazi authorities. Almost two decades later, Gezork recalled his personal feelings back in 1936: "Those of us who in spite of all the success of Hitler resisted him because of our spiritual, moral, and political principles, had to flee the country or landed sooner or later in a concentration camp. We were a small minority." He added a veiled criticism of his former German Baptist colleagues: "The rest were swept away by the success and the glory." Gezork condemned the anti-Semitism behind German Baptist passivity in response to Nazi persecution of the Jews: "Some of them, to be sure, had an uneasy feeling, especially about the terrible treatment which the Jews suffered, but they shrugged their shoulders and said: Well, after all, the Jews needed to be put into their place, a lot of them had it coming to them, and as for the others, that is unfortunate, but could not be helped."[28] In Gezork's mind, voluntary exile was a path to survival, if or when resistance within Germany became untenable. It was also an ethically based refusal to give in to the prevailing spirit of anti-Semitism that was pervasive not only in German society in general but also within the Baptist circles Gezork had frequented.

A Secret Hope

On December 22, 1936, Herbert Gezork sailed from Hamburg aboard the SS *New York*, destined for the port the passenger ship was named after. Traveling alone, he arrived on December 30. His destination was Philadelphia, home of the Eastern Baptist Theological Seminary. Professor William A. Mueller was his contact person.[29] The Manifest of Alien Passengers categorized the thirty-six-year-old minister as a "radio-speaker" and indicated that he had received a United States *reentry* permit on April 1, 1935.[30]

Gezork needed that reentry permit because he had lived in the United States during a portion of 1934 and 1935. He arrived in New York on September 19, 1934, having departed from Bremen on September 11. His immediate destination was Immanuel Baptist Church, a German-language congregation. In his immigration form, the newcomer affirmed that he did not plan to return to Germany, desired to remain permanently in the United States, and intended to apply for citizenship.[31] On November 27, 1934, Gezork filed a Declaration of Intention form to become a citizen of the United States, affirming that he "emigrated to the United States from Berlin, Germany" for the purpose of making a "lawful entry for permanent residence."[32]

Gezork's vocational future played a significant role in his decision to move permanently to the United States. He was called to serve the Immanuel Baptist Church in New York City as pastor, a position he briefly held between mid-September of 1934 through August 1935. During these eleven months, he lived next door.[33]

Further motivation may have come from his experiences at the 1934 World Congress. He secured his visa on August 15, just five days after the meetings concluded. During the congress, he most certainly spoke with Mueller, as both served as translators.[34] No doubt Mueller and Gezork also spent much time together during Gezork's tenure in New York City. It is reasonable to believe that Gezork's perceptions of the congress, as well as of German society at large, influenced him to depart from his home country. Rising anti-Semitism and persecution of German Jews, the speeches of German Baptist leaders at the conference, and the ending of his denominational youth ministry portfolio caused the young minister to lose hope that he had a future in Nazi Germany.

Gezork did not immediately receive American citizenship but instead returned to Berlin in August 1935.[35] His visa may have been on the verge of expiring, or perhaps he was lured back by the prospect of another pastoral position. He may also have had a very personal reason for his return. Ellen Markus arrived in New York's harbor aboard the *President Harding* on May 22, 1937. She was not quite twenty-five years old when she sought permanent residency[36] but not a solitary life in her new country. Waiting for her at the dock was her fiancé, Herbert, and once she was ashore, they wasted no time in becoming husband and wife. Later that same day, they pronounced their wedding vows before Rev. John E. Grypo, Gezork's permanent successor at Immanuel Baptist Church.[37]

In January 1938, Ellen filed her own Declaration of Intention to become an American citizen. Herbert resubmitted his declaration two and a half years later (before his original 1934 application became legally invalid). He claimed that he had been a permanent resident since his original arrival on September 19, 1934 (not mentioning his return to Germany for part of 1935–36). However, in September 1943, this omission was caught and noted in his Petition for Naturalization.[38] Herbert received his naturalization card first, on September 20, 1943; Ellen was granted her citizenship on December 13, 1943.[39] Gezork's secret hope had finally been realized.

RISING AGAIN IN AMERICA

The specter of German National Socialism may have led Herbert Gezork to abandon his friends and colleagues in the German Baptist Union, but with his new wife, Ellen, beside him, a bright future lay ahead in America. After the war, *Missions* introduced an article by Gezork and provided a brief account of his earlier response to Nazism: "In 1936, sensing the ominous rise of nazism [*sic*] and its threat to world peace and human freedom, Dr. Gezork came as a voluntary exile to the United States."[40] Leaving behind his past, Gezork became a rising star in the circles of the Northern Baptist Convention.

South Carolina's Furman University gave Herbert his first academic position in America, in its Department of Religion.[41] Following an investigation of his theological views on topics such as the virgin birth, hell, the infallibility of Scripture and revivals, Gezork was relieved of his teaching responsibilities. He was quoted as stating that the Samson stories were "folktales" and approving of his students' right to question "many of the dogmas of the church."[42] Gezork assumed an interim pastorship for the Clarksburg Baptist Church in West Virginia. His academic career truly took off when he began teaching social ethics at Andover Newton Theological School and Wellesley College in Massachusetts in September 1939.[43]

It did not take long for Gezork to secure speaking engagements. He addressed the Vermont Baptist State Convention on the evening of May 31, 1939. The German Baptist "refugee" spoke on "From Martin Luther to Martin Niemoeller" and offered observations on the "challenge which now confronts all organized Christianity in the land of Hitler."[44] The Resolutions Committee responded by promising to pray for Europe's Baptists.[45] Before the Ministers Council of Boston, Gezork chose the topic of "The Fundamental Conception of Naziism [sic] or Germany under Hitler, and Today's Religious Struggle."[46] In July 1940 he gave a chapel talk at the Northfield Conference of Religious Education, and recounted meeting a German wife and her Jewish husband, who had successfully fled Germany with their daughter. In Germany the girl had been terrorized at school. Shunned by her classmates, she was "hated, spitted in the face and hissed at . . . again and again she was called before the class and put before her fellow pupils as an example of the Jewish race, and a model of all that was bad, evil, low, and ugly." At home she wept and told her mother, "I want to die, I don't want to go to school any longer."[47]

In late 1941 Gezork pronounced solemn judgment on German churches that had been supporting the Nazis. His conclusion may be interpreted as a rebuke of the German Baptist leadership: "Only a compromised Christian church, which has betrayed the fundamental convictions of the Christian faith, could make its peace with Hitlerism."[48] Three years later Gezork revisited this theme in a draft paper, "The Story of the Resistance of the Church to Nazi Dictatorship." While some resisted the agenda of the Nazi movement, other Christians "did not realize what was at stake" or were indifferent. Some (German Baptists?) strove for "a compromise between their Christian faith and their loyalty to the government." At the very least, these leaders were not among those who courageously "opposed and denounced the State-organized persecution of the Jews."[49]

Gezork spoke at an evening plenary session during the Northern Baptist annual convention in May 1944. He focused on "the growing danger to marriage, home, and family in our national life . . . and the explosive frictions and conflicts between racial and cultural groups within our nation."[50] He had in mind the Detroit riots (June 20–22, 1943) in which thirty-four people died and more than four hundred others were injured; Gezork argued for African American civil rights.

Gezork was also concerned about "Christian-Jewish relationships." Noting that 121 domestic organizations that espoused anti-Semitic views existed in 1939, he observed, "There is today more Anti-semitism [sic] in the United States than there was in Germany in the 1920s. Things have happened in our large cities that did not happen in Germany before Hitler came to power. In the Midwest are powerful groups waiting for the end of the war and its accompanying economic dislocations to launch a vicious campaign of anti-Semitism all across the country." Gezork also offered a theological perspective considering the Jewish hope for Israel as a national homeland: "Now Israel is the mystery among the nations. We do not know what God's ultimate plans for this people will be. But we know that there were always two ways to deal with Israel: the barbarian, pagan, satanic way of hating and oppressing; or the Christian way of repenting for the guilt on our own side, of forgiving the guilt on the other side, and of meeting what irritates us, with redemptive love."[51] On July 16, 1944, Gezork shared a message titled "American Ideals—Europe's Hope" on Boston's WORL AM radio channel.[52] In Europe the "abominable Nazis" had "proclaimed that one race is superior to the other, and that the Nordics are the supreme race and therefore destined to rule the world, and that the Jews are the most inferior race and therefore should be exterminated, and all that nonsense." Meanwhile, in Boston Gezork had gained his citizenship and on the day it was conferred, he thought, "This land is my land too." The former rising star of the German Baptist Youth movement had risen again and, in voluntary exile, rediscovered his prophetic voice among Baptists in the United States.

Hope Fulfilled

When the Allied victory was final, Gezork would find himself called back to Germany to investigate the impact and consequences of its Nazi past and the war itself for the United States Defense and State Departments.[53] *Missions* published his preliminary findings in December 1945. Many Germans still expressed support for Hitler or were "stunned and apathetic." Sadly, "perhaps the majority" of Germans showed "very little sense of guilt."[54] Gezork offered an extended summary of how Christians responded to the Nazi persecution of Jews:

> All through the years when Jews were hunted down by the Ge-
> stapo to be sent to concentration camps or to be shipped to
> the extermination camps of Poland, there were Christian people
> who offered them shelter in their homes, hid them from Him-
> mler's henchmen, clothed them and shared their own meagre
> food rations with them. In doing this they daily risked their own
> lives. Anyone who was discovered to be a *Judenfreund*—friend
> of Jews—brought the full fury of the nazi wrath upon his head.
> As such Jews now come out of hiding,—and I met several of
> them,—they cannot praise enough the heroism and kindness of
> their Christian friends.[55]

The journey and witness of the German Baptist Union, and its
churches and clergy, were not mentioned until the conclusion of the
article, almost two pages after the above quote. Gezork excluded
the German Baptist Union from this generally positive summary of
Christian support of Jews. His visits to German Baptist churches
were a "saddening experience for me," he confessed, and not just
because buildings were destroyed and denominational ministries
had been disbanded.[56] What Gezork did not write was perhaps
most damning—he recorded no examples of German Baptists resisting Nazism or aiding Jews.

Gezork never forgot his German homeland and the hard lessons of the Nazi period. Nazism might have been defeated, but in
the 1950s communism threatened to overwhelm Europe and other
parts of the world. Speaking during the second plenary session of
the BWA's Golden Jubilee World Congress in July 1955, he called
upon Baptists to remain independent of the State and be its "moral
conscience." He said totalitarianism must be opposed because it
seeks to "control . . . man's inmost thoughts, his ultimate commit-
ments, his very soul." A Baptist may not "allow Caesar to determine what is his and what is God's; he will reserve that right for his
own free conscience under God."[57] This was precisely what German Baptists in Nazi Germany had failed to do.

In 1959 the former "rising hope" of the German Baptist Union
became the president of the American (formerly Northern) Baptist
Convention. Gezork had reached the pinnacle of his denomination
in the United States. In his 1960 convention presidential address,
he recounted how an American, Barnabas Sears, baptized Johann

Gerhard Oncken, the father of the German and European Baptist movements—who, in turn, baptized Gezork's grandfather. The journeys of German and American Baptists were linked. Conveying his "deep gratitude" for his country of refuge, Gezork recalled, "For when I came here, 24 years ago, escaping from the curse of Naziism [sic] which had thrown its terrible blight upon my native Germany, this blessed land opened its door to me and many others like me, and gave us work and bread and freedom and hope."[58]

Alfred Cierpke: The Prophetic Significance of Jews

COMING TO AMERICA

Seven representatives of the German Baptist Union attended the BWA World Congress in Atlanta in July 1939. Five returned to their home country—Rev. Paul Schmidt, Rev. Friedrich Rockschies, Dr. Hans Luckey, Rev. W. D. Kassul, and Mr. Erich Dahm.[59] Two remained in the United States weeks later when hostilities broke out—Rev. Alfred Arthur Cierpke and his spouse, Irmgard. In contrast to Gezork, the Cierpkes apparently did not intend to become exiles.

As vice president of the North European Baptist Youth Conference, Cierpke wrote an article in October 1938 praising Chamberlain's appeasement initiative. The *Baptist Times* introduced him as "a keen German who is a whole-hearted believer in Herr Hitler."[60] Cierpke himself confirmed his allegiance to Hitler in the opening paragraph. He visualized "Bolshevist curses against my Fatherland and our Fuehrer and Chancellor Adolf Hitler, venerated by all of us." Justifying Hitler's takeover of the Sudetenland, he lauded Chamberlain as an "angel of peace" and equated him with Hitler, "another man of peace and of action, the great Fuehrer and Chancellor" of the German people (and one of the four "great statesmen" of Europe). Cierpke believed that "England and Germany, the two cousins in Europe, should in [the] future understand one another much better than was the case in the past. Now there should be eternal friendship."[61]

The Cierpkes spent some time touring the United States before and after the World Congress began. They departed from Bremen on June 30, 1939, and came to the United States on the *Europa*.[62] The couple arrived on July 6, slightly more than two weeks before the beginning of the congress. They visited Alfred's uncle, Otto Sauermann, who lived in Chicago. The Cierpkes planned to stay in the United States for up to three months and then return to Germany. They declared that they did not wish to apply for United States citizenship.[63]

When returning to their homeland was made impossible by war, the Cierpkes found a new home thanks to Eastern Baptist Theological Seminary, where he enrolled as a student. William Mueller was one of Alfred's teachers, and years later he recommended him for naturalization.[64] They stayed in Philadelphia until May 1940, when they sought to become permanent residents of the United States. The Cierpkes were required to leave the country, reenter, and apply. The Canadian border was not an option, as the English Empire was at war with Germany. So they traveled south, spent a day in Nuevo Laredo, Mexico, and then crossed back over the border in Laredo, Texas, on May 29, 1940.[65] Throughout this period, Cierpke did not express any criticism of the German Baptist Union or concerns about Nazi oppression of Jews in his extensive correspondence with W. O. Lewis.[66]

In May 1941 Cierpke completed his thesis, "Jesus Christ, the Son of God and the Son of Man, the United Personality."[67] In May 1943 he then served as a summer supply pastor for a key German Baptist congregation in Forest Park, Illinois. Dr. William Kuhn, general secretary of the Missionary Society of the German Baptist Churches of North America, resided in Forest Park and later provided Cierpke with a naturalization reference, in which he stated he first met Cierpke at the 1939 BWA Congress.[68]

The Cierpkes moved to Cleveland, Tennessee, in September 1943 so that Alfred could assume his duties as a professor of theology at Bob Jones College, forerunner to Bob Jones University. Their fourth daughter, Lillian Elizabeth, was born on September 17, 1943.[69] While residing in Cleveland, both spouses filled out Petitions for Naturalization. In addition to Mueller and Kuhn, Cierpke's application was supported by Gordon Palmer, the president of Eastern Baptist Seminary.[70] On November 14, 1945, Alfred and Irmgard Cierpke became naturalized citizens of the United States.[71]

It is interesting to note that Cierpke's obituary, written in 1975, claimed that "Dr. Cierpke was well known for his stand against the

Nazis in their treatment of Jewish people. For this reason it was quite dangerous when they left the children in Germany while they were in the United States."[72] Happily, all three of their daughters— Adeltraut, Sieglinde, and Liebhilde—survived the war and were reunited with their parents in 1946.[73]

However, the obituary's claim about Cierpke's opposition to Nazism is problematic. First, as has been shown, events beyond their foreknowledge and control forced the Cierpkes to remain in the United States, and their exile did not seem to be a premeditated personal choice based on religious or political convictions regarding Hitler's mistreatment of the Jewish people. Second, Cierpke's postwar course notes, while providing a positive assessment of Israel's existence in light of biblical prophecy, refrain from offering any serious critique of Nazi mistreatment of the Jewish people.

THE WHITE RACE

Cierpke could not possibly have imagined that he would have an opportunity to return to his homeland so soon following its defeat. In the summer of 1946, with the backing of two Southern Baptist churches, the Conservative Baptist Foreign Mission Society, and North American Baptist General Conference, he visited some fifty displaced persons camps across Europe and claimed to speak before a hundred thousand refugees.

His report published in the *Watchman Examiner* contains several troubling statements, reflecting both his German background and mid-twentieth-century Southern Baptist racial and missiological prejudices. This "new American citizen" conflated his own personal journey with the story of European immigration to the Americas, noting that "Europe is our old home." The racial undertone to this nostalgic statement was made explicit toward the conclusion of the article, where he claimed that Paul's journey to Europe represented a divine call to give Christianity to the white race: "The evangelization of Europe—the cradle of the white race— was thus commanded by the divine Lord of missions, Jesus Christ, and begun by the greatest missionary, the Apostle Paul."[74]

No doubt Cierpke was influenced by the Southern Baptist missionary to Europe, Everett Gill, who espoused a similar racial prejudice in his 1937 book *Europe: Christ of Chaos.*[7] Like Gill, Cierpke wrote as though Jews were invisible. In the camps, he saw only white Europeans who desperately needed to replace Nazi ideology with Christ; in fact, he dwelled on an incident where he outwitted a proponent of Nietzsche. For Cierpke, the era's conflict was between false ideologies of power and Christianity; Jews did not figure into the drama in any central way.[76]

A HOMELAND FOR THE JEWS

In the 1950s Cierpke taught courses on Jewish history, Israel, and Zionism, in light of Jesus' messiahship and Southern Baptist eschatological theology. He composed several bound books on the themes of Jewish history and the establishment of Israel in modern times during his tenure at Temple Baptist Theological Seminary. They appear to be lecture notes, and much of the text is in outline form. Collectively, these works give us insight into his evolving appreciation of the heritage of the Jewish people, their relation to Jesus, the Christian church and end-times theology, as well as Israel's place in the post-Holocaust world. In *Palestine-Israel: The Holy Land Today*, most likely initially bound and distributed in 1953 or 1954, Cierpke summarized his perspective on modern Israel's rebirth:

> Surely no one with eyes to see and ears to hear can deny that the Jewish nation is being revived in a marvelous and miraculous manner, not in some new location, but in the land that God gave to Abraham and his seed by an everlasting covenant. The people that have been scattered to the ends of the earth for nearly nineteen centuries and have been without a home and a temple and a sacrifice, and have endured untold persecutions precisely as predicted by Moses more than 3,000 years ago— that same people have been given back their ancient homeland, and are returning to it by scores of thousands annually, and the land that has lain waste and desolate for centuries is once more blossoming as the rose.[77]

In line with American fundamentalist and grassroots Southern Baptist eschatological understanding, Cierpke affirmed that the establishment of Israel in 1948 was a fulfillment of biblical prophecy—"one of the greatest miracles of history"[78] —and that the Zionist movement was bearing fruit. Most of the volume, and indeed, all Cierpke's published notes, expressed admiration for the Jewish people's resilience and contemporary economic, political, and cultural successes. The texts are philo-Semitic but not particularly original or insightful. More interesting is how Cierpke taught about the Nazi period in his courses, the worst of the "untold persecutions" Jews have endured throughout their history. In brief, he treads lightly.

A core doctrine of Nazi anti-Semitism was that the Jewish people were an inferior race. In contrast, Cierpke rejects the label of race as an adequate descriptor, embracing instead Reconstructionist rabbi Mordecai Kaplan's "peoplehood" definition.[79] European Jews "have known the ghettos of Europe, the persecutions of Hitler, the pogroms of Russia and Poland."[80] The Final Solution of the Nazis was contextualized by making it just one of a variety of anti-Semitic attacks by European countries. It was not explored in detail or depth, and the acquiescence of Baptists in Germany was not addressed.

Anti-Semitism did receive more in-depth consideration in Cierpke's second course book, *Palestine-Israel: God's Miracle Nation*. A drawing before the table of contents pictured a snake named "Anti-Semitism." Tattoos on its skin start, from the rear, as Nazi swastikas and midway across its body morph into the hammer and sickle—representing how the Communists of the 1950s were carrying on the anti-Semitism of the Nazis.

After an episodic review of the Jewish diaspora, Cierpke returned to the theme of Nazi and Communist persecution of the Jewish people. Estimating that 4 million Jews were "gassed, burned, and buried during the reign of Hitler," he recounted an eyewitness account of the gas chambers. Who bore responsibility for these heinous crimes? Most surprisingly, he declared, "Christians all over the world, including America, share heavily and directly in the responsibility for the Jewish pogroms. . . . Cold aloofness of Christians made possible, to a startling degree, the debauchery which permitted Hitler to turn Europe into a Jewish cemetery."[81]

But what about Germany? Cierpke quoted from an unnamed "survivor of Auschwitz" who minimized German complicity, seeing it as a derivative of European Christian anti-Semitism:

German responsibility for those crimes, however overwhelming it may be, is only a secondary responsibility, which has grafted itself, like a hideous parasite, upon a secular tradition, which is a Christian tradition. How can one forget that Christianity, chiefly from the eleventh century, has employed against Jews a policy of degradation of pogroms, which has been extended—among certain Christian people—into contemporary history . . . and of which the Hitlerian has been only a copy, atrociously perfected.[82]

It is unclear if the following paragraph is an extension of the quote or Cierpke's own commentary: "Hitler neither could have nor would have done to the Jewish people what he did if he had not had people who had actively supported him. . . . But basically, the German people as a whole were responsible; and further, the people all over the world were responsible."[83]

Cierpke then rehearsed centuries of episodes of European anti-Semitism, followed by a story of a single anti-Semitic American Christian. Speaking to an American and primarily Southern Baptist audience, he concluded, "While few of us have cast stones at the Jews, we seem to fall into the pattern of Jew-hate, and thus promulgate a situation which permitted a Hitler to lead his followers into an orgy of sin. Their blood is upon us."[84]

The second half of the book rehashes the arguments about anti-Semitism that have already been outlined above. He defined anti-Semitism as "opposition to the Jewish race." Rampant throughout Europe in the nineteenth and early twentieth centuries, "it flared up strongly in Nazi Germany under the dictatorship of Adolph [sic] Hitler in 1933 and later." Immediately, Cierpke shifted his attention to other countries—Iraq, Middle Eastern lands, France, United States, Manchuria, Spain, the Netherlands, and the Soviet Union. His point was clear: Germany was not unique but merely part of a continuing pattern of anti-Semitism.[85]

Cierpke took one last opportunity to discuss Nazism's anti-Semitism from a philosophical perspective. National Socialism "actually elevated to the level of principle, phenomena which had hitherto been regarded as part of our brutish heritage from the past." The Nazis had made evil "aware of itself and turned [it] into a program and guide for the aspirations of humanity." Anti-Semitism was "an integral element in the Nazi philosophy" that made "Nazism fundamentally unclean."[86]

The third volume in the Palestine-Israel series, *The Marvel of the World*, covered much of the same territory as the previous courses. Cierpke devoted a mere half page to discuss the Holocaust period, during which the "persecutions of the Jews under Hitler and Mussolini took place." In an eighteen-line paragraph reviewing Nazi mistreatment and oppression of Europe's Jewish population, there was no specific mention of his homeland, Germany. Statistics on Jewish deportations or deaths, or examples of persecution, were provided for the Baltic countries, France, Belgium, Hungary, Czechoslovakia, Italy, and Norway—allies or occupied countries.[87]

Cierpke appeared unwilling to confront the role that Germany and its citizens specifically played in embracing anti-Semitism and leading the persecution that eventually became the Holocaust. He relativized the responsibility of the German people, assigning blame to other Europeans, Christians in general, and indeed, the whole world. He never claimed that the German people were innocent or without blame, but he did not specifically call them to accountability. Germans participated in an evil movement, but so did others.

Cierpke's reticence to probe the extent to which Germany was uniquely guilty of the most heinous crime in the twentieth century may have been rooted in his personal and religious past. During his American phase, he was philo-Semitic and enthusiastic about the early success of Israel since its rebirth. However, it cannot be denied that in none of his books, which were created after the Holocaust, did Cierpke share about his own journey as a German Baptist in Nazi Germany, apologize for or renounce his earlier support for Hitler, or critique how German Baptists responded to Hitler's anti-Semitism during the Nazi period of Germany's history.

NOTES

1. T. G. Dunning, "Baptist Youth and the Continent," *Baptist Times*, November 19, 1942, 572.

2. Herbert J. Gezork Papers, 1931–1981, biography page, Andover Newton Library Archive.

3. Alfred A. Cierpke obituary, *Journal of the Evangelical Society*, January 1975, 67–68.

4. "Visit of Young German Baptists," *Bedfordshire Times and Independent*, July 22, 1932, 12.

5. "German Baptist Party of Tourists Visit Coventry," *Coventry Midland Daily Telegraph*, July 25, 1932, 1.

6. "Hands Across the Sea—Bond of Friendship with German Baptists," *Bath Chronicle and Herald*, August 6, 1932, 19.

7. "German Baptists in Bristol," *Western Daily Press and Bristol Mirror*, August 2, 1932, 4.

8. "Hiking toward World Peace," *Derby Evening Telegraph*, August 17, 1932, 4.

9. J. W. Weenink, "Het Hitlerism en de Duitsche Baptisten Jongeren," *De Christen*, April 21, 1933, 5177, translation mine. The Dutch article does not use quotes in citing Gezork's writing; all quotes therefore represent Weenink's reporting of Gezork's observations.

10. Weenink, 5178, translation mine.

11. "The German Baptist Meetings," *Baptist Times*, September 7, 1933, 598.

12. Baptist World Alliance, *Occasional Bulletin No. 1—Fifth Baptist World Congress, Berlin, August, 1933*, 6. RUS 12/3 BWA Congress, Berlin 1933, Angus Library and Archive.

13. *Official Programme and Hand-book of the Fifth Baptist World Congress, Berlin, August 4th to 10th, 1934* (Berlin: Baptist World Alliance, 1934), 18; J. H. Rushbrooke, ed., *Fifth Baptist World Congress: Berlin, August 4–10, 1934* (London: Baptist World Alliance, 1934), 249.

14. *Official Programme and Hand-book of the Fifth Baptist World Congress*, 6.

15. "Not Limited to the Home, The Women's Sphere—Baptist Conference in Berlin," *Northern Whig and Belfast Post* (Antrim, Northern Ireland), August 8, 1934, 11.

16. Rushbrooke, *Fifth Baptist World Congress*, 220–21.

17. "Yesterday and Today for Baptists in the New Germany," *Missions*, May 1934, 294–95.

18. "Yesterday and Today for Baptists," 294–95.

19. "Yesterday and Today for Baptists," 295. John C. Shelley claims that Gezork made an address during the BWA Congress that was "sharply critical of Hitler and his regime," resulting in the "dissolving" of the "German Baptist Youth Movement and forbidding Gezork to continue as a Christian pastor." John C. Shelley, "The Gezork Incident," *Furman Magazine* 46, no. 1, art. 4 (2003): 4. This appears to be inaccurate, both regarding the time of the youth activities closure and Gezork's participation in the congress. The Congress Report contains no address from Gezork, and it appears the only opportunity he would have had to do so would have been when he presided over the young people's worship service. It is unlikely he would have used such a platform to criticize Hitler.

20. Andrea Strübind, "German Baptists and National Socialism," *Journal of European Baptist Studies* 8, no. 3 (2008): 11; Bernard Green, *European Baptists and the Third Reich* (London: Baptist Historical Society, 2008), 59–60.

21. James F. Tent, *In the Shadow of the Holocaust: Nazi Persecution of Jewish-Christian Germans* (Lawrence: University of Kansas Press, 2003), 108.

22. Hans Luckey to Herbert Gezork, January 4, 1936; Hans Luckey to Herbert Gezork, May 7, 1936, Elstal Seminary Archive Collection, Berlin, Germany.

23. Herbert Gezork to Hans Luckey, May 26, 1936, Elstal Seminary Archive Collection.

24. Herbert Gezork, *So sah ich die Welt* (Kassel, Germany: Verlag von J. G. Oncken Nachf, 1933), 15.

25. Gezork, 223.

26. Gezork, 232–33.

27. Gezork, 233.

28. Hebert Gezork, "Germany—Key to Europe: A Paper Read to Neighbors of Newton Center," January 12, 1953, 4, Andover Newton Theological Seminary Archive. On page 10 Gezork worried about the rise of Neo-Nazism and its anti-Semitism.

29. "William A. Mueller, Ph.D.," *Watchman-Examiner*, September 24, 1936, 1080.

30. Arriving Passenger List, December 30, 1936, Ancestry.com; https://www.ancestry.com/imageviewer/collections/7488/images/NYT715_5918-0056.

31. Arriving Passenger List, September 19, 1934, Ancestry.com; https://www.ancestry.com/imageviewer/collections/7488/images/NYT715_5549-0518.

32. Declaration of Intent Document for Herbert Gezork, dated November 17, 1934, Ancestry.com; www.ancestry.com/imageviewer/collections/2280/images/47294_302022005557_0509-00690.

33. See http://www.immanuelchurchny.org/our-history/; Declaration of Intent Document for Herbert Gezork, dated November 17, 1934.

34. "Students Met Are 'Enjoyable' Says Mueller," *Richmond Collegian*, February 10, 1950, 3.

35. Passenger List, August 6, 1935, Ancestry.com; https://www.ancestry.com/discoveryui-content/view/97479:9734.

36. Certificate of Arrival on May 22, 1937, for Ellen Markus Gezork (issued January 15, 1938); www.ancestry.com/imageviewer/collections/2361/images/007777224_00495;

Declaration of Intent Document for Ellen Markus Gezork, dated January 26, 1938, Ancestry.com; www.ancestry.com/imageviewer/collections/2361/images/007777224_00496.

37. "What's Happening," *Baptist Herald* 15, no. 13 (July 1, 1937): 194.

38. Petition for Naturalization for Herbert Gezork, dated September 20, 1943, Ancestry.com; www.ancestry.com/imageviewer/collections/2361/images/007778660_01936.

39. Naturalization Card for Herbert Johannes Gezork, September 20, 1943; Ancestry.com; www.ancestry.com/imageviewer/collections/1192/images/M1545_55-3033; and Naturalization Card for Ellen Markus Gezork, December 13, 1943, Ancestry.com; www.ancestry.com/imageviewer/collections/1192/images/M1545_55-3032.

40. Herbert Gezork, "Shadows and Light in War Ravaged Germany," *Missions*, December 1945, 524.

41. "What's Happening," 194.

42. Alfred Sandlin Reid, *Furman University: Toward a New Identity 1925–1975* (Durham, NC: Duke University Press, 1976), 83–84; 92–95; Shelley, "Gezork Incident," 4; Gregory A. Wills, "Progressive Theology and Southern Baptist Controversies of the 1950s and 1960s," *Southern Baptist Journal of Theology* 7, no. 1 (Spring 2003), 4.

43. "Men and Things," *Watchman-Examiner*, March 30, 1939, 325. Gezork became president of Andover Newton in 1950 and served in that capacity until 1965.

44. *1939 Vermont Baptist State Convention Yearbook*, 29.

45. *1939 Vermont Baptist State Convention Yearbook*, 42.

46. Charles L. Paige, "Massachusetts," *Watchman-Examiner*, October 5, 1939, 1108.

47. Herbert Gezork, "Chapel Talk #4, Northfield Conference of Religious Education," July 20, 1940, 2, Andover Newton Theological Seminary Archive.

48. "Men and Things," *Watchman-Examiner*, January 1, 1942, 3.

49. Herbert Gezork, "The Story of the Resistance of the Church to Nazi Dictatorship," draft paper, Summer 1944, 2, Andover Newton Theological Seminary Archive.

50. Northern Baptist Convention Review, "World Affairs," *Watchman-Examiner*, June 8, 1944, 557–58.

51. Herbert Gezork, "Our Christian Witness and Current Problems," speech manuscript for the Northern Baptist Convention, May 23, 1944, 2, Andover Newton Theological Seminary Archive.

52. Herbert Gezork, "American Ideals—Europe's Hope," Andover Newton Theological Seminary Archive.

53. "Men and Things," *Watchman-Examiner*, October 10, 1946, 1030.

54. Gezork, "Shadows and Light in War Ravaged Germany," 524–26.

55. Gezork, 527.

56. Gezork, 528–29.

57. Arnold T. Ohrn, ed. *Baptist World Alliance—Golden Jubilee Congress—London, England—16th–22nd July, 1955 Official Report* (London: Kingsgate, 1955), 44–45; see Derek H. Davis, "Baptists and the American Tradition of Religious Liberty," *Perspectives in Religious Studies* 33, no. 1 (Spring 2006): 41–66.

58. Herbert Gezork, "Blessed Are the Peacemakers," presented to the 1960 American Baptist Convention, June 2, 1960), draft manuscript, Andover Newton Theological Seminary Archive.

59. J. H. Rushbrooke, ed., *Sixth Baptist World Congress Atlanta, GA USA July 22–28, 1939* (Atlanta: Baptist World Alliance, 1939), 303.

60. Alfred 'A. Cierpke, "Thanks to England an Angel of Peace Flew to Germany," *Baptist Times*, October 13, 1938, 765.

61. Cierpke, 770.

62. Bremer Passagierlisten, Staats Archive Bremen, http://212.227.236.244/passagierlisten/passagen.php.

63. Arriving Passenger List, July 6, 1939, Ancestry.com; www.ancestry.com/imageviewer/collections/7488/images/NYT715_6359-0123.

64. William A. Mueller's Deposition of Witness for Alfred Cierpke's Naturalization, September 12, 1945, Ancestry.com; www.ancestry.com/imageviewer/collections/2505/images/40339_1821100522_0978-00045.

65. U.S. Border Crossing from Mexico for Alfred and Irmgard Cierpke, May 29, 1940, Ancestry.com; www.ancestry.com/imageviewer/collections/1082/images/31092_170213-04954.

66. Arthur Cierpke to W. O. Lewis, in the W. O. Lewis Collection (box 5, folder 2.5 /identifier 83), American Baptist Society Historical Archive.

67. Arthur Cierpke to W. O. Lewis, May 16, 1941, in the W. O. Lewis Collection, American Baptist Society Historical Archive.

68. William Kuhn's Deposition of Witness for Alfred Cierpke's Naturalization, August 11, 1945, Ancestry.com; www.ancestry.com/imageviewer/collections/2505/images/40339_18211 00522_0978-00049.

69. Petition for Naturalization for Alfred Cierpke, November 14, 1945, Ancestry.com; www. ancestry.com/imageviewer/collections/2505/images/40339_1821100522_0978-00038.

70. Gordon Palmer's Deposition of Witness for Alfred Cierpke's Naturalization, August 24, 1945, Ancestry.com; www.ancestry.com/imageviewer/collections/2505/images/40339_1821100 522_0978-00043.

71. Petition for Naturalization for Alfred Cierpke and Irmgard Cierpke, dated November 14, 1945, Ancestry.com; www.ancestry.com/imageviewer/collections/2505/images/40339 _1821100522_0978-00038; and www.ancestry.com/imageviewer/collections/2505/images/403 39_1821100522_0978-00052.

72. Alfred A. Cierpke obituary, *Journal of the Evangelical Society*, January 1975, 67–68.

73. Arriving Passenger List of Displaced Persons, 1946, Ancestry.com; www.ancestry.com/ imageviewer/collections/61704/images/0229_81649902_1.

74. Alfred A. Cierpke, "Europe's Haunted Millions," *Watchman-Examiner*, March 13, 1947, 250–51. See also *Watchman-Examiner*, October 24, 1946, 1030.

75. See Lee B. Spitzer, *Baptists, Jews, and the Holocaust: The Hand of Sincere Friendship* (Valley Forge, PA: Judson, 2017), 261–63.

76. Cierpke, "Europe's Haunted Millions," 250–51.

77. Alfred A. Cierpke, *Palestine-Israel: The Holy Land Today* (Chattanooga, TN: self-published, 1953/54), 4.

78. Cierpke, *Palestine-Israel: The Holy Land Today*, 9.

79. Mordecai Kaplan, *Judaism as a Civilization: Toward a Reconstruction of American Jewish Life* (1934; repr. Philadelphia: Jewish Publication Society, 2010); and Kaplan, *The Future of the American Jew* (New York: Macmillan, 1948).

80. Cierpke, *Palestine-Israel: The Holy Land Today*, 27.

81. Alfred A. Cierpke, *Palestine-Israel: God's Miracle Nation* (Chattanooga, TN: self-published, 1954), 15–16.

82. Cierpke, *Palestine-Israel: God's Miracle Nation*, 16.

83. Cierpke, *Palestine-Israel: God's Miracle Nation*, 16.

84. Cierpke, *Palestine-Israel: God's Miracle Nation*, 16–18a.

85. Cierpke, *Palestine-Israel: God's Miracle Nation*, 32–38.

86. Cierpke, *Palestine-Israel: God's Miracle Nation*, 39.

87. Alfred A. Cierpke, *Palestine-Israel: The Marvel of the World* (Chattanooga, TN: self-published, 1954/55), 18.

CHAPTER 10

A Tale of Two Confessions and German Baptist Unfaithfulness

Julius Köbner's Influence on the German Baptist Movement

J. G. Oncken, Julius Köbner, and G. W. Lehmann were the three spiritual parents of the Baptist movement in Germany and through missionary outreach for most of Europe. In 1837 Köbner, the Danish son of a Jewish rabbi, and Oncken began composing a confession of faith for the emerging Baptist movement, and in 1847 it was in final form. In 1848 it was approved as the "Foundation" of the German Baptist Union, with the expectation that it would be "adopted by all the churches which enter this Union."[1] This confession had a widespread influence throughout Europe.

Julius Köbner was the key scribal figure behind the original German Baptist Confession, according to Baptist scholar William Joseph McGlothlin: "Köbner, who was the leading literary representative of the Baptists, was charged with the duty of giving literary form and providing Scripture references for the whole."[2] The Danish Jew's unique imprint on the foundational declaration of faith can be discerned throughout this remarkable document—the 1847 Confession exhibits the greatest degree of Jewish influence of any confession created by the Baptist movement throughout its entire history.

Köbner's Jewish heritage is reflected in the startling opening article of the Confession of Faith[3] concerning the "Word of God." The Old Testament is not only to be revered as God's revelation, but each and every one of its books is Scripture and thus must be taken seriously by Baptists:

> We believe that the Scriptures of the Old Testament—namely the 5 books of Moses, the book of Joshua, the book of Judges, the book of Ruth, the 2 books of Samuel, the 2 books of the Kings, the 2 books of the Chronicles, the book of Ezra, the book of Nehemiah, the book of Esther, the book of Job, the book of Psalms, the proverbs of Solomon, the preaching of Solomon [Ecclesiastes], the Song of Solomon, the books of the prophets Isaiah and Jeremiah, the lamentations of Jeremiah and the books of the prophets Ezekiel, Daniel, Hosea, Joel, Amos, Obadiah, Jonah, Micah, Nahum, Habakkuk, Zephaniah, Haggai, Zechariah and Malachi—as well as the Scriptures of the New Testament—[NT books listed by name]—are truly entered by the Holy Spirit; so these collectively constitute the only true divine revelation to the human race and the sole source of knowledge of God, as must be the sole rule and guideline for faith and lifestyle.[4]

Köbner's affirmation stands in contrast to other mid-nineteenth-century confessions, such as the 1833 New Hampshire Confession, which do not explicitly name each individual book of the Old Testament.[5] Even though other confessions mention the Old Testament, and it is rightly assumed that generic references to the Bible include the Old Testament books, only Köbner's confession places the Old Testament front and center in such a definitive manner. There was one significant historical precedent for Köbner's detailed canonical list. The Second London Confession of 1677 also listed every book, as part of a lengthy defense of the authority of Scripture in contrast to Roman Catholic teachings. The point was not to affirm the Jewish underpinnings of Christian theology and practice, but to define the canon (thus explicitly rejecting the Apocrypha) and assert the divine inspiration of the text.[6]

Article 4 of the 1847 Confession positively highlighted Jesus' relationship to the Jewish law, affirming that "there was never any sin either in the heart of Jesus or in his life, so he rendered an active obedience in that he fulfilled us for the whole divine law, and a passive obedience in that he laid down his body and his soul as an offering for us."[7]

After an extensive review of salvation, the Christian life, the organization of the New Testament church, baptism, and the Lord's Supper, the confession returned to Jewish themes beginning in article 12, "Of the Divine Law." Influenced by rabbinic teaching, Köbner insisted that even in the church age, the Jewish law is relevant and important: "although we live under the dispensation of grace of the new covenant, yet the divine law, as already given in paradise, further explained on Sinai, and glorified in the clearest manner by the Lord Jesus Christ, has not been deprived of power and effectiveness, but now as formerly, has its value and right use."[8]

The confession affirmed three roles for the Jewish law. First, the Torah promoted "God's holiness and righteousness on earth." Second, the law provided a compelling awareness of the "need for mercy and forgiveness." Third, the law served as "a lamp for the born again," guiding disciples into authentic spiritual paths of holy life. In contrast, the ceremonial laws had been fulfilled for in the "sacrifice of Jesus . . . lies the completion of that part of the law." Nevertheless, Köbner insisted that the "ethical, moral part of the law, as it is laid down in the Ten Commandments, we believe that in it the nature and will of God is expressed for all times, and heaven and earth are more likely to pass before even a tittle falls from the law."[9]

Whereas most earlier and contemporary Baptist confessions simply assume that the Sabbath is the Christian version (Sunday observance honoring Jesus' resurrection), the German Baptist Confession of 1847 introduced the Sabbath by explicitly referring to the fourth commandment of the Mosaic law. Köbner valued the Sabbath for its spiritual benefits but did not insist legalistically that Christians observe it on Saturdays. He honored the Christian practice of Sunday observance, with the admonition to utilize it for drawing spiritually closer to God.[10]

Köbner's apostolic legacy, theological contributions, and hymn writing were still honored in the twentieth century. Rushbrooke acknowledged in 1915 that Köbner, Oncken, and Lehmann collectively were the "*Kleebatt*" (coverleaf) of German Baptists, and that the Danish Jew was "distinguished as poet, author and preacher."[11] Similarly, F. W. Herrmann lauded Köbner:

> Through his training in the Hebrew faith, Köbner had acquired
> an extensive knowledge of the Scriptures, and he possessed in

addition a thorough and many-sided education. He was a man of clear and sharp understanding, exceptionally lively imagination, considerable poetic gifts, and fascinating eloquence. By his spiritual songs and by many other forms of literary work he rendered invaluable service for nearly half a century.[12]

In 1929 Rushbrooke characterized Köbner as "a converted Jew of remarkable intellectual and literary powers. He is the author of not a few of the hymns still sung by German Baptists, and he took a leading part in securing a foothold for the Baptist teaching in his native country of Denmark."[13] Within Germany, the memory of Köbner's spiritual legacy was reinforced for a new generation of German Baptists by the publication in 1930 of his biography, written by his daughter, Ruth Baresel.[14] In a review of her book (and another work) for his British Baptist audience, E. A. Payne noted that when Oncken ordained him, Köbner was honored with the title of "Missioner to Germany."[15]

Julius Köbner's distinguished place in the history of the German Baptist movement raises an interesting question: *How could a movement that was founded in part by the son of a Jewish rabbi, reconcile its Jewish-influenced heritage with its hopes to thrive in an anti-Semitic Third Reich?*

Forgetting Jewish Existence

Nazism made a solemn declaration:
"None of the Jewish Book, nor of its translation."
Watching the Book burn, the robot crowd
Stomped, and laughed, long and loud.[16]

The Nazi determination to "create a world without Jews" by destroying the Jewish communities of Europe was not limited to their physical existence. It also involved, as Alon Confino contends, eliminating Jewish intellectual, literary, spiritual, and cultural achievements and contributions in order to create a new Germany and Christianity, divorced from its Jewish roots: "Jewish civilization had to be removed. Germany's historical origins needed to be purified down to the Jews' shared past with Christianity via the canonical text."[17] For the Nazis, this morphed into a spiritual and political obsession, for "the Jews and their historical roots, real or invented, from the Bible down to the modern period, must be eliminated at all costs and whatever the consequences."[18] The burning of Torah scrolls and synagogues, especially during Kristallnacht, not only terrified Jewish residents but also served to place "at center stage" the relationship between Nazism, Judaism, and Christianity: "The Bible was destroyed because it was disturbingly important for the Nazis. In burning it, the Nazis expanded on the idea of eternal racial origins by adding the desire for a clean slate of religious origins. . . . In Kristallnacht the Nazis created at the same time a German national and Christian community that was independent of Jewish roots."[19]

Following Kristallnacht, Friedrich Werner, representing the northern regional German Supreme Evangelical Church Council, had "ordered that the name 'Jehova' and the names of the Jewish prophets must be erased wherever displayed in Protestant churches. The order followed Nazi threats that Christian churches permitting such names to remain would be set afire as were Jewish synagogues recently."[20]

In 1940 a more comprehensive attack against the Jewish roots of Christianity came to light—*Die Botschaft Gottes* (God's Message). Pro-Nazi "German Christians" had created a New Testament "rewritten according to Nazi racial and ethical theories" in which "the person of Christ and the gospel story have been purged from all Jewish associations." Several changes had to be made to present Jesus as an Aryan born in Galilee, and his resurrection was "struck out."[21] Confino provides a chilling description of the Nazi-inspired agenda behind *Die Botschaft Gottes*:

> All references to Jewish names and places were erased from the new text, as were all quotations from the Old Testament unless they portrayed Judaism in a negative light. Also deleted where the genealogical descent of Jesus from the House of David and his fulfillment of any Old Testament prophecy about the Messiah. The new text told the life of Jesus in militarized, masculine, heroic, Nazified language.[22]

A similar "German Christian" effort to transform the Protestant hymnbook was noted by both the *Baptist Times* and the

Watchman-Examiner in 1942. The former observed that "references to the Old Testament should be excluded: 'The words Hallelujah and Jehovah, and even the words Psalter, psalm, and temple, are altered'; the Covenant of God and God's promise may not he mentioned. . . . A 'baptismal' hymn opens with 'O tender child of German blood.'"[23] The American paper quoted another line from the baptismal poem: "We baptize you to service and bravery for devotion and loyalty to the nation in the new age."[24]

German Baptists were no doubt aware of the Nazi campaign to excise Judaism and Jews from Christian historical memory, liturgical practice, and theology. In 1948 Eberhard Schroeder recalled that the Baptist Publishing House was cognizant of the Nazi pressure to eradicate Jewish elements from the restricted set of publications they were still permitted to offer: "The Old Testament was to be treated very cautiously. We as Baptists were interested in renouncing nothing of the principles of the Christian faith, but also tried to avoid unnecessary danger by particular publication of critical themes."[25] In other words, the German Baptist Publishing House succumbed to Nazi pressure and censorship of Jewish-related themes, which naturally impacted how they referred to the Jewish Scriptures.

The 1944 Confession of Faith

G. Keith Parker observes that the 1847 German Baptist Confession "remained basically the same through several revisions until the New Federation when, in 1943–1944, Erich Sauer (for the Brethren) and Hans Luckey (for the Baptists) made a total revision."[26] Similarly, W. L. Lumpkin ties the 1944 revision to the original confession: "A thorough revision of the Baptist Confession of 1847 was made. Two articles on the Word of God were greatly condensed, and the article on 'Election to Salvation' was omitted. The new Confession was considerably shorter than the old."[27]

The 1944 Confession was indeed a radical departure from the 1847 original, both in spirit and theology, and cannot be considered to be a revision undertaken primarily for brevity's sake. Nor were any of the changes necessitated by the German Baptists participating in an expanded fellowship with non-Baptists.[28] The new document was an attempt to adjust the doctrinal position of German Baptists by forsaking its Jewish influences, in conformity with Nazi anti-Semitism and that movement's aim to divorce Christianity from its Jewish roots. This was accomplished by the rearrangement of the confession's structure, the deletion of specific original texts, and the addition of novel language that introduced Nazi perspectives.

The most significant revisions that excised Jewish influence from the 1944 Confession were made to articles 1, 4, 5, and 9.

ARTICLE 1: THE ELIMINATION OF THE JEWISH SCRIPTURES (OLD TESTAMENT)

The 1944 Confession departed in both spirit and structure from Köbner's version from the very outset. Article 1 of the 1847 Confession asserted the spiritual authority and centrality of the Hebrew Old Testament in general, and all of its thirty-nine works in particular, which thus serve along with their New Testament counterparts, as the basis for Baptist life and theology.

The 1944 Confession omitted all mention of the Old Testament as binding on the church and instead substituted a new article. "On God and His Revelation" may be technically theologically orthodox, but its generic reference to "Holy Scripture" eliminated all specific references to the Old Testament and its individual books. The de-Judaization of the article was furthered by its treatment of the Trinity. God the Father was Creator and Lord of the world but was not credited with having a special relationship with Israel as his chosen covenant people. Jesus was "the Son of the living God, who died for us all" (all humanity), but there was no acknowledgment that Jesus was Jewish or Israel's Messiah.

ARTICLES 4 AND 5: JESUS' MESSIANIC IDENTITY

The two confessions differ markedly in their portrayals of Jesus' redemptive mission. In article 4, "Concerning Redemption," the 1944 revision repeated the formula from its opening article, calling Jesus "the Son of God . . . the redeemer of the whole world." He was sent "to the earth" (not Israel) to save "humankind from its alienation from God."

The 1847 Confession and its successors honored Jesus' Jewish context and connection by declaring that through sinless

"obedience," Jesus "fulfilled for us the whole divine law."[29] Köbner's affirmation that Jesus' role as a high priest was based on
Jewish temple practice (Hebrews 7–10). It is missing from the 1944
version. In the earlier confession, Jesus operated messianically within an explicitly Jewish context; in Luckey's version, Jesus has been
shorn of his Jewish roots, and the Jewish context of his redemptive
mission has been lost.

In the revision's article 5,[30] Jesus was no longer tethered to
the Jewish people or Judaism but was generically the Savior of all
people. He did not fulfill a prior Mosaic covenant but brought salvation to humanity because "God wills that all men be saved."[31]
The original article stated that from the beginning of history, it
was the divine will that "Jehovah, the Anointed, should through
his incarnation and his death be the Redeemer."[32] The intentional
and explicit use of a Hebrew-based name (Jehovah/Yahweh) for
the Savior squarely placed Jesus in a Jewish historical-theological
matrix, as did the reference to the incarnation. The Messiah was
born to a Jewish woman.

Article 9: Natural Orders of Creation

Luckey and Sauer consolidated several articles (12–14) into one
new section—"Concerning the Natural Orders"[33] (the new article
9). It contained four concessions to the Nazi viewpoint: the promotion of "natural orders" in place of "divine law," the recognition
of Sunday as a day of rest provided by "the Creator" without acknowledging the prior Jewish Sabbath, the acceptance of Volk as
divinely sanctioned, and the duty of Christians to swear allegiance
even to a totalitarian state.

Article 9 of the 1944 Confession began with a surprising assertion that was a significant theological-political principle historically
articulated by German Lutherans and subsequently appropriated
by the Nazis and the German Christian movement for their own
ends: "We believe that with the creation of the world, God has
also given us certain natural orders [*natürliche Ordnungen*[34]] that
we must fulfill in obedience to His Word."[36] The article discussed
examples of such natural orders—a weekly day of rest, marriage,
family, people, and the state. Holocaust scholar Mary M. Solberg
defines *orders of creation* as "certain structures or institutions God

is said to have established in the early realm to order human life." These include "marriage, family, the economy, the state, and the church. . . . For the German Christians, race—as they understood it—and Volk or Volkstrum were 'orders of creation,' too, and, because they were established by God, were utterly sanctified."[36]

The substitution of natural created orders (even if instituted by God) for divine law, especially as expressed by the Mosaic covenant, was not a part of classical Baptist doctrine. Article 12 of Köbner's confession understood the New Covenant as fulfilling the Old while honoring its timeless principles. The new confession ignored the Jewish law as if it played no role in salvation history. The result was an affirmation of social systems that found their authenticity in a natural order that was compatible with Nazi ideology.

THE FIRST DAY OF THE WEEK. The first example of a natural order that article 9 offered was "a day of rest" (*einen Ruhetag*): "It was the gracious will of the Creator to give us a day of rest and that we should follow the example of the apostolic churches by celebrating the first day of the week on which our Lord rose from the dead as the day of the Lord."[37] It did not mention that the Sabbath had Jewish origins and was a central spiritual practice for them. The word *Sabbath* wasn't even employed to designate the day of rest. In stark contrast, the original confession dedicated a lengthy and detailed paragraph to the Sabbath, clearly situating it within its original Jewish context. Notice how different it was in structure, theme, and tone from its successor:

> All the commands of God among the ten are, therefore, of equal dignity and holiness, and this we believe especially of the fourth commandment regarding the Sabbath. According to its content we hold ourselves obligated to work for six days with persevering diligence and great conscientiousness in the business affairs of our civil calling, using all the powers of our body and spirit for the benefit of the world. But no less does the command obligate us to sanctify one of the seven days of the week wholly to the Lord and on the same to rest from labor, i.e., to cease unqualifiedly all activity which has to do with our livelihood, as also from every other purely worldly work which is not absolutely necessary or demanded by love, according to the example of Christ.[38]

The 1847 Confession was unapologetically respectful of the Jewish origins of the Sabbath, while paving the way for the Christian appropriation of it. In contrast, the 1944 Confession ridded the Sabbath text of its Jewish origin, content, and spirit.

MARRIAGE, FAMILY, AND VOLK. A common German word, *Volk*, took on a much darker meaning under the sway of Nazi ideology. Solberg explains: "Das Volk, or 'the people,' is a perfectly ordinary German term. Like most Germans living in the Third Reich, those who generated these documents embraced this word (and its panoply of variants) in its nazified meaning, which excluded everyone and everything the Nazis considered 'un-German,' especially the Jews. In Nazi-German, Volk could mean 'race' or 'nation.'"[39] One German Christian characterized Volk as "the divinely willed community of German people based on the created orders of race, blood, and soil." The church's mission "must be directed to the community that is the German *Volk*."[40] Furthermore Volk and anti-Semitism were linked: "The Jews are the elect of decay in our Volk. . . . The Jews are our misfortune."[41]

Paul Althaus, a prominent German theologian, affirmed a "twofold revelation of God: in Jesus Christ, and in the divine orders (family, state and Volk)."[42] Like German Baptist leaders, he enthusiastically praised the beginning of the Nazi era "as a gift and miracle of God," while embracing the premise that Volk was an "order of creation."[43] Volk was tied in to both family and state through the glorification of the Aryan race. Thus, Althaus defined Volk as "the community of blood or race [that] has become decisively important for us Germans. . . . It has to do with a specific, closed, blood relationship."[44] Such a relationship could only be passed on through pure Aryan Germans, excluding Jews.

The 1944 Confession of Faith crafted by Luckey and Sauer bore a remarkable similarity to Althaus's understanding of Volk, marriage, and family:

> We furthermore believe that *marriage* was ordained by God so that man and wife may fulfill the will of the Creator in bodily and spiritual fellowship by bringing forth children and helping each other in the struggles of life. We consider monogamous marriage to be a divine order. According to God's Word the adulterer has no part in the Kingdom of God.

> We believe that the *family* and *people* are natural orders of
> God [*Familie und Volk natürliche Ordnungen Gottes sind*[45]]
> which we are not only to accept but which we are also to shape
> according to God's intentions and in whose interest we ought to
> labor in order that the man of God be healthy in body and soul
> and fit for every good work.[46]

These paragraphs represent a shift in theological and confessional perspective—away from traditional Baptist understanding and toward Nazi accommodation. In the Baptist Confession of 1847, marriage was discussed in article 13.[47] Men and women marry to encourage sexual activity within proper relationships (marriage between men and women) and to "avoid fornication." Furthermore, Christians must marry within the faith and seek recognition for the relationship from both the church and civil sphere. Divorce is permissible on the grounds of "adultery and voluntary abandonment." The morality and praxis of sex, marriage, and divorce/remarriage are all regulated by the "Word of God," who "founded/instituted" marriage.

In the 1944 Confession, marriage is described as constituting "a divine order" (*eine göttliche Ordnung*).[48] To casual readers, there might not seem to be much difference between this and the earlier description, but we must remember the article is all about natural orders—a Nazi-friendly category that was not part of historical Baptist theology. Marriage, which formed the basis for family, was then tied to Volk. Marriage and family provided the foundation for a racially pure Volk—the Nazi ideal.

The concept of a social-political Volk within which the Christian church is a subservient institution cannot be found in the 1847 Confession. Marriage, family, and Volk were not natural orders (*natürliche Ordungen*). Marriage and family were spiritual reflections of the will of God, based on biblical revelation; the Nazi concept of Volk cannot be found in the nineteenth-century German Baptist Confession.

SUBSERVIENCE TO THE STATE. The Nazi ideal was of a racially pure people propagated through families of Aryan ancestry (separated from inferior races, especially Jews), who lived under a totalitarian regime enjoying the absolute loyalty of all its citizens.

Althaus maintained that the church should submit voluntarily to totalitarian authority and serve it wholeheartedly: "We Christians know ourselves bound by God's will to the promotion of National Socialism, so that all members and ranks of the Volk will be ready for service and sacrifice to one another."[49]

The final section of article 9 of the 1944 Confession concludes with a discussion of the church's obligation to the political state. The progression of thought regarding natural orders thus goes from marriage to family to Volk to the State, with each sphere encompassing a more comprehensive level of allegiance. The 1944 Confession states,

> We believe that the state is divinely ordered and that we must serve it with all seriousness. For service to our people [Volk] is also service before God. We pray for the magistracy [authorities] that they may justly use the power entrusted to it for the protection of law and the punishment of evildoers. We also swear allegiance to the state, engage in war service, since the magistrate according to God's Word, does not bear the sword in vain. Our faith does not keep us from occupying civil office.[50]

The fusion of state and Volk is indistinguishable from Nazi teaching. No Baptist would have had problems with an assertion that service to humanity is akin to serving God, but an exclusivist understanding supporting nationalistic or racist allegiance as implied by Volk, in the context of the Nazi period, would not have gained any support from the wider Baptist movement.

There appears to be an inconsistency between the 1944 Confession in German and Luckey's post-war translation into English for the wider Baptist (and especially the American) audience. The English version reads, "We also swear allegiance to the state." However, the German text states, "And we swear allegiance to the head [Oberhaupt] of the state,"[51] or, in other words, to Germany's head of state—the Führer! The English translation covered up the confession's apparent acceptance of the Nazi expectation that German citizens would swear personal commitment and loyalty to Hitler.

The 1847 Confession devoted a full article (14) to a more expansive and nuanced discourse on the relationship between the Christian and the political order. It situated the responsibilities of a Christian citizen to one's government and its leadership within a clear biblical context. Based on Acts 4–5, Christians had an obligation to "render unqualified obedience" to society's laws as long as such laws "do not curtail the free exercise of the duties of our Christian faith."[52] This did include military service, but unlike the Nazi era confession, Köbner's acknowledged the legitimacy of the alternative view of some Christians who were conscientious objectors.

The Question of Heresy

The 1944 Confession of German Baptist faith and practice was not an innocently crafted edit of the 1847 Confession, nor was it simply a friendly attempt to produce a general confession to reconcile differences between Baptists and their partners in the Alliance of the Evangelical Free Churches. Rather, the document constituted a radical challenge to a century-long tradition that was supported and undergirded by God's historical interaction with the Jewish people. The teachings of the Jewish Scriptures, as interpreted by Köbner, were foundational for the European Baptist movement during its formative period.

The 1944 Confession was a systematic repudiation of this heritage, in harmony with what was happening in Germany during the Nazi period. Article after article of the original Baptist Confession underwent a literary and theological cleansing of its Jewish roots, with the aim of appeasing the Nazi anti-Semitic desire to eliminate all vestiges of Jewish heritage from German religious life.

The new Confession was a sophisticated and intentional theological and ecclesiastical capitulation to Nazism. It represented the culmination of a decade's worth of German Baptist willingness to welcome, accommodate, submit to, and even represent Nazi authority and power. The activities of German Baptist leaders (including Luckey) from 1933 through 1944 prepared the way for the creation of a confession that might appease the Nazi authorities. In like manner, German Baptist treatment of Jews, largely manifested as passive neglect, prepared the way for the erasing of its Jewish heritage from its key self-defining document.

Respected Holocaust scholar Franklin Littell claimed that the Protestant leadership of Germany "made no effort even to preserve the Jewish foundations of the faith, let alone to show concern for the fate of living Jews."⁵³ Sadly, the same may be said of German Baptist leaders. Littell further asserted that "Christians cannot establish a self-identity except in relation to the Jewish people—past and present, and whenever the Christians have attempted to do so, they have fallen into grievous heresy and sin."⁵⁴ Köbner's confession of 1847 was a fine example of Baptists acknowledging the Jewish foundation of their faith and practice. Luckey's 1944 revision erased the connection between Baptist spirituality and its Jewish roots while embracing Nazi-inspired concepts that were alien to historic Baptist doctrine. For these two reasons, it may be rightly judged as heretical, in Littell's sense: "Deference to political authority rather than obedience to the (admittedly imperfect) creeds and confessions was heretical."⁵⁵

NOTES

1. William Joseph McGlothlin, ed., *Baptist Confessions of Faith* (Philadelphia: American Baptist Publication Society, 1911), 331–32.

2. McGlothlin, 332.

3. The 1847 Confession in German can be found at http://www.reformedreader.org/ccc/germanbaptist.htm.

4. McGlothlin omitted the list, which diluted the paragraph's intent and impact; see McGlothlin, *Baptist Confessions of Faith*, 334.

5. The New Hampshire Confession states, "We believe [that] the Holy Bible was written by men divinely inspired, and is a perfect treasure of heavenly instruction; that it has God as its author, salvation for its end, and truth, without any mixture of error, for its matter." William L. Lumpkin, ed., *Baptist Confessions of Faith* (1959; repr., Valley Forge, PA: Judson, 1974), 361–62.

6. Lumpkin, 248–51.

7. McGlothlin, *Baptist Confessions of Faith*, 336.

8. McGlothlin, 348.

9. McGlothlin, 348–49.

10. McGlothlin, 349–50.

11. J. H. Rushbrooke, ed., *The Baptist Movement in the Continent of Europe* (London: Carey, 1915; repr., BiblioLife, 2009), 12.

12. F. W. Herrmann, "The Movement in Germany: Its Progress and Consolidation," in *Baptist Movement in the Continent of Europe*, ed. Rushbrooke, 13–15.

13. J. H. Rushbrooke, *Some Chapters of European Baptist History* (London: Kingsgate, 1929), 18.

14. Ruth Köbner Baresel, *Julius Köbner: Sein Leben* (Kassel, Germany: J. G. Oncken Nachfolger, 1930).

15. Ernest A. Payne, "Julius Kobner," *Congregational Quarterly* 9, no. 4 (October 1931): 441.

16. "We Shall Not Die: The Jew's Answer to Hitler," in Philip M. Raskin, *The Collected Poems of Philip M. Raskin 1878–1944* (New York: Bloch, 1951), 20.

17. Alon Confino, *A World without Jews: The Nazi Imagination from Persecution to Genocide.* (New Haven, CT: Yale University Press, 2014), 5.

18. Confino, 15.

19. Confino, 121, 126.

20. "More Men and Things," *Watchman-Examiner*, January 26, 1939, 104.

21. "More Men and Things," *Watchman-Examiner*, August 29, 1940, 924–25.

22. Confino, *World without Jews*, 158.

23. "Table Talk," *Baptist Times*, July 23, 1942, 365.

24. "More Men and Things," *Watchman-Examiner*, September 10, 1942, 893.

25. Eberhard Schroeder, "The Baptist Publishing House at Kassel," *Baptist Herald*, February 15, 1948, 9.

26. G. Keith Parker, *Baptists in Europe: History & Confessions of Faith* (Nashville: Broadman, 1982), 56.

27. Lumpkin, *Baptist Confessions of Faith*, 402.

28. It is tempting but in the end unsatisfactory to ignore the significance of the Jewish aspect of the confession's revision while maintaining that the overriding dynamic of the confession was to fashion doctrinal unity between Baptists and the other Free Church constituents, as Edwin Brandt does in "Vom Gemeindeleben der Baptisten," in Günter Balders, ed., *Ein Herr, ein Glaube, eine Taufe: 150 Jahre Baptistengemeinden in Deutschland, 1834–1984: Festschrift* (Wuppertal und Kassel: Oncken, 1985), 188-89. The denominational doctrinal differences cannot fully explain the revisions described in this analysis.

29. McGlothlin, *Baptist Confessions of Faith*, 336.

30. "Election to Salvation" (1847) / "Concerning Regeneration and Sanctification" (1944).

31. Article 5, in *Baptist Confessions of Faith*, ed. Lumpkin, 404.

32. Article 5, in McGlothlin, *Baptist Confessions of Faith*, 337.

33. Article 9, in *Baptist Confessions of Faith*, ed. Lumpkin, 406–7.

34. German Text of 1944 Confession, in *Bekenntnisse der Kirche: Bekinntnistexte aus zwanzig Jahrhunderten*, Hans Steubing with J. F. Gerhard Goeters, Heinrich Karpp, and Erwin Mülhaupt, eds. (Wuppertal, Germany: Brockhaus, 1970), 283.

35. Lumpkin, *Baptist Confessions of Faith*, 406.

36. Mary M. Solberg, ed., *A Church Undone: Documents from the German Christian Faith Movement, 1932–1940* (Minneapolis: Fortress, 2015), 62n7.

37. Lumpkin, *Baptist Confessions of Faith*, 406.

38. McGlothlin, *Baptist Confessions of Faith*, 349–50.

39. Solberg, *Church Undone*, 33.

40. Solberg, 402.

41. Solberg, 413.

42. Matthew D. Hockenos, *A Church Divided: German Protestants Confront the Nazi Past* (Bloomington: Indiana University Press, 2004), 25.

43. Solberg, *Church Undone*, 40; Robert P. Erickson and Susannah Heschel, eds. *Betrayal: German Churches and the Holocaust* (Minneapolis: Fortress, 1999), 23.

44. Erickson and Heschel, 25.

45. German Text of 1944 Confession, in Steubing, *Bekenntnisse der Kirche: Bekinntnistexte aus zwanzig Jahrhunderten*, 283.

46. Lumpkin, *Baptist Confessions of Faith*, 406.

47. McGlothlin, *Baptist Confessions of Faith*, 351.

48. German Text of 1944 Confession, in Steubing, *Bekenntnisse der Kirche*, 283.

49. Erickson and Heschel, *Betrayal*, 24.

50. Lumpkin, *Baptist Confessions of Faith*, 406–7.

51. German Text of 1944 Confession, in Steubing, *Bekenntnisse der Kirche*, 284: "Und wir leisten dem Oberhaupt des Staates den Treueid, . . ."

52. McGlothlin, *Baptist Confessions of Faith*, 351–52.

53. Franklin H. Littell, *The Crucifixion of the Jews: The Failure of Christians to Understand the Jewish Experience* (1975; repr., Macon, GA: Mercer University Press, 1986, 1996), 52.

54. Littell, 66.

55. Littell, 76.

CHAPTER 11

Baptist Reunion

The BWA's Postwar Reconstruction Agenda

Even during the darkest days of the war, the Baptist World Alliance leadership anticipated that its postwar mission to assist Baptists impacted by the conflict would necessitate a rapprochement with Baptists in Axis countries. In June 1942 BWA general secretary Walter O. Lewis counseled that "every effort should be made to restore friendly relations between brethren in all the lands of Europe now at war."[1] Fifteen months later BWA president J. H. Rushbrooke offered through the *Baptist Times* his expectation that Baptist relief work could commence "before the final Armistice."[2] Italian Baptists had already expressed their hope that they would be recipients of Baptist financial aid.

On Tuesday morning, May 1, 1945—one day after Adolf Hitler's suicide—Rushbrooke spoke before the annual assembly of the Baptist Union of Great Britain in support of the BWA's relief plans, which were primarily aimed at aiding Baptist refugees, churches, and institutions. W. Taylor Bowie reported that Rushbrooke spoke of "some of our German brethren, [who] at great peril, protected endangered Jews."[3] No specifics were cited.

The BWA's vision of aiding Baptists across Europe inevitably clashed with the obligation to hold pro-Nazi (and anti-Jewish) German religious leaders accountable for their Nazi-era actions. Cyril Garbett, archbishop of York, warned against reestablishing relations with German church leaders until their past attitudes toward Nazism were clear. The *Baptist Times* agreed: "It would be wrong for us to enter into Christian fellowship with pastors or congregations which have actively supported or defended the Nazi tyranny.

We should be ready to resume fellowship with those who refused to support or defend the Nazis, even though they found themselves unable openly to resist."[4]

Post-War Contacts with German Baptists

On May 7, 1945, the war in Europe was concluded with the un-conditional surrender of the German forces. Two days before the total Nazi surrender to the Allies, Hamburg Seminary leaders Hans Luckey and W. Gutsche mailed a letter to Rushbrooke, Lewis, and William Kuhn. Noting the cutting off of relations between German Baptists and the BWA "through six years of war," they desired to "inform" the BWA about "how things are with us and our work after the terrible storms of the war." The war years were covered in a single paragraph that contained no mention of the Nazi regime's relationship with the Baptist Union or the seminary. Luckey and Gutsche noted that Hamburg absorbed the Lodz seminary "since in the course of the political changes [i.e., the unmentioned Nazi conquest of Poland] instruction was no longer possible."[5]

Throughout the Nazi period, the German Baptist Union had completely "supported and encouraged" the school. However, fol-lowing the "collapse" of the German army, the Union was unable to continue assistance due to its bifurcation under Allied occupation. Accordingly, the seminary leaders requested that the BWA might consider financial assistance. Rejoicing that unspecified "political dangers which have threatened the cause of the Gospel have so far vanished," the writers hoped that a renewal of "great fellowship" with American Baptists might occur.[6]

During the first year of Allied occupation of Germany, British, Northern Baptist, BWA, ecumenical leaders, and Baptist military chaplains made contact with German Baptists to ascertain the con-dition of the churches and to gain an understanding of what hap-pened to them during the war years.

Lloyd A. Hollingsworth, a warrant officer for the United States Army, was among the first Americans to visit Baptist churches in Berlin in July 1945. He reported, "From the evidence that I have been able to gather, it appears that Baptists as a whole never sup-ported the Nazi Party to any extent or actively opposed it. As a re-sult, the German government seems to have left the Baptist churches pretty much alone. I am sorry to say that I found no evidence to report where German Baptists took a firm stand against the persecution of the Jews."[7]

M. E. Aubrey was part of an ecumenical delegation that met with German church leaders in late November and early December 1945. Aubrey had little opportunity to engage in lengthy conversation with German Baptist leaders, but he did meet with Jakob Meister, who was serving as German Baptist secretary in Berlin (while Paul Schmidt still exercised jurisdiction in the rest of the country). Aubrey noted that "Berlin Baptists are anxious to re-establish relations with British and American Baptists." He hoped their "despair" could be turned into "the right sort of hope."[8]

Following his tour of Europe in late 1945 through February 1946,[9] and under pressure to publicly address the issue of German Baptist complicity with the Nazis, Walter O. Lewis apparently refrained from doing so.[10] However, in his American Baptist Foreign Mission Society (ABFMS) personnel file is a paper asking: "What was the attitude of the Baptists toward the Hitler regime during the war?" His analysis, without citing evidence, was threefold:

> By far the great majority of the Baptists were anti-Hitler. Especially did they oppose the slaughter of the Jews. But there was one group, who together with multitudes of people outside of the Baptist ranks hailed Hitler as a sort of Messiah for the German people. Some of the Baptist leaders joined the Nazi Party, but are now ashamed of that alliance. A third group of the Baptists tried to keep in the middle of the road to avoid trouble.[11]

Dr. Edwin Bell, who succeeded Lewis as ABFMS special representative for Europe, spent several months touring Europe during 1945. Bell met with a German Baptist pastor named Driesbach in Munich. Driesbach reiterated what Bell had heard in other conversations about the Baptist dealings with the Nazis. The Nazis sought to "indoctrinate the children and young people with an anti-Church feeling at the Hitler Youth" meetings, which were mandatory, but Driesbach claimed he "tried to counter the effect of this programme by having his young people together on Sunday evening." On the local church level, he asserted that German clergy, including Baptists, "adopted the attitude of neutrality as much as possible . . . in the hope that they might escape involvement with the Nazi Party and that they might be allowed to continue their work in their Churches." The clergy "eschewed reference to political and social questions in their sermons and tried to make their preaching strictly biblical and of the type that would not offend the Nazis."[12]

Bell's conversations with army officers indicated that the "Free Church is in rather a bad way. The impression seems to prevail that there was a fair amount of Nazism in it." Furthermore, Driesbach confessed to Bell that Paul Schmidt was "a Nazi Party member." He claimed that Schmidt told him in October 1944 that "if Germany lost the war, he . . . would have to step down and out of his position of the Secretary for the Baptists."[13]

German Complicity and Conscience

While in Germany, Bell met Stewart W. Herman, an American Lutheran who served as the pastor of the American Church in Berlin until Pearl Harbor was attacked in December 1941. In 1945 the World Council of Churches sent Herman into Germany to assess the Protestant situation.

Herman learned that the Free Churches took little interest in the church struggle against the Nazi encroachment into church affairs in the 1930s and that they "felt a certain amount of satisfaction" that the State-sanctioned churches were under attack instead of themselves. They even "supported the Nazi regime in many ways." With the defeat of Nazism, the Free Churches "betrayed almost no indication that anything of special importance happened in Germany since 1932."[14] But in reality, "Baptist preachers," along with so many other Germans, found themselves willingly caught up by "the spiritual force" of the Nazi revolution.[15]

Herman was startled by a postwar article published in the Baptists' *Bundespost* that was devoid of any sense of repentance or remorse regarding their Nazi-era complicity; it also lacked any sense of responsibility for the plight of the massacred Jewish population. Herman placed responsibility for these omissions squarely on the backs of Free Church leaders, such as the Methodist Bishop Melle and the German Baptist Paul Schmidt, whose leadership roles "had not been spotless during the Nazi regime, but the most alarming thing was that no changes at all—even of heart—were perceptible in the leadership of these two communions."[16]

In October 1945 Martin Niemoeller decried the complicity of the German church under Nazism: "No Christian in Germany has a clear conscience."[17] On December 27, 1945, the *Baptist Times* published an excerpt of a letter from F. W. Simoleit, hailing the German Baptist as "the most widely-known and esteemed of Germany's denominational leaders." In stark contrast to Niemoeller, Simoleit did not display any evidence of a crisis of personal or institutional conscience: "We look upon this calamity as the judgment of God. God has decided, and He will decide, as to who is to blame. . . . We stand upon the ruins of the ever-proud Third Reich. God has crushed it to pieces. Blessed be the name of the Lord—even though we personally could not be blamed for this war disaster and its causes."[18]

Paul Schmidt epitomized how Baptist leaders ignored their ties to Germany's Nazi past in an effort to secure acceptance and compassion from other Baptist conventions. In May 1946 he presented a report, *Unser Weg* (Our Way),[19] to the council of the Federation of Evangelical Free Churches, the Nazi-era union to which Baptists and other small Protestant sects belonged. In *Unser Weg*, Schmidt categorically denied that the Nazis imposed the federation on the Baptists and its partners, maintaining that it was freely entered into while enjoying the favor of the head of the government's Ministry of Churches (even though the Secret Police was against the merger).

Schmidt asserted that in contrast to the struggles of the State churches, "the great political upheaval in Germany in 1933 did not provoke an internal church struggle and strife" for the German Baptist Union. Romans 13 justified subservience to the "Total State" except when the State sought to forbid the proclamation of the gospel. Accordingly, German Baptist churches were able to fulfill their evangelistic mission at the cost of social witness. A few "preachers, for the sake of their clear witness, have aroused the disapproval of the government and had to accept the consequences of responsibility and punishment." During the war, the Secret Police became more aggressive, and some Baptists were targeted: "Indeed, the harder and longer the war went on and the more ungodly the methods of the party and the government grew, the more it inflicted and brought deeper distress upon many of our members, and especially upon the responsible brethren."[20] Schmidt referred to the victory by the Allies as *the Katastrophe*, describing it as a "total collapse in Germany," precipitated by the Allied bombing, that led to a temporary cessation of the federation's work.[21]

Unser Weg addressed the thorny question of German Baptist complicity and passivity during the Nazi period—without ever specifically mentioning the Jewish people. First, Schmidt emphatically rejected the notion of "collective guilt" for what transpired under the Nazi regime. He asked, "Can the church be guilty as a whole if it does not publicly protest against particular sins of State leadership? Can the church of Jesus, by its faithful behavior in proclamation and life, stop the decay of a people and can it be considered as guilty, when there is such a decline of moral forces and so profound a downfall of the people as is the case now?" He claimed that the church "does not have the mission and the strength to preserve and guard a whole people."[22]

Second, the controversial issue of "denazification" was addressed. Schmidt asked, perhaps justifying his own past, "Is belonging to a party disturbing to the life of faith; does someone become guilty in the testimony of Jesus in doing so?" He concluded, "Only where the state power of its own accord interferes with the authority of the [church] community, the community will have to submit if it has exhausted all its means to prevent this interference."[23]

Following the publication of *Unser Weg*, Schmidt wrote to Aubrey in his capacity as the secretary of the German Baptist Union in August 1946, sharing fraternal greetings and projecting a denominational spirit of "brotherly love and eager readiness to face the difficult tasks of the present day."[24] Rather than humbly confessing the failures of the German Baptists during the Nazi era, he asserted that "in the years which lie behind us, we preached the unadulterated Gospel while maintaining the unity of our union." He also referred to the opposition of the State churches to their existence as a free church but made no mention of the Nazi regime's relationship with the German Baptist Union.

Aubrey considered how to reply to Schmidt in correspondence with Dorothy Buxton, an activist and writer who had opposed the Nazis since the early 1930s.[25] In his letter dated August 28, 1946, he surely had Schmidt in mind: "We have to reckon with the curious German mentality, that of people who during all these years have given full support to Hitler and his men and now think they should be treated as ill-used and misled people who deserve the sympathy of the world. Having sown the wind they are reaping the whirlwind."[26]

Private Conversations and Doubts

In his private correspondence with trusted comrades, Rushbrooke received detailed warnings about German Baptist leadership during the Nazi period, and he himself expressed both doubts and sincere anguish over the truth of the situation.

In September and October 1945, Paul Gebauer sent Rushbrooke several letters that surely shook the soul of the recipient, speaking to his worst fears. Gebauer, along with his wife, Clara, had been serving as North American (German) Baptist missionaries in the Cameroons since 1931, and during the war Paul entered the United States Army as a chaplain.[27]

The first letter was also addressed to Gebauer's superior, William Kuhn, the general secretary of the North American Baptist denomination. Dated September 11, 1945, it was hastily composed hours after Gebauer's meetings with Paul Schmidt and others in leadership. Gebauer confirmed that according to Schmidt, the federation was "brought to pass against the wishes of the Gestapo. The Ministry for church affairs helped us in the matter."[28]

A second letter, sent by Gebauer the following day, reflected the missionary's concerns about Baptist support for the Nazis, although he could not prove all the accusations. Gebauer questioned whether the Union and its members had "been loyal to the accepted principles of Baptists; or have they accepted the anti-Christian teachings of the Nazis?" He further was concerned about the German Baptists' "attitude to anti-semitism; what [was] their attitude to Nazi crimes (e.g., in the notorious camps); whether under the influence of nationalism they have deliberately closed eyes and ears; whether they have adopted a 'pietistic' point of view, submitting uncritically to the Nazi authorities?" He added, "If unfortunate answers are given to these enquiries, has there been any substantial body of protest, or is there now any indication of a change of heart?"[29]

Gebauer wondered if the Free Church union was simply a continuation of prior Nazi influence over the Baptist leadership, going back as far as 1933, and if leadership had "been exercised on democratic lines" or had the "Fuehrer principle" been "(in fact or in form or both) adopted?" He heard in the Netherlands that the Hamburg Seminary "had become a hotbed of Nazi influence" and was used for "germanising and nazifying Slav students," while "Hamburg had become a special centre of violent Nazism, and that the Seminary was largely responsible." He wondered if any faculty members were either "members of the Party, or definitely pro-Nazi." Similarly, Gebauer questioned whether it was true that "the 'Siloah' Deaconess Home in Hamburg had a Party member as its head." He even had heard that the "personnel of the Publishing House in Kassel changed in deference to Nazi pressure."[30]

We can surmise from Gebauer's third missive (dated October 10, 1945) that Rushbrooke hoped to visit German Baptist leaders to address Gebauer's concerns. Rushbrooke must have also repeated his belief that in general German Baptists had been faithful to Baptist doctrine during the Nazi period. Gebauer deferentially yet emphatically disagreed. Regarding the possibility of heroic actions by some German Baptists, Gebauer called it "most limited," and offered just one incident: "Prediger Krause from East Prussia, made a public remark about a 1940-attempt on Hitler's life. He got four years for his opinion." Most devastatingly, Rushbrooke's confidence in the fidelity of German Baptist leaders was misplaced, for they certainly were influenced by and willingly supported Nazism:

> Your hope that none "have adopted the Nazi philosophy of life" will be shattered. You have mentioned Hans Fehr. Add to his name others: Prof. Luckey, Pred. Phohl of Hamburg, Paul Schmidt. I would not even agree with you when you state that Paul Schmidt "came to Oxford under pressure;" he came with pleasure. I am fully aware of the activities of the Hamburg Seminary, the Hamburg Group of pastors, the office of the Baptist Union. These are facts that neither goodwill nor prayer can wash away.[31]

Gebauer's negative assessment of German Baptist leadership covered most of the major players in the Union's life:

> I am deeply disturbed by all that I see and hear. Br Gronenberg sees no wrong in his doings. Paul Schmidt knows no repentance. Dr. Speidel dreams about economic plans for his eastern Baptists. Luckey writes to Br Kuhn for help. Rokitta, who did much harm in the Cameroons, assists Paul Schmidt. Gronenberg refers to Rokitta as Der Hurer und Ehebrecher [the whore/fornicator and adulterer]. It is a sad list and it is not all I know and hear. . . . Simoleit? Rockschies? You have heard them in 1934. They have added to their records, since. They are involved.[32]

Furthermore, Gebauer was most disturbed by the postwar unwillingness of German Baptists to express remorse or contrition for their complicity in what occurred under Nazism:

> Thrice, in the presence of witnesses, I have advised Paul Schmidt to resign in order that his saner brethren be given a fair chance to start all over again. He will not even think of resigning. The complete absence of a sense of guilt is most disturbing. This absence is widespread among our Baptists. I have found more willingness to admit failure and guilt among the clergy of the Confessional Church than in any other Protestant camp. As a Baptist I find it most difficult to admit that the Free Churches have and still fail this present Germany.[33]

A similar assessment was offered by a British military chaplain, R. W. Kerr. He sensed that the German Baptist leadership was attempting to retain control over the Baptist Union's future and thus was "getting everything regimented." Kerr dejectedly mused that "Oncken and Köpner [sic] must be stirring uneasily in their graves! Have not yet heard one word of repentance that would indicate any feeling of regret or consciousness that anything untoward has happened in these last ten years; German Baptists will remain a great problem for the Committee of the B. W. A. when it meets."[34]

The reports from Gebauer, Kerr, and Bell compelled Rushbrooke to discuss the German Baptist situation with William Kuhn. Rushbrooke sought to dispel any notion that his criticisms were due to prejudice, since in fact he had a long history of supporting German Baptists: "It was my privilege after the former world war to re-establish contact with them at the earliest opportunity, and I

have at all times taken a stand against any prejudiced representation of their attitude." He even sent Kuhn a copy of his "Victory in
Europe" speech delivered to the Baptist Union in the spring, which
"recognises that some had failed, but affirms (what I still hope is
true) that there was no evidence of apostasy." However, Rushbrooke confessed that the charge of German Baptist "apostasy"
was not unfounded and that German Baptist complicity with the
Nazis was a reality that had to be faced:

> I am bound to report that quite responsible evidence has since
> come to hand that deference to the Nazi government, and even
> active cooperation, have gone much further than I was aware.
> The entire situation has not yet been surveyed, and I do not
> commit myself to any final judgment; but it is a matter for seri-
> ous consideration whether the Baptist organisations in America
> and Britain would not risk grave misunderstanding and criti-
> cism if they took part in the reconstruction of churches and
> institutions in Germany unless and until (assuming the charges
> should, after full enquiry, prove well-founded) there has been a
> definite change of leadership.[35]

The leap from *victimhood* (the self-portrayal by German Baptists)
to *deference* to *active cooperation* was most uncomfortable for
Rushbrooke, and yet he shared his revelations with Kuhn, he said,
"as a confidential intimation of the way in which my mind is most
reluctantly being driven." He thus advised the denominational
leader to "make most careful enquiries before responding to the appeals for financial aid which are probably reaching you as already
they are reaching me."[36]

An Alternative Federation

Five days later, Rushbrooke dashed off a letter to Erik Ruden, general secretary of the Swedish Baptists, requesting his assistance in
verifying another charge—that German Baptist leadership tried to
tempt Northern European Baptists into joining a federation with
German Baptists, sometime between the start of the war (September
1, 1939) and before the Nazi invasions of Denmark[37] and Norway[38]
(April 9, 1941). He was informed that "a letter was addressed to

the Swedish Baptists by the Rev. Paul Schmidt of the Baptist Union of Germany, suggesting a conference of German and Scandinavian Baptists and containing a hint that there should be a lining-up of the Germans and Scandinavians leaving the British and the Americans quite outside." Rushbrooke hoped to confirm that "the letter was sent to Dr. Nordström, and that he definitely turned down the proposal."[39]

Just before Christmas 1945, J. W. Weenink, president of the Baptist Union of Holland,[40] penned an essay in the *Baptist Times* on the Dutch Baptist experience under Nazism. Weenink asserted that Baptists resisted Nazi pressure and influence even before the Netherlands was invaded: "Before the war the Nazis propagated their views with an amazing flow of literature, public meetings and demonstrations, but the charmers made no impression upon the Baptist people in Holland. We were too well informed about the actions the Nazis had taken against the Protestant Churches and the Jews in Germany." The German Baptist initiative continued into mid-1940 when the Dutch leadership was encouraged to meet a German Baptist representative in Zwolle, following Rotterdam's destruction. This unnamed "friend assured us of the sincere sympathy of our fellow believers of Great Germany in the terrible catastrophe which befell our first mercantile city, and the great losses which the Baptists of Holland had suffered." German Baptists offered "(a) free training of our young students in the seminary at Hamburg; (b) a helping hand in rebuilding and re-furnishing the destroyed churches and meeting places; and (c) protection—in case of trouble we could appeal to them." Weenink noted that the "Baptists of so-called Great Germany had deeply disappointed us, and both our national and our Christian honor forbade us to accept their assistance in view of their attitude to Nazi ideals."[41]

At Lewis's request, the *Watchman-Examiner* published an expanded version of Weenink's retrospective. Weenink provided an astounding account of the German delegation's dismay over the Dutch Baptist rejection of their proposals:

> One of the leaders inquired, "But don't you believe that Hitler is sent from God and will win the war?" We replied quietly, "No, never." "I am surprised at what you declare," he said. "Look at all the victories Hitler has won. Do you not know the

Scriptures? What are your reasons for saying what you have said?" We replied that our sole and sure argument is and will be the eternal law of God. . . . During all this conference, a military officer was present and made notes.[42]

Weenink offered a devastating critique of the German Baptists' identification with Nazism: "The Nazis regarded the Baptists as their friends in Germany, and it was assumed they would be friendly in Holland. Some of the Baptist leaders in Germany had openly proclaimed their admiration of Nazi principles. And these leaders sought to win us over to the Nazi side." German Baptist institutions also promoted Nazism to Dutch Baptist seminarians and deaconesses: "Our students who were in Hamburg when the war broke out, and who returned to us at the beginning of the war, told us that, with few exceptions, their professors and fellowship students made life very uncomfortable for them the last few months of their stay in Germany because they refused to accept Nazi views. And some of our young Dutch Baptist sisters, who were training in a Baptist deaconess home in Hamburg, had the same experience."[43]

The charges against the German Baptist leadership, if true, were explosive—potentially fracturing the BWA's core conviction of unity. The alleged episodes indicated that Paul Schmidt and the German Baptist Union were working in league with the Nazi government in reaching out to Baptists in conquered territories and seeking to benefit from German military victories. Rushbrooke had already admitted to Ruden: "I need not tell you that if true, it would seriously affect our relations with the German Baptists—at all events as long as the Rev. Paul Schmidt remains their Secretary."[44]

Rushbrooke was not alone in his private assessment of Schmidt's future. At the end of December 1945, Edwin Bell confided to Rushbrooke that the "Free Church picture in Germany is not especially encouraging at the moment," and that he believed the "German Baptist brethren should take a strong stand, however, in their disavowal of sympathy with and support of the Nazi regime, and that they should put their house in order with respect to some phases of their leadership." Bell clearly was concerned about the unwillingness of any of the German Baptist leaders to resign or be held accountable for their pro-Nazi activities, but nevertheless he held out some hope that "some of their leaders will voluntarily withdraw and relieve the embarrassment of their brethren in their relationships to Baptists on the outside."[45] In a letter to Lewis six months later (June 19, 1946), Bell indicated that "Luckey and other members of the Seminary Faculty . . . and that all the members of the Council who had Nazi connections had resigned," with the exception of Schmidt. According to historian James C. Enns, this report was sufficient to pave the way for the BWA to re-establish connections with German Baptists so that relief and reconstruction aid could be channeled to them.[46]

A Momentous Milestone

Despite all the misgivings expressed in personal correspondence and revelations of German complicity, Rushbrooke continued to publicly support German Baptist reintegration for two reasons. First, as noted above, reconciliation with the German Baptist Union would facilitate the administration of aid to Baptists throughout postwar Europe. Rushbrooke declared that the relief needs of Germany "demanded exceptional action" and that the BWA should take the lead in "dealing with Baptist needs in Germany." Lewis was chosen to act as the BWA's "special representative" for this mission. The second factor was the choice to hold the first postwar world congress in Copenhagen, Denmark. Denmark was an ideal location, both for logistics and for German Baptists to travel.[47]

In August 1946 Rushbrooke and BWA executive committee member H. L. Taylor met with the German Baptist Union Committee and the Plymouth Brethren leaders to discuss "their relations with" "the Nazi Party." They also met with Paul Schmidt.[48] Rushbrooke revealed three "facts" emerging from the conversations that disturbed him: the "fact of hunger" throughout the country; the "deplorable" housing conditions; and the condition of "prisoners of war."[49] The issues of German Baptist complicity with the Nazi regime and their indifference to the suffering of their Jewish neighbors were not mentioned in the column.

A momentous milestone was reached when Rushbrooke cast aside all his private doubts and concerns and provided German Baptists with the cover they needed to whitewash the past and rejoin the international Baptist fellowship. In articles published in the Baptist press between September and November 1946, he finally addressed the issue of German Baptists and the Nazi era.

First, Rushbrooke minimized the extent to which German Baptists were allied with the Nazis. He claimed that German Baptists "are not *pro-Nazi*. The very few ministers who joined the Nazi Party (I did not learn more than four names) did so without sharing any of its anti-Semitism, anti-Biblicism, or anti-Christianity." Rushbrooke revealed no identities and did not indicate why he was so certain of the dubious claim that Nazi-affiliated Baptists had not embraced its anti-Semitism. Gebauer had accused nine individuals by name, and groups, as Nazi collaborators or sympathizers, in his private communications. Rushbrooke then rationalized Baptist passivity by blaming pietistic theology for their political mistakes: "the rarity of public protest on the part of the Baptists was due neither to cowardice nor a pro-Nazi trend, but to a 'pietism' (of what we should call a 'Plymouth Brother' type) which is characteristic of Germans. . . . None of the Baptist ex-Nazis—however nominal was their membership of the party—is now in the Executive Committee of the Union."[50]

Second, Rushbrooke gave personal approval to the German Baptist's merger with smaller free church denominations and to the 1944 Confession of Faith. He did insert a reservation, couched in general terms, that indicated he knew the confession was problematic: "I found it, in general, admirable. Its weakness is on the side of Christian ethic: it asserts, of course, obedience to the secular power (quoting Romans 13); it allows oaths of allegiance and military service; but on the wider responsibilities of a common humanity it is silent."[51] While it is not clear that Rushbrooke recognized the erasure of Jewish influence in the Confession, his reference to "wider responsibilities of a common humanity" may reflect his discomfort with German Baptist silence on the Jewish plight.

In November 1946 the Dutch Baptist newspaper *De Christen* published excerpts from a letter sent by Jakob Meister to Rushbrooke. Meister asserted that German Baptists had always been sympathetic to Jews. He even claimed they rejected the extermination of Jews in concentration camps as "incompatible with the will of God and the conscience under the guidance of the Word of God." He added, "Jewish men and women found shelter, food and support with us. I personally belong to those who, for this matter, have not taken any small risk."[52] Meister further claimed that Rushbrooke also believed that "the German Baptists have indeed shown help towards Jews." The Dutch columnist (simply identified as "L.") responded with a polite but incisive rebuttal of Meister's version of history:

> We would have liked to see Dr. Meister do a little more than wash the German Baptists clean. We believe that the leaders of German Baptist mission behaved in such a way that they were not displeasing to the Nazi authorities. . . . Opportunistic policies drove the leading figures of German Baptists. They fell into the snares of Nazism for the simple reason that they were too nationalistic. Their nationalism damaged their Christianity. Their Germanism was not under Christ's. They were rooted a little too deep in the earthly Fatherland and therefore they were spiritually nearsighted. Their discernment was insufficiently developed and therefore they did not notice what was going on in National Socialism.[53]

The Dutch respondent judged that the German Baptists' "attitude from the beginning was too accommodating" and that they had no excuse for failing to recognize "why National Socialism was objectionable." Therefore, caution should be applied before uncritically accepting German Baptists back into the BWA: "We want to forgive what has been done to us and reach out to them with the hand of the community, but for deeper fellowship to be possible, then the brothers on the East must let us know that they reject the National Socialist principles as such, because the totalitarian demand imposed on man by the State affects Christ's crown rights."[54]

Undeterred by such criticism, Meister continued to lobby for renewed fellowship between German Baptists and Baptists around the world. Avoiding the past era entirely, he offered examples of German Baptist suffering and need, and praised Rushbrooke's visit in the summer of 1946: "His presence, his addresses, and the possibility of personal speech and conference have contributed much to the strengthening of mutual relations."[55]

In 1947 Meister expanded his campaign to portray German Baptists as *victims* of the Nazi era. German Baptists and their fellow neighbors were victims of the ravages of war who faced homelessness, a lack of necessities, and destroyed church buildings. Humanitarian relief and evangelical campaigns were vital. Jews, both dead and living, were invisible.[56]

Reintegration into the Baptist Family

After a lifetime of remarkable achievements, Dr. James Henry Rushbrooke, former general secretary and president of the Baptist World Alliance, experienced a stroke on January 26, 1947, and then passed away on February 1.[57]

Rushbrooke's final message to the Baptist community, published posthumously, was an invitation to attend the upcoming Seventh World Congress, scheduled for July 29 through August 3 in Copenhagen, Denmark. He sensed that many were uneasy about welcoming German Baptist delegates to the congress, as it would confirm the reintegration of the German Baptist Union into full fellowship with the rest of the global Baptist family. Rushbrooke advocated for their inclusion even though German Baptists had not expressed any repentance for their actions during the Nazi era; ironically, he wrote that admitting the Germans would demonstrate "the reality of Christian brotherhood that knows no distinctions of race." The unity of Baptists trumped the justice demands that would have held the German Baptists accountable for their Nazi-era performance. Rushbrooke argued that the German Baptists' "painful sense of isolation and the need of strong encouragement through strong and intimate Christian fellowship" was the "supreme and sufficient reason for an early Congress."[58]

A German Baptist delegation of fifty members did arrive in Copenhagen. The Danish government required that "none of the entering German Baptists had been associated with the Nazi Party." It is unclear who vouched for these leaders. The Germans came without adequate apparel and "their expenses in Denmark had to be defrayed by the Baptist World Alliance." The First Baptist Church of Richmond in Virginia, the American Baptist Foreign Mission Society, and Baptists in England provided donations. With their travel and personal needs tended to, the Germans "renewed their contacts and shared again in the inspiration of the world fellowship of Baptists."[59]

On the opening day, Jakob Meister represented the German Baptists in the roll call of nations, and on Friday, August 1, he led a German-language breakout session titled the "Witness of the Church of Jesus Christ in a Time of Confusion."[60] Meister's greetings during the roll call are not included in the official book, but a copy is in the Elstal Archive. After acknowledging the "painful interruption of our [Baptist] solidarity by the war" and the joyous reunion taking place in Copenhagen, Meister offered an unspecific statement of regret that was in line with other German Baptist statements: "We humble ourselves under the guilt that our people have borne through the tyranny of recent years. The mighty hand of the judging God weighs heavily on our country, our people and our communities. We believe that after all, an hour of divine visitation has begun for all peoples." Most significantly, Meister avoided references to Jews and the Holocaust.[61]

Eberhard Schroeder, the director of the German Baptist Publication Society, presented at the Layman's Conference on Thursday, July 31. His speech illustrated the main themes of the German Baptists' postwar campaign to become reintegrated into the wider Baptist fellowship without being held accountable for their actions during the Nazi period. Schroeder revealed that he was chosen to present by none other than the recently deceased and universally admired BWA president. If Rushbrooke desired German participation in the congress, who could object? He humbly thanked the congress "that a German representative is allowed to speak at all." Schroeder acknowledged that Germany was "guilty" for the suffering it inflicted, but there was no recognition of its specific guilt for the Holocaust. He cast German Baptists as victims who required aid: "Brethren from many countries have also supported our needy congregations by sending food and clothes, and thus saving many from starvation."[62] To be sure, German suffering was widespread, but Schroeder was silent regarding the millions of Jews who died or who barely survived and were still in dire need.

Fortunately, the Copenhagen congress did not ignore the tragedy of the Jewish Holocaust.[63] Several historic resolutions were passed, making this gathering one of the most important milestones in the history of the Baptists and the Jewish people.

On August 3 the congress approved a Manifesto on Religious Freedom composed by the Commission on Religious Freedom. The manifesto declared that Christians should exercise "independent judgment" from presumably totalitarian regimes and strive to "maintain this God-given freedom not only for ourselves, but for all men everywhere." Baptists were duty-bound to "extend the rights of conscience to all people, irrespective of their race, colour, sex, or religion (or lack of religion)." The implication was clear: German Baptists during the Nazi era should have expressed solidarity with and concern for persecuted Jews. The BWA's disappointment in German Baptist complicity with the Nazi agenda and their passivity toward the Jews was diplomatically expressed in the statement's "Standing Firm in the Faith" subsection: "We rejoice with those our brethren who have resisted gloriously all attempts to subject the living Word of God to the will of totalitarian States or other outside pressures. We would that all, within our great worldwide fellowship, might have chosen this same course." The German Baptists' rationale for submitting to Nazi authority was rejected: "When any conflict arises between the State and our religious convictions," Baptists must "place the will of God before the dictates and decrees of men." Despite German Baptist claims that their movement enjoyed freedom during the Nazi era, the consensus of the congress was that "there can be no true religious liberty in a tyrannical State."[64]

Two resolutions passed on August 2 also repudiated the German Baptists' perspective. The Resolution on Race Relations affirmed that the "personalities of all races must be insisted upon by Christians." The attribution of *personality* to all races was a pointed affirmation that Jews and nonwhite peoples (such as African Americans and Asians) were made in the image of God and deserving of political and social equality and civil rights. Accordingly, "un-Christian practices and abuses of people, such as lynchings, race extermination, economic and racial discrimination, unfair employment practices, and denial of political rights are contrary to the principles of Christianity."[65]

The historic Resolution concerning the Jews called "upon Baptists throughout the world to manifest the Spirit of Jesus Christ, Himself a Child of Israel, and to do everything in their power to alleviate the sufferings of the Jews." The horror of the Nazi era was described in graphic terms, and the resolution expressed solidarity with the Jewish victims but did not specifically call out German Baptists:

> Aware of the unprecedented suffering through which the people
> of Israel have passed during recent years, millions of them being

exterminated by the most inhuman means; aware also that these sufferings are not yet at an end, but that hundreds of thousands are still in concentration camps or wandering homeless from land to land; aware, further, that the poisonous propaganda and destructive designs of anti-Semitism are still at work in many lands: this Congress puts on record its sense of sorrow and shame that such conditions prevail.[66]

British Baptist scholar Keith G. Jones has concluded that after the Second World War, "there was a general desire, particularly in BWA circles, to restore friendly relations as soon as possible" with the German Baptists.[67] By the conclusion of the 1947 congress, this aspiration had largely been achieved. Despite the statements passed, a serious attempt was not undertaken to hold German Baptists accountable for their submission to Nazism and their lack of support for the Jewish people who died in the Holocaust. Nazi-era leaders were able to continue serving their Union, were invited to serve again on BWA committees and commissions, and cooperated with the BWA in relief projects.

NOTES

1. W. O. Lewis, "Work on the Continent," *Baptist Times*, June 18, 1942, 307.
2. J. H. Rushbrooke, "Relief of Distress in Europe—Significance of Italy," *Baptist Times*, September 16, 1943, 6.
3. W. Taylor Bowie, "The Church Facing Its Tasks," *Baptist Times*, May 10, 1945, 6.
4. "Fraternising with German Christians," *Baptist Times*, May 24, 1945, 2–3.
5. H. Luckey and W. Gutsche to Rushbrooke, Lewis, and Kuhn, May 5, 1945, in BWA Europe Box 2A Folder #3—Germany (1946–1953), in Angus Library and Archive.
6. H. Luckey and W. Gutsche to Rushbrooke, Lewis, and Kuhn.
7. Lloyd A. Hollingsworth, "German Baptists," *Watchman-Examiner*, December 6, 1945, 1178.
8. M. E. Aubrey, "Baptists in Germany," *Baptist Times*, December 20, 1945, 6.
9. "Table Talk: Dr. Walter O. Lewis," *Baptist Times*, January 31, 1946, 5.
10. Bernard Green, *European Baptists and the Third Reich* (London: Baptist Historical Society, 2008), 217.
11. "The Situation in Europe: First Hand Impressions by Dr. W. O. Lewis, General Secretary of the Baptist World Alliance," undated article manuscript in Lewis's personnel file (undated), American Baptist Historical Society Archive.
12. Edwin Bell, "Observations regarding the Existing Situation in Germany," 1945, Angus Library and Archive.
13. Bell, "Observations regarding the Existing Situation in Germany."
14. Stewart W. Herman, *The Rebirth of the German Church* (New York: Harper and Brothers, 1946), 20.
15. Herman, 51.
16. Herman, 138–39.
17. Quoted in "Editorial: Niemoeller Indicts Church," *Watchman-Examiner*, November 8, 1945, 1079.
18. "Letters: Dr. F. W. Simoleit," *Baptist Times*, December 27, 1945, 7.

19. Paul Schmidt, *Unser Weg: als Bund Evangelisch-Freikirchlicher Gemeinden in den Jahren 1941–1946* (Original Verlag J. G. Oncken Nachf., Stuttgart Gedruckt, 1946. Digital copy: bruederbewegung.de, 2009).

20. Schmidt, *Unser Weg: als Bund Evangelisch-Freikirchlicher Gemeinden in den Jahren 1941–1946*, 6–10.

21. Schmidt, *Unser Weg: als Bund Evangelisch-Freikirchlicher Gemeinden in den Jahren 1941–1946*, 11–13.

22. Schmidt, *Unser Weg: als Bund Evangelisch-Freikirchlicher Gemeinden in den Jahren 1941–1946*, 15.

23. Schmidt, *Unser Weg: als Bund Evangelisch-Freikirchlicher Gemeinden in den Jahren 1941–1946*, 15–16.

24. "A Message from the Secretary of the German Baptist Union," *Baptist Times*, August 8, 1946, 4.

25. Keith Robbins, "Church and Politics: Dorothy Buxton and the German Church Struggle" in *Church, Society and Politics*, ed. Derek Baker (Oxford: Basil Blackwell, 1975), 419–43.

26. M. E. Aubrey to Buxton, August 28, 1946, in M. E. Aubrey Folder, Angus Library and Archive.

27. Alan Effa, "The Legacy of Paul and Clara Gebauer," *International Bulletin of Missionary Research 2006* 30, no. 2: 92–96.

28. Paul Gebauer to J. H. Rushbrooke and William Kuhn, September 11, 1945, Angus Library and Archive.

29. Paul Gebauer to J. H. Rushbrooke and William Kuhn, September 12, 1945, Angus Library and Archive.

30. Gebauer to Rushbrooke and Kuhn, September 12, 1945.

31. Paul Gebauer to J. H. Rushbrooke, October 10, 1945, Angus Library and Archive.

32. Gebauer to Rushbrooke, October 10, 1945.

33. Gebauer to Rushbrooke, October 10, 1945.

34. R. W. Kerr to J. H. Rushbrooke, October 13, 1945, Angus Library and Archive.

35. J. H. Rushbrooke to William Kuhn, October 22, 1945, Angus Library and Archive.

36. Rushbrooke to Kuhn, October 22, 1945.

37. See Bo Lidegaard, *Countrymen: The Untold Story of How Denmark's Jews Escaped the Nazis* (New York: Knopf, 2013).

38. See Arne Hassing, *Church Resistance to Nazism in Norway 1940–1945* (Seattle: University of Washington Press, 2014).

39. J. H. Rushbrooke to Erik Ruden, October 27, 1945, Angus Library and Archive.

40. See Helle Horjus, "The Union of Baptist Churches in the Netherlands and the Rise of Nazism," *Trajecta* 27 (2018): 353–71.

41. J. W. Weenink, "The Baptists of Holland and the Nazis," *Baptist Times*, December 13, 1945, 8. See Green, *European Baptists and the Third Reich*, 106–8.

42. J. W. Weenink, "The Baptists of Holland and the Nazis," *Watchman-Examiner*, February 14, 1946, 156–58.

43. Weenink, "Baptists of Holland and the Nazis," *Watchman-Examiner*, 156–58.

44. Rushbrooke to Ruden, October 27, 1945.

45. Edwin Bell to J. H. Rushbrooke, December 27, 1945, Angus Library and Archive.

46. James C. Enns, *Saving Germany: North American Protestants and Christian Mission to West Germany, 1945–1974* (Montreal: McGill-Queen's University Press, 2017), 97, 247, note 165. Günter Balders records that Luckey was both appointed and then resigned (without supplying a reason) from the directorship of the seminary in 1946, while the school's two other key professors, Carl Neuschäfer and Julius Jansen, "retired for reasons of age." Günter Balders, "Kurze Geschichte der deutschen Baptisten," in Günter Balders, ed., *Ein Herr, ein Glaube, eine Taufe: 150 Jahre Baptistengemeinden in Deutschland, 1834–1984: Festschrift* (Wuppertal und Kassel: Oncken, 1985), 136.

47. J. H. Rushbrooke, "Baptist World Alliance Next World Congress in Copenhagen," *Baptist Times*, June 13, 1946, 6; "Seventh Baptist World Congress," *Baptist Times*, July 11, 1946, 3.

48. "Dr. Rushbrooke in Germany," *Baptist Times*, August 29, 1946, 6.

49. J. H. Rushbrooke, "Germany: Disturbing Facts," *Baptist Times*, September 5, 1946, 8.

50. J. H. Rushbrooke, "Baptists in Germany: A Conspectus," *Baptist Times*, September 12, 1946), 8; part 2 of the column appears in the September 19, 1946, issue. A column (incorporating both parts) appeared in *Watchman-Examiner* under the title "Baptists in Germany," October 10, 1946, 1038–39.

51. Rushbrooke, "Baptists in Germany: A Conspectus," 8.

52. "Een Boodschap van Duitse Baptisten," *De Christen*, November 22, 1946, 3, my translation.

53. "Een Boodschap van Duitse Baptisten," 4, my translation.

54. "Een Boodschap van Duitse Baptisten," 4.

55. "Conditions in Germany," *Watchman-Examiner*, March 13, 1947, 258.

56. Jakob Meister, "The German Scene," *Watchman-Examiner*, September 11, 1947, 929–30; Jacob Meister, "What Gospel for a Broken Nation and a Hopeless People?", *Missions*, June 1947, 362–63.

57. "Men and Things," *Watchman-Examiner*, February 6, 1947, 122; "Death of Dr. James H. Rushbrooke," *Watchman-Examiner*, February 13, 1947, 153.

58. J. H. Rushbrooke, "Copenhagen Awaits Baptists," *Watchman-Examiner*, February 13, 1947, 156–57.

59. "Copenhagen Commentary," *Missions*, October 1947, 469.

60. Walter O. Lewis, ed., *Seventh Baptist World Congress: Copenhagen, Denmark July 29–August 3, 1947* (London: Baptist World Alliance, 1948), app. B, 90.

61. The full text of the greeting in German can be found in Heinz Szobries, ed., *Schuldbekenntnisse aus dem Bund Ev.-Freikirchlicher Gemeinden und anderen Kirchen in Deutschland nach 1945* (Wustermark: Oncken-Archive Elstal, 2013), 53–54.

62. Eberhard Schroeder, "The Responsibilities of Baptist Laymen," in *Seventh Baptist World Congress*, ed. Lewis, app. B, 124–28.

63. See Lee B. Spitzer, *Baptists, Jews, and the Holocaust: The Hand of Sincere Friendship* (Valley Forge, PA: Judson, 2017), 426–30.

64. Lewis, *Seventh Baptist World Congress*, 118–20.

65. Lewis, 98–99.

66. Lewis, 99.

67. Keith G. Jones, *The European Baptist Federation: A Case Study in European Baptist Interdependency: 1950–2006* (Milton Keynes, UK: Paternoster, 2009), 195.

CONCLUSION

Baptists and the Jewish People

In September 1971, Hans Luckey was asked to reflect on the response of the German Baptists during the time of the Third Reich. It is a revealing and rather disturbing interview. He claimed that following the war, "the absence of an official [German Baptist] confession of guilt" was due to "a lack of public will." Luckey asserted that even Jakob Meister's roll call statement in Copenhagen elicited condemnation from people who "didn't want to know anything about an apology." Frankly, nothing in Luckey's own words in the interview resembled a humble or sincere confession. He categorically denied that he and other German Baptist leaders had "taken the side of National Socialism in an ideological way." The interview is, in many ways, an exercise in self-justification. It lacks any expressions of care for Jewish people who suffered so deeply during the Holocaust, and shrugs off the pietistically-inspired German Baptist disinterest in their past. Luckey stated, "The Baptists let the dead bury their dead. Mission is everything."[1]

Vergangenheitsaufarbeitung

The Holocaust, as the "most traumatic experience of Western Europe" in the twentieth century, has provided a "most searching test of Christian integrity."[2] The historical narrative presented in this book compels us to face a moral and ethical reckoning. Roland Fleischer, a German Baptist scholar, acknowledged in 2019 that "For Baptists and Free Churches more generally their stance towards the Jews during the Third Reich is one of the most disgraceful chapters in their history. Their failure to recognize the Holocaust for what it was is still a horrid wound, and even now engenders shame because of a guilty silence: the subject 'Baptists and Jews 1933–1945' has been ignored or suppressed for too long."[3]

Philosopher Susan Neiman has provided a fascinating account of how contemporary German society has sought to come to grips with its Nazi past. She details how *Vergangenheitsaufarbeitung*[4]—reappraisal of the past—may help a society to confront, learn from, and thus come to terms with the past. Historians surely play a crucial role in *Vergangenheitsaufarbeitung*, for the events, facts, and narratives historians present set the stage for an honest reappraisal to take place. Historian Gertrude Himmelfarb, addressing the historian's craft and its impact on understanding the Holocaust, has delivered a "rebuke to historians, philosophers, and literary critics" who have trivialized, relativized, deconstructed, or denied the anti-Semitism of the Nazi era and its culmination in the Shoah.[5]

In this volume and its predecessor, I have sought to highlight the intertwined narratives of the leading Baptist individuals and ministries that confronted the challenge of Nazi anti-Semitism, with a focus on Baptists from Great Britain, France, Germany, the United States, and the Baptist World Alliance. My hope is that these works, added to the research of other historians and scholars, may serve to support and encourage an authentic global Baptist embracing of *Vergangenheitsaufarbeitung*.

By engaging in an honest reappraisal of the Holocaust period, Baptists today may remember and honor Baptists who acted in solidarity with Jews during the Holocaust, while at the same time acknowledging the inconvenient truth that many Baptists failed to respond appropriately to Nazism. Although every Baptist convention and organization, including the BWA, would benefit from engaging in historical reckoning, no doubt, the most difficult burden falls on the heirs of the Nazi-era German Baptist Union and its leadership.

Victoria J. Barnett, in her study of Holocaust bystanders, notes several characteristics of those who were passive or complicit as the Nazis pursued their unholy agenda against the Jews. Some were anti-Semitic, but not all. Many were more concerned with their own self-preservation than with helping Jews to survive. Even if they did not know all the details, many knew or surmised that crimes against the Jewish people were being committed. However, most passive bystanders felt that they were powerless to change what was transpiring, comparing their weakness to the strength of the powerful Nazi movement.[6]

Barnett's bystander model might serve as a constructive platform from which Baptists could delve deeply into the journey of *Vergangenheitsaufarbeitung.* Her discussion on "indifference" speaks directly to the German Baptist experience. Barnett defines "indifference" as "the mark of the bystanders who remain passive, who avoid involvement and thereby step out of the wheel of history." Indifference might be manifested as "a moral stance, a psychological attitude, or actual behavior"[7] of individuals or organizations. During the Nazi period, indifference could lead to "organizations and world leaders who, while they may have felt pangs of conscience about the plight of the Jews, put those emotions aside in the interests of political and military pragmatism."[8]

Pragmatism influenced the actions of not just German Baptists, but leaders of the Baptist World Alliance as well. Rushbrooke, Lewis, and their fellow BWA colleagues accepted and facilitated the premature reintegration of the German Baptist Union and its leadership, effectively releasing them from spiritual, ethical, and moral accountability. Following their lead, the Baptist denominations of the Allied nations (the major donors) turned away from the due diligence investigations called for by German Baptist actions during the Nazi period and pushed forward with cooperative arrangements (financial and material aid) and renewed fellowship. No one had the appetite to probe for the full truth about German Baptist complicity, and the resulting silence and inaction introduced, regarding the Jewish people and their near destruction, a loss of concern and memory.

Struggling with Memories

In *The End of Memory: Remembering Rightly in a Violent World,* Miroslav Volf speaks about "redeeming the past" while treating "memories of wrongs responsibly," because "redemption and right remembrance" are interconnected. We must seek the truth and forsake the temptation to create false memories. When Baptist historians write about the Holocaust period, we must "commit ourselves to render truthfully what happened in the past." This is a "moral obligation" as well as an "obligation of justice"[9] despite the difficulties we may face in confronting our movement's shortcomings and failures.

If Fleischer is correct in his assessment that German Baptist treatment of the Jews during the Nazi period has not been definitively addressed, and I believe he is right, then German Baptists, as well as Baptists in general, should not yet claim that we have fulfilled the aims of *Vergangenheitsaufarbeitung* or have redeemed the past.

Over the past eight decades, a few preliminary but insufficient steps have been taken. Between 1974 and 1977, German Baptists from both sides of the Cold War divide produced a joint confession of faith that moved away from the 1944 Confession's silence on Jews and Judaism: "In our belief in Jesus Christ, whom God brought forth from Israel in due time, we recognize Israel as God's chosen people. . . . God's election and calling of Israel have not been nullified by their unfaithfulness and disobedience. In God's preserving the Jewish people down to the present we perceive a sign of his faithfulness and mercy."[10] The recognition of the Jewishness of Jesus and the chosenness of the Jews is welcome, but the statement's reference to Israel's "unfaithfulness and disobedience" is troubling, implying that their suffering might have been deserved.

The second paragraph of the section rejected any notion of an "Aryan Jesus" and affirmed that Jesus could not be separated from the people of his birth; he is both "Christ for the Gentiles" and the "Messiah of Israel." However, the statement does not fully reject supersessionism[11]—the assertion that the Jewish covenant has been "dissolved" in light of the New Testament era of the church: "The new covenant, in which God has established his rule of grace for all men, dissolves the old covenant and at the same time brings it to fulfillment. Jesus Christ is the Savior of the world, as he is the Messiah of Israel."[12] The priority of the New Testament over the original covenant was reasserted in section 6: "The Old Testament bears witness to us of God's dealings with his people Israel and of God's will for all mankind. The Christian community understands the Old Testament from the perspective of God's revelation in Christ and sees it as pointing toward that revelation; for Christ is the goal and the end of the law."[13]

While the new confession addressed general theological issues that were central to German Baptist apostasy during the Nazi era, it did not offer an apology to the Jewish victims of Hitler for German Baptist anti-Semitism, passivity, and complicity. Fleischer admits that German Baptists did not publish "an official statement on hostility toward Jews and the persecution of Jews," including specifically Kristallnacht, until 1978. The statement may be interpreted as a sincere first step at truthful remembrance:

> On 9 November 1938 the synagogues burned in Germany. A large number of Jewish citizens were abused, arrested and sent to concentration camps. Jewish shops were destroyed and looted. For Christians and non-Christians in Germany, the 9th of November is a day of deep shame and sadness. Since that day, the burden of great guilt has been on our people. Through anti-Jewish prejudices, lack of interest and unwillingness to help, many—even unconsciously and unintentionally—contributed to the National Socialist state being able to take the path of the so-called "final solution" to the Jewish question. When our Jewish citizens were threatened and persecuted, many stood by and remained silent under the pressure of the totalitarian regime. We remember all the more gratefully the few who took care of persecuted Jews, risking their lives. . . . We, the elderly, do not want to hide the injustice that has happened before our youth. We therefore ask God again through his son Jesus Christ for forgiveness for the injustice done by our people. At the same time, we want to reaffirm our solidarity with the Jews and recognize the permanent election of Israel by God (Romans 11:2–36).[14]

On August 1, 1984, German Baptist leader Günter Hitzemann, on behalf of the Free Church congregations in Germany, shared a statement before delegates of the European Baptist Federation. Acknowledging that German Baptist history could not shy away from "the turmoil of the period under National-Socialist domination," the declaration expressed "shame and grief, particularly when we recall the persecution and mass extermination of the Jews. Because of this, our national guilt, we are dependent upon the forgiveness of God." The statement then sought to rationalize German Baptist support of the Nazi regime:

> To recognize the evil from the beginning was more difficult than it seems in retrospect today. There were those amongst us who

saw through the then regime, warned against it and bravely opposed the injustice. But we did not ally ourselves openly with
the struggles and suffering of the Confessional Church and likewise failed to set ourselves unequivocally against the violation
of the divine commandment and precepts. It weighs heavily
upon us that we, as the German Federation, often succumbed
to the ideological temptations of the time and did not show
greater courage in professing truth and justice. Even after the
collapse of the Hitler regime, it was only individuals, and not
officially the Union of Evangelical Free Church Congregations,
who voiced an opinion on these events.[15]

While attempting to admit errors, this expression of remorse
falls short of the mark. Devoting just one sentence to specifically
acknowledge the enormous tragedy of the Holocaust for Europe's
Jews seems inadequate. The specific sins Baptists committed against
the Jews deserve to be enumerated in detail (such as passively
watching measures of discrimination imposed on Jews by the government throughout the 1930s, doing nothing to help Jews during
Kristallnacht and even trying to profit from their losses, representing the Nazi cause in international venues, putting forth the 1944
Nazi-conforming Confession, and permitting Nazi supporting leaders such as Paul Schmidt to continue in office).

As this and other historical studies have demonstrated, it was
not "difficult" to "recognize the evil from the beginning." Nazism,
totalitarianism, and anti-Semitism were soundly repudiated by the
BWA and its most prominent international leaders before, during,
and after the 1934 World Congress in Berlin, while German Baptist
leaders enthusiastically expressed support for Hitler and his revolution. German Baptist leaders not only rejected the counsel of their
American and British colleagues; they justified Nazi rule in their
newspapers and speeches. This unwillingness to repudiate their
complicity with Nazism continued even after the war was over.

Although the 1984 statement has been portrayed as a German
Baptist apology that brought the story to a close, it was not. The
apology was offered to the European Baptist Federation, which in
turn confessed that "the history" of the Nazi era "lies heavily upon
us, but at the same time there is mercy and forgiveness through the
Cross of Christ."[16] The European Baptist Federation's reply did not
reference Jews or their suffering.

However, the complicity of German Baptists during the Nazi era was not primarily a transgression against its European Baptist compatriots—it was first and foremost a grievous betrayal of their Jewish friends, neighbors, and fellow Jewish believers in Christ. The harm experienced by European Baptists, though real, was not equal to the sufferings of the Jewish people. Thus, although it was appropriate to ask forgiveness from the rest of the European Baptist community for their offenses, the declaration—or a more thoughtful version of it—should have been addressed *specifically to the Jewish communities of Germany and Europe.*

Pathways toward Reconciliation

Miroslav Volf's call to engage in a truthful remembering represents an initial advance toward bridging the gulf between those who have harmed others and their victims: "To remember truthfully . . . is to render justice both to the victim and to the perpetrator and therefore to take a step toward reconciliation."[17]

A humble reading of how Baptists responded to anti-Semitism during the Third Reich surely calls us to confess shortcomings and failures in rising to the standards Baptists profess, even while humbly honoring accounts of loving and sacrificial actions Baptists performed on behalf of the Jewish people throughout Europe under Nazi occupation. Baptists across the world did reject Nazi anti-Semitism through both words and deeds, but more could have been done. Other Baptists were guilty of being either passive bystanders or complicit, to the shame of the entire Baptist family. Accordingly, the whole Baptist family bears a responsibility to repent and seek reconciliation with the Jewish world.

In 2003 German Baptist scholar Erich Geldbach asserted that "the point of departure for thinking about a reasonable Baptist-Jewish relationship must be the recognition of the Holocaust,"[18] and noted that the post-Holocaust era church's reconsideration of its relationship with the Jewish people necessarily involved a reflection on Baptist heritage and teaching, as well as missionary praxis. Geldbach pointed to *Dienste in Israel* (Service in Israel), which was founded in 1975 and continues to send volunteers to Israel today, as an example of contemporary German Baptist philo-Semitism.[19]

Turning to the future, Baptists are called to continue journeying toward reconciliation with the Jewish community.[20] It is not sufficient for Baptist leaders and scholars to converse with one another and seek forgiveness and reconciliation within the Baptist family. The Jewish people suffered the most harm, and it is to this community that Baptists must turn and seek forgiveness, reconciliation, and friendship.

Historians most certainly will play an important role if Baptists are willing to embrace the challenge of *Vergangenheitsaufarbeitung* (the reappraisal of the past to discover truth). The historical narrative of Baptists and the Nazi era is not yet complete; there are many stories still to be remembered and evaluated. We need to rediscover the heroes and heroines that can inspire us to strive for higher levels of faithfulness and virtue. We must humbly acknowledge the shortcomings of our historical response to anti-Semitism and confess that among us are individuals and institutions that fell far short in expressing the righteousness, justice, compassion, and love of the God we claim to follow.

Furthermore, the recovery of historical truth is not complete until we learn wisdom from it and discern new pathways to express and embody that wisdom in the ongoing transformational quest toward a more just and peace-filled world. The questions we ask ourselves after reading historical accounts such as this one represent the first steps down such pathways. Consider these questions that may guide us in applying the lessons of the past to contemporary concerns:

1. How might German Baptists in particular, and the rest of the Baptist family more generally, honestly, and courageously face historical truth and repent for our failure to be more faithful in expressing solidarity with the Jewish people and opposing anti-Semitism during the Nazi era?

2. Baptists and other people of goodwill struggled to counter the rise of anti-Semitism during the Nazi era. What should be our responses to the rising tide of anti-Semitism in today's world? More generally, how should Baptists confront racism in all its varied manifestations?

3. How might Baptists as a global family creatively reach out to the Jewish people and offer friendship in a

post-Holocaust world? Does our history offer points of contact to build relational bridges and provide opportunities for honest conversation, even if the issues are difficult to face and overcome?

4. The Holocaust took place before most of this book's readership reached adulthood; many of us were not alive during that time period. What is our responsibility to address and rectify the actions of past generations? Is there such a thing as collective or transgenerational guilt? How do we seek forgiveness and reconciliation for events that occurred during previous generations?

5. How do Baptist core convictions (such as soul freedom, separation of church and state, conscience, political liberty, and personality) inform Baptists of our responsibilities and responses when situations arise that challenge these convictions in today's world?

6. Rushbrooke's fundamental concern for Baptist unity and fellowship trumped his sincere fight against anti-Semitism. What do we do when two or more Baptist core convictions come into conflict with one another?

Seeking trust, reconciliation, and authentic friendship between the global Baptist family and the Jewish people will no doubt take time. In light of our history during the Holocaust period, the burden of responsibility necessarily falls on the Baptists to initiate and invite the Jewish world into new avenues of relationship, dialogue, and sharing. Anniversaries of significant events often may serve as catalysts to memory preservation and thoughtful reflection and reconsideration, as well as celebration and mourning. The year 2034 marks the one-hundredth anniversary of the BWA World Congress in Berlin and the passage of the historic racialism resolution condemning anti-Semitism. I cannot think of a better venue and time for the global Baptist movement to remember truthfully and further the journey toward reconciliation with God's chosen people than Berlin in 2034.

NOTES

1. Hans Luckey, Interview: Wir sind widerlegt worden (September 1971), in *Schuldbekenntnisse aus dem Bund Ev.-Freikirchlicher Gemeinden und anderen Kirchen in Deutschland nach 1945*, ed. Heinz Szobries, 60–64.

2. K. W. Clements, "A Question of Freedom? British Baptists and the German Church Struggle," in *Baptists in the Twentieth Century: Papers Presented at a Summer School July 1982*, ed. Clements (London: Baptist Historical Society, 1983), 96.

3. Roland Fleischer, "The German Baptists and Their Conduct Towards Jews and Jewish Christians, Especially during the Third Reich," in *People of God: Baptists and Jews over Four Centuries*, ed. John H. Y. Briggs and Paul S. Fiddes (Oxford: Center for Baptist Studies in Oxford Publications, 2019), 193.

4. Susan Neiman, *Learning from the Germans: Race and the Memory of Evil* (New York: Farrar, Straus and Giroux, 2019), 7, 17.

5. Gertrude Himmelfarb, *On Looking into the Abyss: Untimely Thoughts on Culture and Society* (New York: Vintage Books, 1994), xi.

6. Victoria J. Barnett, *Bystanders: Conscience and Complicity during the Holocaust* (Westport, CT: Praeger, 2000), 36–51.

7. Barnett, 117–18.

8. Barnett, 122–23.

9. Miroslav Volf, *The End of Memory: Remembering Rightly in a Violent World* (Grand Rapids: Eerdmans, 2006), 41–55.

10. Pt. 1, sec. 5, in G. Keith Parker, *Baptists in Europe: History & Confessions of Faith* (Nashville: Broadman, 1982), 62. In a German-language version published in 1975, this is section 4. All quotes here are from Parker's later translation.

11. For a discussion of supersessionism, see R. Kendall Soulen, *The God of Israel and Christian Theology* (Minneapolis: Fortress, 1996).

12. Pt. 1, sec. 5, in Parker, *Baptists in Europe*, 62.

13. Pt. 1, sec. 6, in Parker, *Baptists in Europe*, 63. In a German-language version published in 1975, this is section 5.

14. "Kristallnacht 1938," *Die Gemeinde* 48 (1978): 11; quoted in Roland B. Fleischer, "'Das verachtete Volk der Juden': Baptisten, die Pogromnacht 1938 und das Verhältnis żum Judentum," in *Freikirchenforschung* 17 (2008, S.): 221, translation mine.

15. Supreme Council of the Association of Protestant Free Church Congregations in Germany, *Declaration of the Protestant Free Church Congregations in Germany*, August 1, 1984; https://www.ccjr.us/dialogika-resources/documents-and-statements/protestant-churches/eur/declaration-of-the-protestant-free-church-congregations-in-germany. The statement and the European Baptist Federation's reply in German may be found in *Schuldbekenntnisse aus dem Bund Ev.-Freikirchlicher Gemeinden und anderen Kirchen in Deutschland nach 1945*, ed. Heinz Szobries, 65–67.

16. Both the German declaration and the European Baptist Federation's response can be found in full in Bernard Green, *European Baptists and the Third Reich* (London: Baptist Historical Society, 2008), 232–34. See also Nicholas M. Railton, "German Free Churches and the Nazi Regime," *Journal of Ecclesiastical History* 19, no. 1 (January 1998): 138–39.

17. Volf, *End of Memory*, 56.

18. Erich Geldbach. "Baptist-Jewish Relations: Some Observations from a German Point of View," *Baptist History and Heritage* 38, no. 2 (Spring 2003): 20.

19. See the organization's website, https://dienste-in-israel.de.

20. Franklin H. Littell's *The Crucifixion of the Jews: The Failure of Christians to Understand the Jewish Experience* (1975; repr., Macon, GA: Mercer University Press, 1986, 1996) is a thoughtful example of seeking reconciliation.

Bibliography

Primary and Secondary Books and Articles

Adams, R. J. Q. *British Politics and Foreign Policy in the Age of Appeasement 1935–1939*. Stanford, CA: Stanford University Press, 1993.

Allen, William Lloyd. "How Baptists Assessed Hitler." *Christian Century* (September 1-8, 1982): 890–94.

Bajohr, Frank. "The 'Folk Community' and the Persecution of the Jews: German Society under National Socialist Dictatorship, 1933–1945." *Holocaust and Genocide Studies* 20, no. 2 (Fall 2006): 183–206.

Balders, Günter, ed. *Ein Herr, ein Glaube, eine Taufe: 150 Jahre Baptistengemeinden in Deutschland, 1834–1984: Festschrift*. Wuppertal und Kassel: Oncken, 1985.

Baptist World Alliance. *Liederbuch für den Fünften Weltkongreß der Baptiften* (Hymn Book for the Fifth Baptist World Congress, Berlin 1934). Berlin: Baptist World Alliance, 1934.

_____. *Official Programme and Hand-book of the Fifth Baptist World Congress, Berlin, August 4th to 10th, 1934*. Berlin: Baptist World Alliance, 1934.

Baptist World Alliance Youth Committee. *Christ Our Life: A Permanent and Illustrated Record of Addresses Given and Resolutions Passed at the Second Young Baptist International Congress, Zurich, 1937*. London: Baptist World Alliance, 1937.

Baresel, Ruth Köbner. *Julius Köbner: Sein Leben*. Kassel: J. G. Oncken Nachfolger, 1930.

Barnett, Victoria J. *Bystanders: Conscience and Complicity during the Holocaust*. Westport, CT: Praeger, 2000.

_____. *For the Soul of the People: Protestant Protest against Hitler*. Oxford: Oxford University Press, 1992.

Baumel-Schwartz, Judith Tydor. *Never Look Back: The Jewish Refugee Children in Great Britain, 1938–1945*. West Lafayette, IN: Purdue University Press, 2012.

Blocher-Saillens, Madeleine. *Témoin des années noires: Journal d'une femme pasteur—1938–1945*. Edited by Jacques-E. Blocher. Paris: Les Editions de Paris, 1998.

_____. *Une femme dans la grande guerre: Journal de Madeleine Blocher-Saillens*. Edited by Franck Belloir. Paris: Editions Ampelos, 2014.

Bowie, W. Taylor. "'Baptists Speak to the World,'" *Baptist Quarterly* 10, no. 1 (January 1940): 44.

Briggs, John H. Y., ed. *A Dictionary of European Baptist Life and Thought*. Milton Keynes, UK: Paternoster, 2009.

Briggs, John H. Y., and Paul S. Fiddes, eds. *Peoples of God: Baptists and Jews over Four Centuries*. Oxford: Centre for Baptist Studies, 2019.

Brown, Eva. "The Baptist World Congress at Berlin." *Baptist Quarterly* 7, no. 4 (October 1934): 154–61.

Bulletin de la Société d'Histoire et de Documentation Baptistes de France: Histoires D'Une Famille 1 (2007). Paris: La Société d'Histoire et de Documentation Baptistes de France, 2007.

Cabanel, Patrick. *De la paix aux résistances: Les protestants en France 1930–1945*. Paris: Fayard Histoire, 2015.

_____. *Juifs et protestants en France, les affinités electives XVIᵉ–XXIᵉ siècle*. Paris: Fayard Histoire, 2004.

Chalamet, Christophe. *Revivalism and Social Christianity: The Prophetic Faith of Henri Nick and André Trocmé*. Eugene, OR: Pickwick, 2013.

Cierpke, Alfred A. *Palestine-Israel: God's Miracle Nation*. Chattanooga, TN: self-published, 1954.

_____. *Palestine-Israel: The Holy Land Today*. Chattanooga, TN: self-published, 1953/1954.

_____. *Palestine-Israel: The Marvel of the World*. Chattanooga, TN: self-published, 1954/1955.

Claesberg, Veit. *Der pastorale Leiter als Prophet: Der Baptistenpastor Arnold Köster (1896–1960) im Widerstand gegen den Nationalsozialismus*. Elstal, Germany: Oncken-Archiv, 2018.

Clements, Keith W. *Baptists in the Twentieth Century: Papers Presented at a Summer School July 1982*. London: Baptist Historical Society, 1983.

Coleman, Fred. *The Marcel Network: How One French Couple Saved 527 Children from the Holocaust*. Washington, DC: Potomac Books, 2013.

Confino, Alon. *A World without Jews: The Nazi Imagination from Persecution to Genocide*. New Haven, CT: Yale University Press, 2014.

Conway, John. S. *The Nazi Persecution of the Churches 1933–45*. 1st American ed. New York: Basic Books, 1968.

De Jong, L., and Joseph W. F. Stoppelman. *The Lion Rampant: The Story of Holland's Resistance to the Nazis*. New York: Querido, 1943.

De Russet, Alan. "Baptists and Germany." *Baptist Quarterly* 10, no. 2 (1940): 79–84.

Defries, Harry. *Conservative Party Attitudes to Jews 1900–1950*. London: Frank Cass, 2001.

Dulauroy, Yves-Emmanuel and François Recamier. "'La Maison'—La Pouponnière de Nurieux." *Histhoíría* 8 (2015): 22–28.

Enns, James C. *Saving Germany: North American Protestants and Christian Mission to West Germany, 1945–1974*. Montreal: McGill-Queen's University Press, 2017.

Erickson, Robert P. *Complicity in the Holocaust: Churches and Universities in Nazi Germany*. Cambridge: Cambridge University Press, 2012.

Erickson, Robert P., and Susannah Heschel, eds. *Betrayal: German Churches and the Holocaust*. Minneapolis: Fortress, 1999.

Fath, Sébastien. "Another Way of Being a Christian in France." *Baptist History and Heritage* (January 2001).

_____. "Evangelical Protestantism in France: An Example of Denominational Recomposition?" *Sociology of Religion* 66, no. 4 (Winter 2005): 399–418.

_____. *Les baptistes en France (1810–1950): Faits, dates et documents.* Cléon d'andean, France: Éditions Excelsis, 2002.

_____. "L'Etat face aux enjeux 'autorité-pouvoir' chez les baptistes: l'exemple français, 19ème–20ème siècle." *Social Compass* 48, no. 1 (2001): 51–61.

_____. "Le pasteur évangélique Ruben Saillens et le judaïsme." *Archives Juives* 40, no. 1 (2007): 45–57.

Fleischer, Roland B., "'Das verachtete Volk der Juden': Baptisten, die Pogromnacht 1938 und das Verhältnis zum Judentum." *Freikirchenforschung* 17 (2008, S.): 196–221.

_____, ed. *Der Streit über den Weg der Baptisten im Nationalsozialismus.* Elstal, Germany: Onchin-Archiv Elstal, 2014.

Franklin, James H. *In the Track of the Storm: A Report of a Visit to France and Belgium, with Observations regarding the Needs and Possibilities of Religious Reconstruction in the Regions Devastated by the World War.* Philadelphia: American Baptist Publication Society, 1919.

Geldbach, Erich. "Baptist-Jewish Relations: Some Observations from a German Point of View." *Baptist History and Heritage* 38, no. 2 (Spring 2003): 20–37.

_____. "The Religious Situation in Germany: Past and Present." *American Baptist Quarterly* 23, no. 3 (September 2004): 238–57.

Gezork, Herbert. *So sah ich die Welt.* Kassel, Germany: Verlag von J. G. Nocken Nach, 1933.

Glaser, Mitchell Leslie. "A Survey of Missions to the Jews in Continental Europe 1900–1950." PhD diss., Fuller Theological Seminary, 1998.

Goertz, Lisa. *I Stepped into Freedom.* London: Lutterworth, 1960.

Goldhagen, Daniel Jonah. *Hitler's Willing Executioners: Ordinary Germans and the Holocaust.* New York: Vintage, 1997.

Gottlieb, Amy Zahl. *Men of Vision: Anglo-Jewry's Aid to Victims of the Nazi Regime 1933–1945.* London: Weidenfeld and Nicolson, 1998.

Graf-Stuhlhofer, Franz. Öffentliche *Kritik am Nationalsozialismus im Grossdeutschen Reich: Leben und Weltanschauung des Wiener Baptistenpastors Arnold Köster (1896–1960).* Neukirchen-Vluyn: Neukirchener, 2001.

Green, Bernard. *Crossing the Boundaries: A History of the European Baptist Federation.* London: Baptist Historical Society, 1999.

_____. *European Baptists and the Third Reich.* London: Baptist Historical Society, 2008.

_____. *Tomorrow's Man: A Biography of James Henry Rushbrooke.* London: Baptist Historical Society, 1996.

Gushee, David P. *Righteous Gentiles of the Holocaust: Genocide and Moral Obligation.* 2nd ed. St. Paul, MN: Paragon, 2003.

Heinz, Daniel, ed. *Freikirchen und Juden im »Dritten Reich« Instrumentalisierte Heilsgeschichte, antisemitische Vorurteile und verdrängte Schuld.* Göttingen: V & R Unipress, 2011.

Herman, Stewart W. *The Rebirth of the German Church.* New York: Harper and Brothers, 1946.

Heschel, Susannah. *The Aryan Jesus: Christian Theologians and the Bible in Nazi Germany.* Princeton, NJ: Princeton University Press, 2010.

Hilberg, Raul. *Perpetrators, Victims, Bystanders: The Jewish Catastrophe 1933–1945.* New York: Harper Perennial, 1993.

Hockenos, Matthew D. *A Church Divided: German Protestants Confront the Nazi Past.* Bloomington: Indiana University Press, 2004.

Hoffman, Conrad. "The Challenge of Our Jewish Neighbors." *Baptist Quarterly* 6, no. 6 (1933): 255–59.

Horjus, Helle. "The Union of Baptist Churches in the Netherlands and the Rise of Nazism." *Trajecta* 27 (2018): 353–71.

Jones, Keith G. *The European Baptist Federation: A Case Study in European Baptist Interdependency: 1950–2006.* Milton Keynes, UK: Paternoster, 2009.

Jones, Richard. *The A.B.C. of Jew Baiting: An Address Given at Hawthorn Baptist Church, Pontypridd (Wales) on April 23rd, 1939.* Tiptree, Wales: Anchor, 1939.

Josephs, Jeremy, with Susi Bechhöfer. *Rosa's Child: The True Story of One Woman's Quest for a Lost Mother and a Vanished Past.* London: I. B. Tauris, 1999.

Kastein, Josef. *History and Destiny of the Jews.* New York: Viking, 1933.

Kerstan, Reinhold. *Blood and Honor.* Elgin, IL: Cook, 1983.

Köbner, Julius. *Das Lied von Gott: Ein didaktisches Gedicht in acht Theilen.* (The Song of God: A Didactic Poem in Eight Parts). Hamburg: Verlag von Ludwig, 1873. Reprint, Whitefish, MT: Kessinger Legacy Reprints, 2018.

_____. *Glaubensstimme der Gemeine des Herrn: Lieder-Sammlung.* Hamburg: J. G. Oncken, 1860. Reprint, London: Forgotten Books, 2018.

_____. *Manifest des freien Urchristentums an das deutsche Volk* (1848). Berlin: WDL-Verlag, 2006.

_____. *Wasser aus dem Heilbrunnen.* Berlin: Bethel, 1906.

Le Quesne, C. T. "The Significance of the Berlin Congress." *Fraternal* 17 (January 1935): 2–6.

Leisten, Hans-Joachim, ed. *Wie alle andern auch: Baptistengemeinden im Dritten Reich im Spiegel ihrer Festschriften.* Hamburg: WDL-Verlag, 2010.

Lewis, Walter O. *Seventh Baptist World Congress: Copenhagen, Denmark July 29–August 3, 1947.* London: Baptist World Alliance, 1948.

Lidegaard, Bo. *Countrymen: The Untold Story of How Denmark's Jews Escaped the Nazis.* New York: Knopf, 2013.

Lipstadt, Deborah E. *Antisemitism: Here and Now.* New York: Schocken, 2019.

Littell, Franklin H. *The Crucifixion of the Jews: The Failure of Christians to Understand the Jewish Experience.* Macon, GA: Mercer University Press, 1975. Reprint, Macon, GA: Mercer University Press, 1986, 1996, 2000.

Locke, Hubert G., ed. *The Church Confronts the Nazis: Barmen Then and Now*. New York: Edwin Mellen, 1984.

Lord, F. Townley. "The Achievement of Personality in a Material World." *Baptist Quarterly* 8, no. 5 (1937): 227–35.

_____. *Achievement, a Short History of the Baptist Missionary Society 1792–1942*. London: Carey, 1942.

_____. *Baptist World Fellowship: A Short History of the Baptist World Alliance*. Nashville: Broadman, 1955.

_____. "Some Modern Views of the Soul." *Baptist Quarterly* 5, no. 2 (1930): 66–73.

Lumpkin, William L., ed. *Baptist Confessions of Faith*. Valley Forge, PA: Judson, 1974.

MacFarland, Charles S. *The New Church and the New Germany*. New York: Macmillan, 1934.

Macy, Paul Griswold, ed. *The Report of the Second World Conference of Christian Youth, Oslo, Norway, July 22 to 31, 1947*. Geneva: World Council of Churches, 1947.

Mathews, Basil. *The Clash of Colour: A Study in the Problem of Race*. London: Edinburgh, 1924; 3rd ed., October 1938.

_____. *The Jew and the World Ferment*. New York: Friendship, 1935.

_____. *Through Tragedy to Triumph: The World Church in the World Crisis*. New York: Friendship, 1939.

McGlothlin, William Joseph, ed. *Baptist Confessions of Faith*. Philadelphia: American Baptist Publication Society, 1911.

McKinney, Blake. "'One Lord, One Faith, One Baptism' in the Land of ein Volk, ein Reich, ein Führer: The Fifth Baptist World Congress (Berlin 1934)." *Church History* 87, no. 1 (March 2018): 122–48.

Moorehead, Caroline. *Village of Secrets: Defying the Nazis in Vichy France*. New York: Harper, 2014.

Neiman, Susan. *Learning from the Germans: Race and the Memory of Evil*. New York: Farrar, Straus and Giroux, 2019.

Ohrn, Arnold T. ed. *Eighth Baptist World Congress Cleveland Ohio July 22–27, 1950 Official Report*. Philadelphia: Judson, 1950.

_____. *The Gospel and the Sermon on the Mount*. New York: Revell, 1948.

Oldham, J. H. *The Oxford Conference (Official Report)*. Chicago: Willett, Clark, 1937.

Paldiel, Mordecai. "The Altruism of the Righteous Gentiles." *Holocaust and Genocide Studies* 3, no. 2 (1988): 187–96.

_____. *Churches and the Holocaust: Unholy Teaching, Good Samaritans and Reconciliation*. Jersey City, NJ: KTAV, 2006.

_____. *The Righteous among the Nations: Rescuers of Jews during the Holocaust*. New York: HarperCollins, 2007.

_____. *Sheltering the Jews: Stories of Rescuer Survivors*. Minneapolis: Fortress, 1996.

Panicacci, Jean-Louis. *L'Occupation itlaienne: Sud-Est de la France, juin 1940–septembre 1943*. Rennes, France: Presses Universitaires de Rennes, 2010.

Parker, G. Keith. *Baptists in Europe: History & Confessions of Faith.* Nashville: Broadman, 1982.

Parkes, James. *The Jew and His Neighbour: A Study in the Causes of Anti-Semitism.* London: Student Christian Movement Press, 1930; rev. ed. 1938.

Payne, Ernest A. *Baptists Speak to the World: A Description and Interpretation of the Sixth Baptist World Congress, Atlanta, 1939.* London: Carey, 1939.

_____. *James Henry Rushbrooke, 1870–1947: A Baptist Greatheart.* London: Kingsgate, 1954.

_____. "Julius Kobner." *Congregational Quarterly* 9, no. 4 (October 1931): 438–45.

_____. "Review: A Life of Kobner." *Baptist Quarterly* 5, no. 6 (1931): 281–84.

_____. "Review—Julius Kobner and the German Baptists." *Baptist Quarterly* 4, no. 8 (1929): 380–82.

Pierard, Richard V., ed. *Baptists Together in Christ 1905–2005: A Hundred-Year History of the Baptist World Alliance.* Birmingham, AL: Samford University Press, 2005.

Poujol, Jacques. *Protestants dans la France en guerre 1939–1945: Dictionnaire thématique et biographique.* Paris: Les Éditions de Paris, 2000.

Railton, Nicholas M. "German Free Churches and the Nazi Regime." *Journal of Ecclesiastical History* 19, no. 1 (January 1998): 85–139.

Randall, Ian M. *Communities of Conviction: Baptist Beginnings in Europe.* Schwarzenfeld, Germany: Neufeld, 2009.

Randall, Ian M., Toivo Pilli, and Anthony R. Cross, eds. *Baptist Identities: International Studies from the Seventeenth to the Twentieth Centuries.* Eugene, OR: Paternoster, 2006.

Reid, Alfred Sandlin. *Furman University: Toward a New Identity 1925–1975.* Durham, NC: Duke University Press, 1976.

Robinson, H. Wheeler, *Corporate Personality in Ancient Israel.* Philadelphia: Fortress, 1967; rev. 1980.

Rosenfeld, Gavriel D. "Who Was 'Hitler' before Hitler? Historical Analogies and the Struggle to Understand Nazism, 1930–1945." *Central European History* 51, no. 2 (2018): 249–81.

Rushbrooke, J. H., ed. *The Baptist Movement in the Continent of Europe.* London: Carey, 1915. Reprint, BiblioLife, 2009.

_____, ed. *Fifth Baptist World Congress: Berlin, August 4–10, 1934.* London: Baptist World Alliance, 1934.

_____, ed. *Sixth Baptist World Congress Atlanta, GA July 22–28, 1939.* Atlanta, GA: Baptist World Alliance, 1939.

_____. *Some Chapters of European Baptist History.* London: Kingsgate, 1929.

Sands, Philippe. *East West Street.* New York: Vintage, 2017.

Schmidt, Paul. *Unser Weg als Bund Evangelisch-Freikirchlicher Gemeinden in den Jahren 1941–1946.* Stuttgart: J. G. Oncken Nachf., 1946. Digital copy, bruederbewegung.de, 2009.

Sebba, Anne. *Les Parisiennes: Resistance, Collaboration, and the Women of Paris under Nazi Occupation*. New York: St. Martin's Press, 2016.

Semelin, Jacques. *The Survival of the Jews in France 1940–44*. Trans. Cynthia Schoch and Natasha Lehrer. Oxford: Oxford University Press, 2018.

———. *Unarmed Against Hitler: Civilian Resistance in Europe, 1939–1943*. Translated by Susan Husserl-Kapit. Westport, CT: Praeger, 1993.

Semelin, Jacques, Claire Andrieu, and Sarah Gensburger, eds. *Resisting Genocide: The Multiple Forms of Rescue*. Translated by Emma Bentley and Cynthia Schoch. New York: Oxford University Press, 2013.

Shelley, John C. "The Gezork Incident." *Furman* Magazine 46, no. 1 (2003): art. 4.

Sherman, A. J. *Island Refuge: Britain and Refugees from the Third Reich, 1933–1939*. Berkeley: University of California Press, 1973.

Solberg, Mary M., ed. *A Church Undone: Documents from the German Christian Faith Movement, 1932–1940*. Philadelphia: Fortress, 2015.

Spanring, Paul. *Dietrich Bonhoeffer and Arnold Köster: Two Distinct Voices in the Midst of Germany's Third Reich Turmoil*. Eugene, OR: Pickwick, 2013.

Spicer, Kevin P., ed. *Antisemitism, Christian Ambivalence, and the Holocaust*. Bloomington: Indiana University Press, 2007.

Spitzer, Lee B. "Baptists, Barth, and the Crisis of Conscience Initiated by the Emergence of Nazi Anti-Semitism." *American Baptist Quarterly* 34, nos. 3–4 (Fall and Winter 2015; published April 2017): 343–62.

———. *Baptists, Jews, and the Holocaust: The Hand of Sincere Friendship*. Valley Forge, PA: Judson, 2017.

———. "The Nazi Persecution of the Jews and Scottish Baptist Indignation." *Baptistic Theologies* 9, no. 2 (November 2017): 68–74.

Stassen, Glen H., and David P. Gushee, *Kingdom Ethics: Following Jesus in Contemporary Context*. Downers Grove, IL: InterVarsity, 2003.

Stein, Leo. *I Was in Hell with Niemoeller*. New York: Revell, 1942.

Steubing, Hans, with J. F. Gerhard Goeters, Heinrich Karpp, and Erwin Mülhaupt, eds. *Bekenntnisse der Kirche: Bekinntnistexte aus zwanzig Jahrhunderten*. Wuppertal, Germany: Brockhaus, 1970.

Strübind, Andrea. *Die unfreie Freikirche: Der Bund der Baptistengemeinden im "Dritten Reich."* Berlin: Neukirchener, 1991.

———. "German Baptists and National Socialism." *Journal of European Baptist Studies* 8, no. 3 (2008): 5–20.

Szobries, Heinz, ed. *Schuldbekenntnisse aus dem Bund Ev.-Freikirchlicher Gemeinden und anderen Kirchen in Deutschland nach 1945*. Wustermark: Oncken-Archive Elstal, 2013.

Talbot, Brian R. *Building on a Common Foundation: The Baptist Union of Scotland 1869–2019*. Eugene, OR: Pickwick, 2021.

———, ed. *A Distinctive People: A Thematic Study of Aspects of the Witness of Baptists in Scotland in the Twentieth Century*. Eugene, OR: Wipf and Stock, 2014.

———. *The Search for a Common Identity: The Origins of the Baptist Union of Scotland 1800–1870*. Carlisle: Paternoster, 2003.

Tent, James F. *In the Shadow of the Holocaust: Nazi Persecution of Jewish-Christian Germans*. Lawrence: University of Kansas Press, 2003.

Thobois, André. *Cent ans de l'Église baptiste de l'avenue du Maine à Paris 1899–1999*. Paris: Croire et Servir, 1999.

———. *Henri Vincent: infatigable serviteur du Christ, passionné d'évangélisation*. Paris: Croire et Servir, 2001.

Unsworth, Richard P. *A Portrait of Pacifists: Le Chambon, the Holocaust and the Lives of André and Magda Trocmé*. Syracuse, NY: Syracuse University Press, 2012.

Voigtländer, Nico, and Hans-Joachim Voth. "Nazi Indoctrination and Anti-Semitic Beliefs in Germany." *Proceedings of the National Academy of Sciences* 112, no. 26 (June 2015): 7931–36.

Wilkinson, Alan. *Dissent or Conform? War, Peace and the English Churches 1900–1945*. London: SCM Press, 1986.

Wills, Gregory A. "Progressive Theology and Southern Baptist Controversies of the 1950s and 1960s." *Southern Baptist Journal of Theology* 7, no. 1 (Spring 2003): 12–31.

Wyman, David S. *The Abandonment of the Jews: America and the Holocaust, 1941–1945*. New York: New Press, 1984, rev. 2007.

Zimmerman, Sandra. *Zwischen Selbsterhaltung und Anpassung: Die Haltung der Baptisten und Brüdergemeinden im Nationalsozialismus*. Germany: Brüderbewegung, 2004; www.bruederbewegung.de/pdf/zimmerman.pdf.

Zuccotti, Susan. *The Italians and the Holocaust: Persecution, Rescue, and Survival*. Lincoln: University of Nebraska Press, 1996.

———. *Père Marie-Benoît and Jewish Rescue: How a French Priest Together with Jewish Friends Saved Thousands during the Holocaust*. Bloomington: Indiana University Press, 2013.

———. "Père Marie-Benoît and Joseph Bass: The Rescue of Jews in Marseille and Nice, 1940–1943." *French Politics, Culture & Society* 30, no. 2 (Summer 2012): 53–65.

Special Collections

Baptist World Alliance

Baptist World Alliance Executive Committee Minutes, American Baptist Historical Society, Mercer University.

Correspondence and Papers of Hans Luckey, Elstal Seminary Archive Collection, Berlin.

Correspondence and Papers of J. H. Rushbrooke (1933–47), Angus Library and Archive, Regent's Park College, University of Oxford, Oxford, England.

Papers and Correspondence of Walter O. Lewis, American Baptist Historical Society, Mercer University.

Baptist Conventions

The Baptist Convention of the Netherlands *De Christen* newspaper (1933–48).

Baptist Times, a weekly newspaper representing the voice of the British Baptist community. The number of relevant articles for each year is in parentheses: 1933 (43); 1934 (69); 1935 (27); 1936 (15); 1937 (33); 1938 (68); 1939 (40); 1940 (33); 1947 (3).

Baptist Union Annual Assemblies Handbooks for the period of 1933–48 (inclusive), published by the Baptist Union. Each book contains national convention minutes, reports, resolutions, and selected speeches. Memoirs of key individuals can be found in the 1943, 1948, and 1959 handbooks.

Baptist Union of Great Britain and Ireland Minute Books.

Correspondence of M. E. Aubrey, Angus Library and Archive, Regent's Park College, University of Oxford, Oxford, England.

Correspondence of Ernest A. Payne (1928–1967), Angus Library and Archive, Regent's Park College, University of Oxford, Oxford, England.

Missions, a magazine published monthly by the Northern Baptist Convention.

The Scottish Baptist Union: *The Scottish Baptist Union Year Books* (1933–48) and *The Scottish Baptist Magazine* (1933–48).

Other Sources

Association of Jewish Refugees (London), *AJR Journal* (1949–2018).

The British Newspaper Online Archive (https://www.britishnewspaperarchive.co.uk).

Chosen People Ministries Online Archive.

Jewish Chronicle (London), the journalistic voice of the Jews in Great Britain. The number of relevant articles for each year is in parentheses: 1929 (1); 1933 (1); 1934 (5); 1935 (1); 1936 (2); 1937 (1); 1938 (1); 1939 (2); 1941 (2).

Watchman-Examiner, an independent Baptist newspaper representing an evangelical/conservative perspective.

Index